P9-EER-026

Praise for *Executive Greed*

"The author courageously points his finger at one of the worst illnesses of modern capitalism. He builds a bridge between the theoretical models taught in business schools and the daily practices of business life, where top executives seem to have 'forgotten' the basics of good management in favor of their greed for personal financial gain. His considerations help the reader understand where executive greed originates and how it hurts all stakeholders. The book also provides valid suggestions on how to control executive greed and limit its dramatic consequences, with no fear of shaking up the corporate executive establishment. Something which, nowadays, is well worthy of consideration!"—Riccardo Spinelli, Post-doc Research Fellow, Department of Economics, University of Genoa

"Dr. Kothari delineates the cozy incestuous relationship between the boards and senior executives for mutual gain that perverts the interests of individual shareholders. The horrific impact of executive greed on both companies and countries is explicitly explored. Practical solutions for corporate governance reforms are advocated. All board members, executives, and legislators should scrutinize this study to understand and to avoid the 'dark side' of the free enterprise system which triggers cataclysmic economic crises."—William Bradley Zehner II, PhD, Fellow at the IC2 Institute, and Associate Professor of Management at St. Edward's University

"*Executive Greed* is a fast paced read on "doing the right things" in corporate America instead of "doing things right...for stockholders, that is." From short-sighted, short-termed strategy to treating humans inhumanely, *Executive Greed* seeks to explain the causes, effects, and cures for placing stockholders over an organization's stakeholders. A good read for today's business student to grasp the current business and economic situation facing America and the world."—Charles Fenner, PhD, SUNY

"*Executive Greed* is an excellent and thought provoking read. It is a reality check, and a must read for CEO's, corporate leaders, managers and business school academics. It analyses the short-termism of today's corporate leaders and delivers numerous strategic business-for-tomorrow success tools for CEO's. The book's innovative and competitive customer-focused solutions are highly suitable for corporate long-termism, and for the ongoing growth in shareholder value."—John Hamilton, Associate Professor and Director of E-Business, James Cook University

Executive Greed

HD
31
K63
2010
web

Executive Greed

Examining Business Failures that Contributed to the Economic Crisis

Vinay B. Kothari

palgrave
macmillan

JF

EXECUTIVE GREED
Copyright © Vinay B. Kothari, 2010.
All rights reserved.

First published in 2010 by
PALGRAVE MACMILLAN® in the United States – a division of St. Martin's
Press LLC, 175 Fifth Avenue, New York, NY 10010.

Where this book is distributed in the UK, Europe and the rest of the world,
this is by Palgrave Macmillan, a division of Macmillan Publishers Limited,
registered in England, company number 785998, of Houndmills, Basingstoke,
Hampshire RG21 6XS.

Palgrave Macmillan is the global academic imprint of the above companies
and has companies and representatives throughout the world.

Palgrave® and Macmillan® are registered trademarks in the United States,
the United Kingdom, Europe and other countries.

ISBN: 978-0-230-10401-3

Library of Congress Cataloging-in-Publication Data is available
from the Library of Congress.

A catalogue record of the book is available from the British Library.

Design by MPS Limited, A Macmillan Company

First edition: July 2010

10 9 8 7 6 5 4 3 2 1

Printed in the United States of America.

This book is dedicated to my wife, Connie, my daughter Madison P. F. Goodwin, and the rest of my family for their love, inspiration, encouragement, and support.

Contents

Table

Preface

In 2009, the insurance giant AIG (American International Group), along with Merrill Lynch and a number of other American firms, stood for corporate greed. Their CEOs were handing out huge bonuses for themselves as well as for their cronies, angering the society at large. Americans were enraged by the news of executive bonuses in the firms that were being bailed out by the government. Without the billions in government assistance, most of these businesses would not have survived. Even though many managers of these firms were responsible for their firms' financial decline, they were rewarding themselves as if they deserved high compensations for their disastrous business decisions, policies, and actions. The financial excesses brought these executives worldwide notoriety and public ridicule.

The highly publicized cases are only the few drops in the vast pool of executive greed. There are thousands of executives earning high compensations unjustifiably in countless big companies. The reported incidents shed light on how corporate leaders in the United States and elsewhere have been enriching themselves, legally or unlawfully, at the expense of consumers, employees, distributors, suppliers, stockholders, and the society at large.

In most cases, business decision-makers at the top have contributed directly to their firms' business problems. However, instead of accepting responsibility for their flawed strategies and practices, these business managers continue to reward one another at the top with high salaries, bonuses, and severance packages. In large firms, many corporate executives act as if they are accountable to no one; they behave as if they are entitled to high compensations—even in times of their firms' most serious circumstances.

The corporate leaders have been able to get away with their irresponsible behavior for years without much scrutiny from the government or other responsible parties, such as the public accounting firms, rating agencies, trade associations, and research firms. The business press has been blind, beating frequently the corporate drums. All the watchdogs seem to overlook the corporate misdeeds. Some, in fact, act as collaborators simply to protect their own personal or organizational financial interests. Political contributions and aggressive lobbying by business have strong influence on the regulatory atmosphere.

Even after Barack Obama won the White House and the Democrats enjoyed a clear majority in both houses of Congress in 2009, there was no strong political will to implement the most beneficial health care and financial regulatory reforms for the society at large. As usual, business has been very successful in crushing or watering down any regulatory reforms.

The recent economic crises suggest a troubling situation of moral decline. Over the past few years, too many business and civic leaders have been found guilty or have come under suspicion for immoral or illegal conduct.

It is not difficult to understand what takes place when the business and government leaders behave as collaborates for personal gains and are not held accountable. The self-serving leadership behavior becomes clearly evident when its economic and social consequences are disastrous.

In less than 25 years, there have been three major economic crises, each one much more serious than its predecessor(s) and each a result of personal greed. Each time, the leadership behavior seems to be more self-centered, reckless, and severe. The absence of sound regulations or law enforcement entices greedy business leaders to pursue self-interests more than corporate or public interests.

The S&L (savings and loan) scandal of the 1980s in the United States shocked the financial markets. The imprudent real-estate lending practices for high profits then had made several financial institutions vulnerable to heavy losses. To minimize the economic disaster, the government had to intervene and bailout many S&L institutions. Hundreds of financial firms and thousands of homeowners suffered. The sharp decline in personal wealth had shaken the public confidence and, in order to prevent similar economic crises in the future, the demand for regulatory reforms grew.

The impact of the S&L scandal was shortened by the advancement in computing and telecommunication technologies. In the 1990s, several technical innovations ignited the entrepreneurial spirits and contributed to economic growth. The Internet accelerated the expansion of global markets. The increasing cross-border demand for capital, technology, workers, and consumer goods and services generated political pressures for international regulatory reforms and cooperation. Trade barriers began to crumble, leading to greater deregulation worldwide.

The changing business climate led to exaggerated business and investment expectations. Growth potentials were magnified, especially for those businesses associated with the information and "e-" (electronic) technology revolutions. Backed by venture capital, many young and technology-savvy entrepreneurs entered the marketplace hoping to become rich overnight with their initial public offerings (IPOs). Each initial or new stock offer to the public was so high in price that it could not be justified with any proven sales and income records. Most investors had no clear understanding of e-technologies or their business potential. The skyrocketing stock prices of tech firms and speculation appeared to invalidate the old financial concepts, theories, and models. New financial strategies were emerging fast for quick gains. Economic history and common sense did not matter. Nobody wanted any government oversight or regulation to squash the prevailing market optimism.

The e-party evidently did not last long. Near the turn of the millennium, the "dot-com" bubble busted, costing billions in stock market losses and wiping out thousands of retirement funds and individual dreams. The financial and economic consequences were more serious and widespread, in comparison with those of the S&L crisis.

Slowly, the world recovered from the "dot-com" bust with the progress in technology—just to face another crisis in less than a decade. This time, far worse and unprecedented since the 1930s worldwide Great Depression.

The twenty-first century "subprime" crisis has turned out to be a worldwide problem, not just an American problem, threatening major financial institutions and overall economic well-being across national boundaries. The disastrous economic situation could alter the international political stability and cooperative economic spirit. Governments worldwide were left with no option except to intervene to avoid the consequences of economic calamity.

The U.S. government spent billions to prevent the collapse of giant financial institutions like the Citibank and the AIG. The government had to take over and sell out Bear Stearns, Lehman Brothers, and Merrill Lynch, and it had to take over General Motors (GM)—the largest corporation in the world not too long ago. The cost to the U.S. taxpayers for financial bailouts is estimated to be in trillions. In the United Kingdom, Germany, and elsewhere, the national governments had to step in with all sorts of financial programs and bailout money to save their major financial institutions, businesses, and economic well-being. Without the huge government assistance programs, most economies would have collapsed.

Once again, millions of individual saving accounts, retirement funds, and personal dreams shrunk or vanished with the decline in the stock markets and jobs. Loss in real-estate values increased home foreclosures and homelessness. As the feeling of helplessness and hopelessness began to spread, there emerged a nonconsumption mentality—a real shift in American social phenomenon.

All across the globe, the economic growth had slowed down. Some countries appeared to be far worse off than others, but almost everyone had been affected by the subprime blunder. There had been a widespread fear that the economic downslide could linger on for a long time and that there could be massive unemployment and human suffering. To combat the crisis and stimulate economic growth, the recently elected president in the United States implemented a mass infusion of government funding and incentive programs. While the U.S. government deficit rose, the unemployment increased to nearly 10 percent; in California, it rose to more than 12 percent. Many more became underemployed with lower income.

There is plenty of evidence to suggest that each of the past three major economic crises is related to unbridled personal greed at the highest level in the corporate world. While corporate executives enrich themselves using their management positions, everyone else pays the heavy price. The self-serving corporate leadership behavior aimed at get-rich schemes is unhealthy and detrimental to the society's economic well-being. What we have observed is the management preoccupation with personal wealth maximization without any regard for the security, stability, and growth for the institutions they manage. Most corporate leadership decisions and actions may be legal, but they are not morally justifiable.

The situation is not limited to a specific country or region. Not too long ago, the financial markets in India were shaken when Satyam Chairman resigned after admitting that the accounting records of this leading tech firm had been falsified to inflate the corporate financial performance and position. In Germany, the Chief of Deutsche Post, a giant firm, resigned after he came under investigation for tax evasion; he was among several German business leaders suspected of criminal business practices. In Lebanon, hundreds of small investors apparently have lost their land and retirement savings in pursuit of high returns promised by a reputable and politically connected businessman, named Salah Ezzedine; the Associated Press describes the Lebanese situation as similar to the Bernie Madoff scandal in the United States.

There are reports of hundreds of inappropriate leadership actions worldwide. The number of U.S. executives found guilty in the past decade or two is astonishing. These executives led large corporations such as Enron, WorldCom, and Tyco. Among their misdeeds are forgeries, backdating of stock options, using secret slush funds or fictitious employees, lying to the auditors or regulators, inflating corporate revenues and incomes, overstating cash flows, and understating liabilities.

Such acts have one simple executive objective: boost stock prices to enhance personal earnings and benefits.

Executive get-rich-quickly schemes, both legal and illegal, are costly. Often the organization pays the price and vanishes; other stakeholders continue to suffer the consequences year after year. Enron, WorldCom, Global Crossing, Countrywide Financial, and IndyMac are among the examples of costly and disgraceful management behavior.

The sad social fact is, many of the disgraced business leaders were hailed as great mentors—worthy of high praise, social recognition, and honor. Their leadership attributes and styles were glorified by the media, and they became part of case studies in business school classes and management training rooms. They were the focus of some "best seller" books on leadership.

Too many books indeed are written on the subject of what makes a good leader, often on the basis of leadership that later turned out to be disastrous for the firms or the stakeholders. These books advance false impressions about individual contribution to business success. What such books say is far from the truth. Most corporate executives are not worthy of their attributed "indispensability." Corporate leaders do contribute to success by virtue of their corporate positions, but success is not entirely due to them, or as much as what these books and executive compensations suggest.

Management guru Peter Drucker pointed out a long time ago that management is no more than getting things done through people. Yes, it is people working together who contribute to an organization's success. The fate of business is in the hands of its people at all levels and throughout its supply and distribution chains. All across the organization, people hold the power over the implementation of the leadership plans and decisions, and they could affect the actual outcome.

When the organizational leadership facilitates the productive human motivation and effort across the organization with the right incentives and adequate resource support, people would rise up; they would release their energy and use their power positively for success. On the other hand, without the appropriate work environment and incentives, people would not perform to the best of their abilities.

The reality is that corporate leaders pursue self-interests and fail to ignite the human motivation and energy. As a result, businesses suffer. No one leader controls the organizational success. No one individual deserves all the credit for the organization's accomplishments. Yet, we bestow all the rewards for success on those whom we call "great leaders" or "visionaries." The so-called outstanding leaders are treated as royalty until they falter. Thereafter our well-reputed leaders are dethroned and ridiculed.

But, who pays the price? Not these so-called visionaries or great leaders. When they fail, when the time comes for them to depart, they get heavily rewarded through their severance packages. We treat corporate leaders as if they are worthy of high rewards—even in times of business decline and fall.

Ours is a misguided business world!

Most highly paid corporate managers in big firms are not founders of their organizations, nor are they innovators. They do not perform highly skilled leadership tasks. They do not possess any extraordinary or unique skills or attributes. Often they assume their leadership positions in well-established and well-run companies that are strong in core competencies. Sometimes, a business firm may experience difficulties because of its management's past mistakes. But as long as a troubled organization is intact and not harmed at its core, all it takes for its managers is to repair the mistakes and move on. It does not take a genius. A commonsense approach can solve many business problems. What makes them deserving of extremely high compensation—much more than everyone else within the organization? Nothing!

There are a few exceptional situations or individuals deserving high rewards or compensations. Corporate founders, entrepreneurs, and "real" innovators make contributions worthy of extraordinary, high rewards. Nobody can dispute the economic impact of individuals like Henry Ford, Arthur Sloane, Bill Gates, Sam Walton, Steve Jobs, and Jeff Bezos. Such individuals did—or do—deserve their fortune as well as fame. Their economic contributions are unique and noteworthy.

Unlike business entrepreneurs and innovators, however, "professional" corporate managers do not contribute significantly to business. Yet, they are rewarded highly—frequently on the basis of wrong premises. Their leadership performance is evaluated mostly on the basis of the corporate current profitability and stock price appreciation, not on the results over a long period of time, nor for individual contribution toward long-term corporate survival and growth.

The way the corporate managers are compensated is inherently flawed.

To maximize their own personal salaries and bonuses, corporate decision-makers focus on the firm's current revenue increases and cost-cuttings and ignore the corporate core skills and product development for long-term competitive strengths. This type of leadership behavior leads eventually to business disasters.

The problem, in essence, is that corporate leaders are expected to fulfill their long-term fiduciary responsibilities and duties, but they are compensated lavishly for their short-term "operational" results or accomplishments. The recent economic crises provide us with ample evidence of the consequences of this reality. The fallacy of contemporary executive compensation practices is highlighted below by a brief list of some business realities concerning business survival and growth:

1. Business success does not solely depend on the corporate CEO or its top managers.
2. A business firm could succeed, in spite of its leaders.
3. A business firm fails largely because of its leadership, not because of its people below or across the organization.
4. While business failure is a leadership phenomenon, organizational success is a group phenomenon characterized by joint, productive efforts throughout the organization.
5. Because most "professional" corporate executives are highly educated and experienced, a business failure is not usually related to management or leadership incompetence.
6. Business failures are avoidable with careful and effective planning and implementation—even under the most adverse business conditions. Because external environmental factors affect all competing firms in the marketplace, only the internal or company factors could create and provide a competitive edge.
7. To anticipate competitive problems and overcome them as they arise, it takes the right leadership motivations, proactive leadership thinking and orientation, and careful management policies and actions.
8. Corporate managers have the fiduciary obligation and responsibility to enhance their firm's long-term security, survival, and growth. When executives are not compensated in relation to their long-term obligations, they tend to ignore their fiduciary duties, and they fail to perform to the best of their abilities in pursuit of their own individual immediate financial benefits. This has become evident in recent economic crises and serious business problems.
9. Most corporate leaders do not deserve their high compensation (salaries, bonuses, and severance packages) from the perspectives of their limited contribution during their short –tenures, ranging on average from a few months to under ten years.
10. Mergers and acquisitions leading eventually to business failure may be carefully planned and carried out by corporate managers for their own financial gains.

The list could go on and on.

In the field of management, there are many widely held popular beliefs that are not related to the business realities. Many beliefs are no more than myths. We must understand and recognize this situation. This book explains why and how corporate executives succeed in exploiting their leadership positions for their own personal gains. The author explores and analyzes various aspects of corporate leadership and management to show what the corporate business realities are.

Basically, the author underscores the leadership motivation, behavior, and decision-making behind various corporate strategies, policies, and practices. Even though executive compensation, not management incompetence, is identified as the primary cause of management failure to compete in the long run, this book is not a manual on "executive compensation." The book just explains how compensation-based motivations affect various executive decisions and actions. It highlights how sound business principles are ignored in pursuit of self-serving needs. Furthermore, it suggests what needs to be done to minimize corporate disaster.

As the book points out, "professional" corporate managers often preach about team efforts and the importance of team-playing, and they use all the buzzwords that they have learned from the business schools and management gurus. However, when it comes to sharing financial rewards, there is not much available for the team players below the executive level. While the CEOs and other senior executives and staff continue to earn high year after year, everyone else gets much less in reward and can barely keep up with the ever-rising cost of living. No wonder we have low work morale, high number of product quality flaws, and deteriorating services!

The book highlights a number of ways corporate managers fail to adequately compete in the global marketplace in the long run. The "Why and how" management failures take place is explained throughout the book. Several external players, such as legislators and regulators, are identified in the book as contributing factors toward the failure of corporate managers.

Clearly, we have a leadership crisis. In order to deal with our serious business problems, we have to understand the underlying reasons for management shortcomings.

Here is what two great thinkers suggest:

Dale Carnegie: "Develop success from failures. Discouragement and failure are two of the surest stepping stones to success."

Confucius: "Our greatest glory is not in never falling, but in rising every time we fail."

Today, we are faced with many challenges worldwide. We must rise up to prevent and minimize the social costs and human suffering. Our economic resources are scarce, but our social and ecological needs are infinite, limitless. The stakes are too high. We have already observed and experienced the consequences of leadership greed in our society.

This book hopes to generate a useful dialogue among and between the management practitioners, academics, public policy makers, and the society at large.

Because hundreds of business problems and corporate failures have been reported widely in the press over the past few years, the author intentionally does not include many examples in the book. It is not necessary to repeat the highly publicized managerial moral and legal missteps. If the reader is interested, there are numerous instances easily accessible online. Appendix 2 in the book includes a few examples.

The chapters in the book are organized to make the material easy to follow. Each chapter is designed to stand on its own. Thus, some overlapping between the chapters is considered essential, unavoidable, and intentional. No specific academic or management background is required for the reader to follow the subject materials in the book.

For this book, the author draws from a number of business concepts, theories, and practices—some more popular than others. Because the book is not primarily aimed at academics, no attempt is specifically made to attribute any specific concept to its rightful contributor(s). Management thinkers and researchers like Peter Drucker and Michael Porter need no special recognition; they are already well-known for their outstanding contributions in the field of management. The book may certainly reflect the influence of many scholars. For the interested readers, the book includes a list of recommended readings in the field of business and management.

Needless to say, many of the author's perspectives and insights on leadership and corporate management are the result of his extensive educational background and considerable academic as well as business experience.

Acknowledgments

Many individuals have provided encouragement and useful guidance in the completion of this book. Several management practitioners and academic colleagues volunteered to review a portion or portions of the book for critical comments and suggestions. The names of reviewers are listed separately. This list is partial and does not include some individuals specifically from the business community. Many individuals prefer anonymity for confidentiality reasons. The author gratefully acknowledges each individual's generous offer to participate, support, and contribute in some way in the book's development and review process. Many individuals undoubtedly spent countless hours, much greater time and efforts than others, to provide detailed and useful suggestions and corrections. The author is especially very grateful to them and wishes that he could show his appreciation in person. Perhaps their paths will cross someday.

The author has tried to integrate the reviewers' priceless suggestions in the best possible manner. However, the author is solely responsible for any conceptual or grammatical errors or omissions. The views, positions, or perspectives expressed in the book are those of the author, and they are not endorsed by any specific individual or academic or business organization.

The list below includes the names of the academic and professional colleagues who recently responded to the author's call for voluntary participation in the review and revision process of this book. The response was overwhelming. Most of these university professors and business managers spent numerous hours going over the materials carefully, evaluating the contents, pinpointing several questionable underlying premises (assumptions) and conceptual flaws, making grammatical corrections and comments, and offering recommendations. Because of time constraints, not all of them were asked to review the whole manuscript; instead, they were requested to review a chapter, or two, or a section, on an individual basis. Irrespective of their level of participation, the author gratefully acknowledges their personal involvement, kind cooperation, and sincere and honest critiques. Their suggestions were extremely useful. Any omissions, errors, or conceptual flaws in the book are those of the author, and these colleagues should not bear any scholarly responsibilities.

Special thanks to the following academic colleagues for their encouraging and kind words and support for this book project: *Dr. Subhash C. Jain*, Professor and Director of Center for International Business Education and Research, University of Connecticut, USA; *Dr. William Bradley (Brad) Zehner II*, IC2 Fellow at the IC2 Institute (Innovation, Creativity and Capital), The University of Texas at Austin and Associate Professor of Global Management, St. Edward's University, USA; *Dr. Lyn S. Amin,* Professor Emerita of Marketing and International Business, Saint Louis University, USA; *Professor Nicholas Grigoriou,* Principal—Monash College Guangzhou Program, C/—Hua Mei International School, Guangzhou, People's Republic of China; *Dr. Charles Fenner,* SUNY (State University of New York), USA; *Dr. John Robert Hamilton,* Associate Professor and Director of E-Business, James Cook University, Australia; *Dr. Juan Carlos Barrera,* Assistant Professor of International Business, Elmhurst College, Illinois, USA; *Dr. Nazly K. Nardi,* Consultant and Adjunct Professor, School of Business and Management, Kaplan University, Florida, USA; *Dr. Jopie Coetzee,* currently working full time on a book on leadership, formerly, Senior Lecturer International Business, The University of South Africa, South Africa; *Professor Eduardo Garrovillas,* Jose Rizal University, Philippines; *Dr. D. S. Rana,* Professor of Management, College of Business, Jackson State University, Mississippi, USA; *Dr. Riccardo Spinelli,* Postdoctorate Research Fellow, DITEA—FacoltÃ di Economia, UniversitÃ degli Studi di Genova, Italy.

Also, special thanks to *Laurie Harting,* Associate Editor at Palgrave-Macmillan Publisher, and her staff—including *Laura Lancaster,* Editorial Assistant; *Matt Robinson,* Production Editor; and *Imran Shahnawaz,* Project Manager—for their courteous and professional conduct throughout various stages of book publishing.

Sincere thanks to the following for their support in the review process:

Jehad Saleh Aldehayyat, Al-Hussein Bin Talal University, Jordan

Muhammad Amjad Lancashire Business School, University of Central Lancashire, UK

William P. Anthony, Florida State University, USA

Juan Carlos Barrera, Center for Business & Economics, Elmhurst College, Illinois, USA

Dave Beaudry, Southern New Hampshire University (SNHU), USA

Alexander Brem, University of Erlangen-Nuremberg, Germany

Richard Brunet-Thornton, Canada

Andrés Mauricio Castro Figueroa, Universidad del Rosario, Bogotá, Colombia

Raul Chavez, University of Mary Washington, Fredericksburg, Virginia, USA

Tsun Chow, Roosevelt University, USA

Jopie Coetzee, Graduate School of Business Leadership, University of South Africa, South Africa

Shivakumar Deene, Karnataka State Open University, Manasagangotri, Mysore, India

Serdar S. Durmusoglu, University of Dayton, USA

Gary Dusek, Nova Southeastern University, USA

Charles Fenner, State University of New York (SUNY), USA Eduardo P. Garrovillas, Jose Rizal University, Philippines

Madison Payal Goodwin, Hewlett Packard, USA

Nicholas Grigoriou, Monash College Guangzhou (Huamei International School), Guangzhou, People's Republic of China

S. Jeyavelu, Indian Institute of Management (IIM), Ahmedabad and Kozhikode, India

Abu Bakar A. Hamid, Universiti Teknologi, Malaysia

Hamid H. Kazeroony, William Penn University, USA

Azhar Kazmi, Dept. of Management & Marketing, King Fahd University of Petroleum & Minerals, Saudi Arabia Omar J. Khan, Maine Business School, The University of Maine, USA

Shaista E. Khilji, George Washington University (GWU), Washington, D.C., USA

Larry L. Kurtulus, Roosevelt University, Schaumburg, Illinois, USA, C. Lakshman, Management Consultant, USA

Maria Lai-Ling Lam, Malone University, USA

Natalja Martjanova, Aston University/ABS, Aston Triangle, Birmingham, UK Cleamon Moorer, Jr., Trinity Christian College, Palos Heights, Illinois, USA

Wojciech Nasierowski, University of New Brunswick, Fredericton, N.B., Canada

Nazly K. Nardi, Nova Southeastern University, USA

Francine Newth, Providence College, USA

Lam Nguyen, Webster University, St. Louis, USA

Colin Ong, MR=MC Consulting, Singapore

Opas Piansoongnern, Shinawatra University, Thailand Daya Shanker, Deakin University, Melbourne, Australia

Daljit Singh, Northcentral University, Prescott Valley, Arizona, USA

Juan Carlos Sosa Varela, School of Business & Entrepreneurship, Turabo University, Gurabo, Puerto Rico

Michelle Ingram Spain, Walsh University, USA

John Staczek, Thunderbird School of Global Management, Arizona, USA

Lily Lavanchawee Sujarittanonta, Chiang Mai University, Thailand

Asli Tuncay-Celikel, Isik University, Turkey

Bindu Vyas, McGowan School of Business, King's College, Pennsylvania, USA

Paul K. Ward, Management Consultant, Washington, D.C., USA

Brad Zehner, University of Texas at Austin and St. Edward's University, USA

PART I

General Overview

CHAPTER 1

Introduction

Sometimes a noble failure serves the world as faithfully as a distinguished success.
Edward Dowden

The corporate business world is in crisis. Not just in business but in other sectors as well, our leaders are performing well below our normal expectations. They are not managing our scarce and valuable economic resources in the most productive way. Many major problems characterize our institutions such as businesses, hospitals, public schools, universities, research institutes, social organizations, and governmental entities. Discontent with leadership and management is evident everywhere.

Recent Business Events and Key Management Issues

This organizational problem has surfaced in the past few years. It is highlighted in the highly publicized business failures, government bailouts, and other economic events. Prior to the twenty-first-century "subprime" crisis and its aftermath worldwide, there were the Saving and Loan (S&L) scandal and the dot-com bust of the 1980s and 1990s. Of the last three major economic crises in the past 25 years, the subprime has been the worst. There are dozens of examples of big business problems and failures.

Companies such as AIG (American International Group), Merrill Lynch, Bear Stearns, Countrywide Financial, Lehman Brothers, Satyam, WorldCom, Global Crossing, IndyMac, and Enron represent many of the large businesses with some serious leadership problems. At the political level, too, poor planning and bad management become clearly evident in the postwar chaos in Iraq. Rising health care costs and deteriorating quality of education in the United States are indicators of ineffective utilization of economic resources and inadequate and disastrous social policies.

What is so alarming is the fact that most large corporations and other institutions suffering from poor management performance are led and run by the individuals who are highly intelligent and skilled, who are professionally well trained and developed, and who possess considerable leadership and management experience.[1] These professional managers do understand the basic principles of management and do know the importance of strategic thinking, planning, and implementation. In spite of their knowledge, though, there is a lack of effective management to accomplish the organization's desired mission.

As a result, their organizations are not able to carry out their vision and reach the long-term destinies and goals. Across all sectors of our society, our leaders are not effectively fulfilling their fiduciary duties and responsibilities. In large corporations, the situation is much more serious. Effective strategies and plans are few in numbers; frequently, they are poor in quality or altogether missing.

When the corporate managers fail, others bear the responsibilities and pay the heavy price one way or another. Everybody has some stakes in business well-being. When a big firm is in trouble, its consumers, employees, creditors, stockholders, suppliers, distributors, and the public at large suffer the consequences. When the government has to bailout a large business or financial institution, the taxpayers pick up the tab.

Often after a big business disaster, we wonder and ask: Why? Why couldn't its managers perceive the problems ahead and do something? Why couldn't they think, plan ahead, and have effective business strategies? Why did they take unnecessary chances? Why couldn't they develop and offer better products and services at competitive prices? Why couldn't they hold on to their productive employees? Why did they overlook or neglect their firm's long-term competitive strengths and capabilities? Why weren't they concerned about their company's security, survival, and success in the years to come? Why were they so preoccupied with their current corporate profitability and current stock prices, and not worried about their future problems? In short, what were these corporate CEOs and executives thinking of and doing, and why?

Important strategic questions are not raised in most cases until and unless a corporation is in serious trouble. For decades General Motors (GM), Ford, and Chrysler have been aware of their strategic issues related to rising oil prices, U.S. dependence on foreign oil, and international competition. Yet these industry giants ignored their strategic challenges for years and, because of their size and market dominance, were able to get away with it. Only recently, in light of their financial problems and business bankruptcies, we have begun to wonder what happened and why their leadership did not do something years earlier to avoid their competitive problems.

Because most corporate managers are well trained and highly capable of managing their firms, the leadership crisis is certainly not related to management incompetence. The root causes or underlying problems evidently lie somewhere else. The most obvious: executive greed, management's fast pursuit of personal financial gains (individual compensation package) in any way possible.

Many incidents of high executive compensations; unlawful or immoral leadership behaviors; and unsound management decisions, policies, and actions have been reported over the past few years by the news media worldwide. The news stories underscore several key issues facing the corporate world. Among them are the following:

- Executive greed and self-serving business practices for personal financial gains
- Declining leadership ethical and moral values
- Incapability of corporate managers to act responsibly in the deregulated environment
- Too much preoccupation with corporate current or immediate operational profitability and stock price appreciations via fast sales increases and cost cuttings
- Considerable management disregard for the corporate long-term survival, growth, and success
- Indifference to the needs of corporate stakeholders (consumers, employees, etc.)
- Failure to effectively carry out management long-term fiduciary duties and responsibilities
- Failure of corporate boards, legislators and regulators, rating and certifying agencies, and others to provide adequate supervision and guidance
- The absence of proper "checks and balance"
- Too much conflict of interests and cross-collaborations for personal financial gains and other reasons

Executive Greed and Financial Motivations

There is plenty of evidence in the news media and elsewhere to suggest that the corporate managers often use their corporate positions for their own personal gains. Their self-centered management behavior is detrimental to their business, its survival, and future growth. The disastrous and imprudent lending practices undertaken for personal gains, indeed, failed many major financial institutions; such practices led to numerous government bailouts and financial assistance programs

The leadership chase for high personal compensation via quick corporate profitability is evident in corporate policies and practices. The business reality is that, in pursuit of their own self-interests, corporate decision-makers take shortcuts. Instead of improving the long-term competitive strengths and advantages of their business, they focus on the current sales revenues and immediate cost-cutting. They lower prices to increase sales and/or they implement cost-reduction measures such as reducing product/service quality, employee and staff layoffs, research and development (R&D) budget cuts, cuts in human resource development and training programs, improper plant maintenance and modernization, and postponing investments for product and market developments. In essence, to improve their corporate profitability fast, the corporate managers lay the ground for future business problems and disaster.

For corporate managers, there is not much to lose. Their short-term focus improves the operational picture temporarily and, as a result, enables them to earn and enjoy extraordinary financial compensation (salaries, bonuses, frills, and perks) immediately during their tenures. When they fail to gain the expected results, they may lose their job but get rewarded with huge severance packages. Financially, the top leaders are well taken care of; their generous retirement benefits and lavish severance packages guarantee their future financial well-being. It is a win-win situation for the professional managers. Such compensation practices explain the reasons for risky, short-term focused business practices, as well as the reasons for short executive tenures ranging from few months to fewer than ten years in most instances.

Management Contribution: Realities and Consequences

That's the state of our business reality. We reward failures. The executive reward systems encourage risky and careless management behaviors. They produce a high level of management indifference to competitive problems in the years to come. When the management focus is only on immediate operational performance, it eventually leads to business disaster. Many competitive and financial challenges emerge down the road, which may be too late to handle effectively. The firm in trouble may vanish or get gobbled up by its stronger rivals. Corporate managers sometimes improve their operational profits quickly in order for their firm to get acquired. The reason: most mergers and acquisitions (M&As) generate lucrative compensations for their corporate executives. It does not matter if the acquired firm eventually loses its competitive edge and corporate identity. Financially, corporate managers stay ahead one way or another. But the firm's other stakeholders bear the heavy cost.

One of the ironies of the business world reality is that corporate leaders are heavily rewarded in spite of their failure to protect the corporate long-term interests. Executive compensations, in reality, entice the CEOs and other senior members to overlook their long-term fiduciary duties and obligations.

The culprit in business failures is greed. Business problems are a by-product of executive actions dictated by the individual self-serving financial motivations.

For personal gains, business leaders are ready to do anything—even cross ethical, moral, and legal boundaries. At the moment, the number of executives who have been put in jail in recent years or who are under judicial investigation for unethical or criminal business conduct is phenomenal.

Political contribution and heavy lobbying by business are part of corporate strategies and are frequently used by corporate managers to minimize their regulatory and legal problems. To some extent, as the growing evidence suggests, corporate management is not averse to corrupting both the political processes and financial markets; together, business executives and regulators enable one another to pursue their own individual financial gains and personal interests.

One of the ironies of the business reality is that when corporate executives are paid exuberantly, there is an implicit recognition or underlying assumption that corporate success solely depends on its top management, its CEO and his/her lieutenants. This is obviously far from the truth. Management guru Peter Drucker pointed out a long time ago that management is getting things done through people. No organization succeeds or flourishes without its people all across; at all levels, it takes collaboration and cooperation. Within the organization, people hold the power to determine how the strategies and plans handed down from the top are implemented and carried out. Their motivations and the quality of their participation affect the outcomes. Thus, contrary to what the leadership perceptions and beliefs are, the organizational success is a collective phenomenon. Corporate managers do decide, guide, and contribute toward their organizational results, but they do not deserve—or they cannot claim—the sole credit for the firm's success.

The fact is, corporate leaders contribute more significantly toward the business failure than its success. When the appropriate resources are not provided to the operational levels by the decision-makers, or when the workers are not appropriately motivated, rewarded, and empowered to use their best effort and discretion, the organization suffers from leadership flaws and it fumbles. The serious business problems are usually the result of bad management decisions and practices. As long as managers do not interfere with their unsound policies, procedures, and micromanaging, workers could—and frequently do—overcome minor leadership shortcomings and competitive pressures from outside.

There are too many myths about leadership that falsely enhance the management's contribution and worth, and compound business problems regarding executive compensations.

In 2008, stocks were in downfall, losing billions and billions in investors' dollars. Nevertheless, there was no slump in executive compensations. More than 20 of Fortune 500 corporations' executives were paid twice their 2006 earnings. In 2007, Sovereign Bancorp Inc.'s CEO received 285 percent increase in compensation while his company lost more than 55 percent of its stock value a year later. The median executive salary across the Fortune 500 companies was $8.4 million at the time many families were losing their homes in mortgage foreclosures and their corporations were downsizing. In just a few years, the top executive annual compensations in big corporations and financial institutions jumped from under 50 to over 500 times their average worker salaries.

Corporate CEOs and others justify their high salaries by rewarding one another at the top fairly well. By keeping team "players" well compensated, corporate CEOs insure their senior staff's loyalty and support necessary to carry out the management game plans without much opposition.

The Management Club—Collaborators

All of the self-serving management plans go on under the watchful eyes of the corporate boards, the guardians and protectors of corporate stockholders and their interests. Even though corporate boards are there to supervise and guide corporate managers, they fail to provide required checks and balances. There is plenty of evidence to suggest that the corporate boards tend to go along with management policies, plans, and actions without very close scrutiny. Why?

There are several factors that prevent the board from performing its fiduciary duties. Cross-board memberships, nominations of board directors by corporate executives, insufficient time commitment from the board members, and the board directors' personal financial motivations and other self-interests are part of the explanations or reasons for the lack of adequate board oversight.

The board's failure empowers corporate managers to pursue their own interests at the expense of the corporate stockholders. Too often board members become their management's collaborators. In many ways, the corporate board system has evolved to serve the top executives much more than it does the primary stakeholders. Everything that the corporate executives do with their board's approval mostly for their own personal gains is official, proper, and possibly, within the legal boundaries.

As the growing evidence suggests, there are many others who have failed to provide adequate oversight and, in reality, have become collaborators in pursuit of their own self-interests. They include politicians, legislators, regulators, rating agencies, management consultants, investment bankers and advisors, and certifiers such as public accountants.

Many such individuals have been enticed by the corporate managers. These collaborators rather protect their own financial and nonfinancial interests, and join the "management club." Instead of fulfilling their moral and fiduciary obligations, these team players prefer to do what the corporate managers want them to do. As "club" members, the collaborators ignore their responsibilities for closer oversight and supervision. They create a probusiness regulatory climate through deregulation, favorable legislation, and lack of law enforcement. They provide government assistance programs and financial bailouts. They approve of high executive compensation and justify unsound business plans. They build a regulatory facade. Above all, they serve at the pleasure of their corporate benefactors by pretending to represent the public interest.

All of this has become evident over the past few years in the extraordinary risk-taking by so many businesses—and financial institutions, in particular. The subprime crises and billions of dollars in government assistance are only just indicators of individual greed and strategic management failure.

Almost everybody who has the responsibility to encourage and ensure good business conduct seemingly serves as collaborator in one way or another. This is one of the reasons why executive compensations appear to be ever rising, and any attempt to stop them from rising is strongly opposed and often crushed by corporate leadership through business lobbying and financial means. Because of some public protest and government-imposed restrictions on executive compensations, many corporate leaders evidently have either turned down the offers of government bailouts or preferred to pay back the billions in bailout money that they received.

What we see is nothing but the pursuits for personal financial gains by the leadership in business, government, education, health care, and other social institutions.

Inequity at Work and Unhealthy Work Environment

The professional managers in large organizations remain financially well off. What trickles down below from the top in the management hierarchy, however, is not much in financial terms. The gap between the average worker and top management compensations has been rapidly widening over the past few decades. The CEOs, senior executives, and other top management team members in many big firms annually earn as much as 550 times the average employee salary in their organizations, compared to 40 to 50 times a decade or two earlier.

There is something wrong with this scenario. Otherwise, there would not be deteriorating employee morale and diminishing worker productivity. The quality of worker output is evident in ever-rising workplace accidents, product defects, medical errors, consumer complaints, employee absenteeism, non-work-related Web surfing at work, work pretense, and other forms of waste of productive hours. It is not unusual to find so many individuals pretending to work while accomplishing nothing worthwhile in doing their job. Most businesses are faced with the problems of people underperforming, because of their lack of employee drives and motivations.

The work environment has become unsatisfying. It is deteriorating fast and becoming less and less productive with the widening gaps in worker and management salaries and fringe benefits. Business suffers when there is a feeling of financial inequity at the operational levels, when there are no good incentives to work hard. Because the corporate managers fail in sharing financial rewards equitably, they crush work incentives and motivations.

When corporate engineers and scientists, sales people, operational managers and supervisors, and other hard-working employees—who actually contribute toward the development of successful products and markets and thus contribute in reality toward corporate profitability—get stepped over and overlooked and remain underappreciated and undercompensated, they become dissatisfied. They get demotivated and lose their productive drive. As soon as the situation becomes intolerable, they either quit their employment or begin to underperform. When this happens, business suffers from the loss or underutilization of valuable corporate resources. Sooner or later, the firm is in trouble.

No corporation could succeed without its core human skills or competencies at the operation levels that truly and directly contribute toward business success. Human productive motivations and efforts make the difference in the marketplace. When the corporate managers become indifferent and ignore employee motivations and incentives, they should be held accountable—not rewarded undeservingly. They should not earn high rewards for the cost-cuttings that lead to unhealthy and inequitable work environment. Even though corporate managers do play an important part by virtue of their decision-making responsibilities and powers, their contribution to corporate survival and growth is not substantial, not worthy of high compensations and financial rewards in relative terms.

Nonetheless, corporate managers manage to get the biggest piece of the reward pie. Even in times of losses in corporate revenues, markets, and incomes, the leaders continue to receive large compensations as if they deserve better retention payments than anybody else. The leadership or management contribution and indispensability are usually exaggerated.

There are many reasons why business fails or encounters life-threatening competitive challenges. But the root cause can be traced down to top corporate management or leadership. Indeed, it is difficult to justify the high compensations of most "professional" corporate managers.

Certainly, not many corporate managers are like Henry Ford (Ford Motors), Arthur Sloan (General Motors), Bill Gates (Microsoft), Sam Walton (Wal-Mart), Steve Jobs (Apple), Larry Page (Google), Sergey Brin (Google), Jeff Bezos (Amazon.com), and Tom Watson (IBM) —to name a few entrepreneurs, innovators, risk-takers, and creative managers. These well-known individuals' contributions and their impact on our lives remain indisputable; they have made themselves worthy of their fame and fortune.

Most professional corporate managers have not contributed nearly as much in reality. Yet, they wish for, and do earn, an obscene amount of undeserved money, claiming or believing falsely that they are entitled to big salaries, bonuses, and severance packages. The feeling of entitlement seemingly prevails even among some corporate leaders who have led their organizations toward the paths of disaster and ruin.

It is not difficult to imagine how the leaders of Enron, Bear Stearns, Merrill Lynch, and countless other big failed powerhouses thought of their compensations. They took advantage of their management positions to enrich themselves as well as their collaborators just days before their company's doomsday.

Understanding Management Fiduciary Failure

Even though the business failures are associated with a host of factors, both external as well as internal to the organization, they could be traced back largely to the leadership personal values, financial motivations, and unsound strategic management decisions and actions.

From the fiduciary perspectives of strategic management, disastrous business problems are the result of (1) failure to compete or (2) failure of "enviable success." "The failure to compete" is not hard to understand. This failure is a result of myopic and reactive corporate management behavior. Simply speaking, management fails when it has not been able to gain a competitive advantage in the marketplace in relation to price and/or quality, and when management cannot deliver satisfaction beyond customer expectations.

The second type of failure is quite the opposite of the failure to compete. "The failure of enviable success" is smaller in numbers and not very obvious, but not unheard of. When corporate management delivers too much customer satisfaction and earns extraordinary profits continuously over a period of time, its performance gets noticed with envy. The firm becomes a good investment target and may get acquired. As a business unit in a larger organization, the firm may lose its previous competitive edge from the fact it no longer enjoys its former structural informality, flexibility, and creativity. Eventually, the acquired firm may lose its competitive edge, its drive, identity, and survival.

Many successful and founding entrepreneurs resist the temptations of big financial takeover offers, mainly in order to maintain their own freedom and to preserve their organizations. Professional corporate managers, on the other hand, intentionally undertake short-term profit measures in order to have their business get acquired and, in the process, receive lucrative personal financial rewards, and possibly, better executive positions in the larger acquiring firm or somewhere else.

Whether planned or not, any fiduciary failure of corporate managers for personal gains is costly in the long run to its various stakeholders. Many such failures have become evident over the past several years. They are at the center of our contemporary business crisis characterized by slow economic growth, rising home foreclosures, rising unemployment and financial insecurity, diminishing personal savings and retirement benefits, and diminishing standards of living.

We will look at the nature of management failure in greater details in the next chapter and thereafter. We will further explore some key strategic management areas and issues and point out how and why corporate managers, along with their collaborators, contribute to competitive problems and business failure. We will also highlight the effectiveness of specific management decisions, policies, and actions as they relate to the formulation and implementation of business strategies and plans for long-term corporate survival and growth in the competitive global marketplace.

The chapters in the book represent a certain conceptual framework. Nonetheless, each chapter is designed so that the reader could read any one chapter at any time, in any order, without losing the essence of the subject matter.

Finally, it is important to understand that business failures are preventable. But to do so, first we must recognize that there is a serious leadership crisis in corporate America and elsewhere. Instead of focusing on or learning what makes a great leader, it is more important to understand the motivations and actions that are detrimental to business security and success in the long run. Once we acknowledge the problem and understand the consequences of leadership's fiduciary failure can we reverse the trends that have emerged over the past decade or two!

Today we are faced with numerous challenges of scarce economic resources and infinite social needs. We cannot meet our social challenges, such as global warming, successfully unless we understand and address the underlying problems of management shortcomings. As the book explores certain strategic management problems, it sheds light on some potential solutions, specifically in areas related to executive greed, compensation, and self-serving decision-making behavior.

Notes

1. Business leaders are interchangeably referred to as corporate leaders, executives, managers, management professionals, or professional managers throughout the book.

Most of these individuals hold graduate college degrees, such as MBA (Master of Business Administration), MHA (Master of Health Administration), MEd (Master of Education in Administration), and MPA (Master of Public Administration). Some of them also are professionally certified as CPA (Certified Public Accountant) or CFA (Certified Financial Analyst). Almost all of them belong to one or more professional, trade, or academic organizations, including American Management Association, American Marketing Association, and SAM (Society for Advancement of Management).

CHAPTER 2

Nature of Management Failure

Failure is, in a sense, the highway to success, inasmuch as every discovery of what is false leads us to seek earnestly after what is true, and every fresh experience points out some form of error which we shall afterwards carefully avoid.

John Keats

Extent and Quality of Strategic Efforts

Management failure is associated with a host of factors, some external and others internal to the organization. There are several personal, interpersonal, organizational, and external factors that can affect management performance in different areas.

One of the important tasks of corporate leaders is to analyze the dynamics of the external environment. This done, they must plan and act on the basis of the findings. The dynamic and competitive global marketplace makes strategic management extremely important for the organization's long-term security, survival, growth, and overall success. Not doing so, not identifying and anticipating the potential strategic opportunities and problems, is poor management. Not making and implementing effective plans and decisions is a failure of corporate managers. Misjudging the competitive strengths relative to those of the rivals puts the firm at a disadvantage; it is like choosing the wrong "battlefield" to fight.

Whether or not certain factors that contribute to failure are beyond management control does not matter. Lack of corporate control is irrelevant in the competitive marketplace. Almost all of the similar external factors confront and affect others—including the firm's direct and indirect competitors.

When the organization lacks a competitive edge because of its bad management planning, execution, and control in the past, its management has failed. When management fails to motivate employees or is unable to get them "on board" with the strategic plan, it has failed.

Lacking adequate contingency plans in case of "unexpected" results or circumstances is a sign of management failure. When the organization is not adequately prepared to handle "surprises," its leaders have done poor planning. Even national leaders have failed when they were not effectively prepared to deal with emerging problems. The Bush administration's failure was clearly evident in the developments in Iraq immediately after the rapid victory of the U.S. military invasion.

The use of effective management skills and judgments is much more essential in a constantly changing environment, in contrast to when the environment is fairly static and predictable. The global marketplace has never been very static or certain. Actions that are aimed at short-term results and are not part of the strategic plan for the future cannot guide the organization effectively in the long run.

Corporate leaders may find it difficult to analyze and anticipate events and factors outside their organization and over which they have no direct control. Nonetheless, they have to plan, act, and adapt to the changing competitive environment. When managers resist changes and fail to adapt, business suffers.

When corporate leaders fail to undertake what is important and required, when they fail to develop a learning, adaptive, and productive organizational culture to meet the competitive challenges of today and tomorrow and the distant future, they cannot accomplish the desired and expected long-term results and lead the organization to its ultimate destiny.

Often the organizational plans are dictated from the top and pushed down. This is not the ideal way to manage for most organizations. If the plans evolve from the bottom and move up, there is a ready acceptance across the way. The high levels of participation, involvement, and motivation make the plans easier to implement. No effective plans would succeed unless there is a willingness and readiness to accomplish the desired results throughout the organization.

The organization's structure, its delegation of decision-making and operational authorities and responsibilities, its policies and processes, its employment approaches and practices, its compensations and incentives systems, and other organizational features could affect how the plans are formulated and implemented. Performance measurement standards and actual evaluations too determine the quality of organizational efforts.

If at any stage in the process there is neglect or inadequacy, the expected results are difficult to accomplish. When lower levels in management show insufficient interest in cooperating and collaborating, the organization would not move forward with success, though business may not necessarily fail.

In the absence of effective strategic management, the organization may be able to compete for a while, but it would not be able to develop its long-term corporate core strengths and advantages that are essential to compete, prosper, and survive as an ongoing entity. The key point is that management must compete on the basis of the firm's strategic core competencies, not on the basis of past success, nor on the basis of what is expedient for quick gains.

Strategic management failure could threaten not only the organization's well-being but also its very survival. Bear Stearns, Merrill Lynch, Countrywide Financial, WorldCom, Chrysler, and General Motors are just a few recent examples of the consequence of strategic management failure—even in the large and well-established businesses.

Types of Marketplace Failures

To understand how business could ultimately fail, it is important to look at corporate managers' major fiduciary shortcomings. In terms of the organizational long-term survival and success perspectives, basically there are two types of management failure:

1. Failure to compete
2. Failure of, what may be referred to as, "enviable success"

As mentioned briefly in the previous chapter, "the failure to compete" is not hard to understand. It is everywhere in the marketplace. This failure is a result of myopic and reactive management behavior that attempts to respond to competitive strategies and tactics. Such behavior is usually unsuccessful because of the lack of leadership foresight and careful planning. Simply speaking, management fails when it has not been able to gain a competitive advantage in relation to price and/or quality and it cannot deliver satisfaction beyond customer expectations. When the business organization has a competitive disadvantage in any way, its management has failed unless it overcomes this problem rapidly and effectively.

The second type of failure, here referred to as "the failure of enviable success," is quite the opposite of the failure to compete. The failure of enviable success is not unheard of. Yet, it is not usually understood or looked upon as a failure. When this failure occurs and its adverse consequences are felt, it surprises many stakeholders and it makes them wonder why a formerly very successful firm happens to fail later on.

When management delivers too much customer satisfaction and the firm earns extraordinary profits continuously over a period of time, beyond a year or two or three, its performance gets noticed in the marketplace. The financial markets react positively with stock price appreciations. The firm is looked upon with envy in the business community. Its management policies and practices become the "benchmarking" standards and get adopted by other firms for competitive reasons. Moreover, the firm's consistent outstanding profit performance over some time makes the organization a good investment or takeover target. Subsequently, the firm may get acquired and lose its identity.

As a business unit in a larger organization, the acquired firm experiences different management realities. There are constraints imposed by the big organization's strategic objectives and/or management policies. The former flexibility, creativity, adaptability, and other advantageous characteristics may have been compromised or destroyed by the acquiring firm's size and its bureaucratic management approaches and practices. The result is the inability of the acquired firm to remain as competitive as in the past.

Since the firm encounters organizationally imposed conflicts and weaknesses, its previous competitive ability diminishes. Also, as competitors learn, imitate, and gain capacity to compete, the previously existing competitive advantages weaken. Because the acquired firm no longer enjoys its former competitive advantage, its future success is no longer certain.

The company's enviable success prior to its acquisition thus has devolved later into the failure of the first kind—the failure to compete with an edge over its rivals. In other words, the enviable business performance could lead to changes in ownership interests and objectives, as well as to changes in capabilities to compete in the marketplace. Too much success actually may turn out to be a serious disaster threatening the organization's very own existence in the long run.

Many successful business entrepreneurs and founders experience enviable results and do encounter takeover threats. But they frequently resist the temptations of huge financial gains in order to preserve their own corporate pride, identity, and independence, as well as their entrepreneurial creativity and flexibility.

Corporate "professional" managers, on the other hand, sometimes plan for best profit results over the short period in order to get their firm acquired. They know that their current performance would get noticed and it would enable them to earn higher compensation or better position after acquisition. To glorify their financial worth, they try to exceed their stockholders' and stock markets' expectations as quickly as possible through sales increases and cost-cutting.

The quality of management performance is typically measured on the basis of the corporate current or immediate profit results or the actual operational goal accomplishments. Any improvement in current profitability is viewed as success, especially if it exceeds market expectations. The discrepancy or difference between the actual results and expected results is used as the performance measure. If the actual outcome exceeds the expected planned results, everyone is happy with management. No one dares to complain.

Usually, there are no complaints about the "enviable" success—until the organization becomes an acquisition target and gets acquired, until its identity as an entity vanishes and its various stakeholders start to pay the actual price and suffer the adverse consequences of previous success. For instance, when the acquiring firm undertakes postacquisition consolidations of jobs, manufacturing facilities, and products, many employees and the community at large bear the price of layoffs and plant shutdowns; they are among the first victims of "enviable" success.

Corporate management professionals like the "transient" success and prefer to grab the available acquisition opportunities for quick personal financial rewards and/or possible upward career promotions.

It is not inconceivable that highly educated, experienced, and competent professional corporate managers may actually aim for, plan, formulate, and implement strategies for fast enviable results in order that their firm may be acquired at a later date for huge personal gains. They may intentionally undertake available short-term measures (cut costs, enhance revenues) to significantly improve the corporate profitability over a few quarters or years, leading their firms toward future failure.

Venture capitalists prefer and frequently contribute to management pursuits for fast profit-oriented objectives that are not in the best long-term interests of the firm and its other stakeholders.

Management fails when a business firm plans for and pursues a specific goal or outcome, irrespective of its implications in the long run for the organization. From the perspectives of stakeholders' long-run expectations and interests, momentary short-term results may be viewed as management failure if there has been a neglect of actual commitment and resource support for the development of long-term corporate competitive capabilities, strengths, and competencies for the future. When the firm ignores the development of markets, product, and core strengths, simply to improve its immediate profitability, its management is being shortsighted.

If corporate leaders have not undertaken needed efforts to develop better human resources, better technologies, better manufacturing processes and facilities, and conducive working conditions, any current corporate success could not be sustained in the long run. A business firm ultimately cannot hold on to or develop its markets if it cannot continue to offer the market-desired products, services, and prices.

Consequences of Strategic Failure

All management failures have consequences that range from insignificant business problems to total business disaster.

When a business firm does not generate a positive cash flow, the failure may be bearable as long as there is no substantial loss and operational cash or credit is available. But when the loss is substantial, when it uses up all the organization's cash reserve and credit lines, when there are not enough liquid assets and stock options to cover the organization's maturing debt, the problem becomes serious. The insolvency may force the firm into bankruptcy and out of business. This could happen when the firm experiences a deteriorating market share over a period of time and the cash flow begins to slow.

Management failure must be viewed in relation to the impact of managerial decisions, policies, plans, and actions—both in the short run and in the long run.

Usually corporate managers attempt to improve the cash flow immediately by planning and implementing a variety of quick cost-cutting and revenue-enhancing actions. The momentary gains on the surface may be impressive but could be deceiving. Yet they are used to evaluate and describe the management performance as "good." Only in the future looking backward, the impact of quick-fix measures is truly comprehended.

Normally, the term "failure" is not considered appropriate if the operational outcome is positive and improves the actual cash flow, even temporarily, because such an outcome appears to be favorable to the organization's health and well-being. As a matter of fact, the improved financial situation is regarded highly in favor of management; the decision-makers are rewarded with bonuses and enhanced compensation packages; they are showered with all sorts of financial and nonfinancial recognition for the job well done.

But if the corporate leaders fail to improve operational results as planned and expected, everybody clearly understands the management shortcoming; immediate actions follow to correct the situation. Usually, no effective corrective measures are taken quickly from the perspectives of corporate long-term problems and potential business disaster as a result of management shortcomings or failure.

The problem is that it is erroneous to describe management failure strictly as discrepancy between the actual and the planned or desired short-term outcomes. The extent of management goal accomplishments only in one (negative) direction and not in the opposite (positive) direction is not sufficient.

The short-term operational results, reflected as operational income (sales minus costs) or cash flow, beg issues such as future competitive organizational skills and products. The current profitability may not indicate whether or not the corporate leaders have strengthened or weakened the organizational ability to compete over a long period of time. Operational income or cash flow could depend on a number of factors, including the cash utilization and accounting (record-keeping and reporting) practices.

The short-term operational results are not good measures of long-term strategic decisions if they are not aligned with long-term goals.

Because the benefits or adverse consequences of certain management decisions in some distant future are inherently uncertain and invisible at present, there is too much reliance on the operational income and cash flow that can be comprehended and measured.

It is easy for corporate managers to maneuver and improve operational results fast, and they may do so for many reasons. Long-range strategic planning is much more difficult, and the resource allocation hard and painful for the uncertain distant future or markets.

The fact is there is no such thing as certainty about the external environment (except uncertainty, of course!).

More frequently than not, most corporate leaders delay or postpone long-range planning as much as possible and avoid unnecessary long-term thinking. When they do plan, they frequently do not support their plans with adequate resources. They do not prefer to take chances with costly activities like R&D and investments for new competencies, products or markets, which drain cash immediately but may or may not pay off in the future.

In times of general economic downturn or current corporate cash flow problems, corporate managers could justify holding back investments into the future, claiming to defend or improve their immediate company financial situation. Special or justifiable cases for decreasing resource commitment exist, but such decisions are detrimental for corporate well-being if rivals continue to improve their competitive strengths and capabilities in spite of the unpredictable future outcomes.

There is not much uncertainty or possibility of errors in accomplishing self-serving good operational results fast. Corporate managers can effectively indulge in some shuffling and allocate the resources to quickly improve business profitability so as to earn high executive compensations. They do not have to depend on uncertain future results in the dynamic marketplace.

When we consider a business organization as an ongoing entity, it becomes clear that we must view and define management success or failure in relation to the needs of the organization in the long run, not in terms of a year or two. We have to measure the quality of management performance in terms of its contribution or accomplishments toward the corporate security, growth, and overall success, in the future.

Question of Intent

At this point, let's ask some important questions: Is the absence of long-term orientation and focus in planning and implementation intentional or not intentional? Is the failure of strategic management avoidable? Is the strategic failure even planned?

In his book *Managing the Risks of Organizational Accidents*, James Reason talks about human failures as "errors" and "mistakes" and classifies them as "skill-based errors," "rule-based mistakes," and "knowledge-based mistakes." He suggests that the skill-based and knowledge-based mistakes are "unintended failure of 'execution.'" But the rule-based mistakes are not "unintended."

Because most corporate managers are well educated and highly experienced, they do possess the requisite management skills and knowledge, and they do understand the concepts, principles, or "rules" of prudent management.

When management decisions knowingly violate well-established or sound business "rules," their actions are certainly not "unintentional." Corporate leaders are well aware of their intentions and behaviors.

The problem is their intentions are more personal and less organizational. No doubt, this is detrimental to the organization in the long run—if not in the short run.

It is not difficult to conceive that most management decisions and actions are "deliberate," and frequently they are significant "deviations from safe operating procedures, standards, or rules." Often there are "routine violations," resulting in "cutting corners" and "shortcuts" in skilled tasks. It is not unusual to find that some corporate leaders even regard their certain violations as "necessary" (even though unethical or against the law) to get the job done and accomplish the desired results.

In most cases, managerial decisions and actions are deliberate and intentional. The adverse consequences of their neglect or misjudgments in long-range planning and execution are the undesirable outcomes that underscore nothing but leadership failure. Their shortcomings are the by-product of their self-serving intentions and rule violations for personal financial gains. This is not in the best corporate interest.

Factors Contributing to Management Failure

Another way to understand the nature of management failure is to analyze the extent to which each of the following factors contributes to business failure: managers or leaders as individual (the CEO, other corporate executive or manager, board director, or staff member), managers or leaders as leadership team or group member (board of directors, top management, committees, etc.), the organization itself and its internal environment, its own nature and complexity, and other environmental dynamics facing the organization.

There are several individual factors that affect the individual's personal motivations and his/her business decisions and actions. Among the specific personal traits and characteristics are financial and career needs and desires, as well as one's cognitive capabilities and limitations. Egoism can be a major factor. Operational-performance-based compensations and related career promotions are very strong personal drivers; indeed, the immediate corporate results could impact the individual's financial health, his/her financial and job security, and his/her progression on the career path.

The individual position in a corporate leadership or management team, committee, or group exposes him/her to an environment that represents directly or indirectly a variety of peer or group pressures. The individual security within the organization and the safety of his/her position in the team or group or in management could be affected and determined by the way the individual behaves, acts, reaches, and supports corporate decisions. As a team player, the individual may be compelled to support or endorse the decision or decisions of others with which he or she may not fully concur.

If the CEO, the team peers, and/or some superiors are focused on or committed to specific short-term actions and results, even if the aimed path is apparently detrimental to the organization's competitive advantages, strengths, and interests in the long run, there is not much room for personal or individual choice. Any contrary opinion or dissent could jeopardize one's own financial and professional well-being.

An individual is in a precarious situation when a forceful, superior leader or team tries to influence the decision-making process and, in one way or another, thrusts upon others an idea or decision or a behavioral code. Often specific group-thinking, values, and norms are pushed through, and the conformity is expected.

There may thus emerge individual decisions and actions as a united team effort or as a group consensus or approval. In case of failure, consequently, the responsibility may be shared and the blame could be spread and passed on to others in the group or to the group as a whole; no one solely could be held accountable and reprimanded, and no one has to bear the consequences or pay the price alone.

Sometimes the corporate CEO or his/her executives may have some strong preconceived notions before the planning and execution process begins. Then, the information search becomes narrower in scope, supporting evidence is sought out, few other alternatives and options are superficially considered and examined, opposing views are discouraged or blatantly crushed if necessary, the collective progress is closely monitored, and the final decisions and plans are cleverly skewed.

Team efforts have a tendency to ignore or overlook the "rules" of good management. For expediency and harmony, less than ideal choices may get adopted, putting the business organization at risk. Self-interests and organizational pressures tend to overwhelm and dominate the collective efforts. Hence, the best plans that could meet the challenges of the competitive marketplace are not considered and discarded in favor of some immediate fixes and self-serving goals. Because playing as part of the management "team" or "club" enhances individual safety, suboptimal choices occur, evolve, and get supported.

Management failure is an individual or collective phenomenon within the organization.

The organizational and external environmental characteristics and complexity too contribute to management failure because they affect the availability and quality of information essential for effective planning and execution. The dynamic features of both the internal and external environments make the utilization of relevant and pertinent information extremely difficult, affecting the quality of leadership decisions and actions. The inadequate information often forces the corporate leaders to think short term and focus on the operational results on a year-to-year basis, which have a higher probability of success, which seem more feasible or do-able, and which are beneficial right away at least to the individual himself or herself.

There is also another management justification for the short-term operational focus and planning: When the apparent or visible immediate negative or adverse consequences are considered and avoided, or at least minimized through specific measures, the chosen course of management actions presumably is viewed as adequate and very appropriate in light of the current market situation.

To sum it up, the individual, group, role-playing, organizational, and external factors (including competitors and their moves) affect the quality and availability of information, economic resources, decision-making processes and intents, and decisions themselves.

Essentially, what corporate leaders deliver is less than ideal or desirable in strategic planning and implementation. They do not deliver what most corporate stakeholders wish for and expect—that is, steer the organization right on the difficult and long path toward success and survival.

Strategic Shortcomings in Specific Functional Areas

From the perspectives of all those with a stake in the firm—stockholders or owners (particularly those with only few shares ownership), employees, suppliers, distributors, customers, and the society at –large, corporate CEOs and other top managers are not effectively fulfilling their fiduciary and moral obligations with their short-term business objectives and approaches. These leaders essentially fail in the following ways:

- To clearly recognize and define the organization's vision and destiny based on corporate ethical and moral values and aspirations
- To effectively analyze and identify long-term profitable and sustainable market potentials and opportunities based on corporate core competitive strengths, advantages, and capabilities

- To formulate effective long-term business strategies and plans
- To overcome ethnocentric attitudes and approaches, especially in the global markets, and adapt to market characteristics and needs
- To counteract competitors' strategic moves fast, forcefully, and proactively
- To develop effective corporate strategic goals through active participation of people across the organization and communicate such goals down the organizational hierarchy to employees
- To ensure strategic resource-planning and management related to the acquisition, development, allocation, and utilization of key resources—such as capital, R&D and proprietary assets, management information systems, human resources, manufacturing and service processes and physical facilities, suppliers and distributors, creditors and investors, financial advisors and management consultants, advertising agencies, public relations firms and lobbyists, sympathetic legislators and regulators, and public goodwill and support
- To enhance individual motivation, talent, work excellence, and productivity through effective business policies that are fair, equitable, and acceptable across the organization
- To decentralize decision-making and delegate appropriate authority and responsibility; in other words, failure to empower lower-level managers, supervisors, and workers in order to promote and enhance innovation and creativity
- To maintain and develop organizational worker knowledge and skill through education, training, job-rotations, etc.
- To develop flexible, adaptive, learning and participative organizational structure—business units, divisions, departments
- To put in place customer-relationship management
- To evolve stakeholders-relationship management

Overall, instead of thinking and planning strategically ahead and being proactive, corporate managers react when the serious competitive problems emerge in the marketplace.

Numerous recent business failures and events suggest that there is no clear management vision or long-term view as to where the business organization wants to be and where it wants to head. When there is no well-defined viewpoint and understanding with regard to the organizational mission or what "business" the organization really is in, the leadership lacks the right overall strategy. The business flounders, adds products and services haphazardly, fails to develop effective organizational processes and practices, fails to develop excellence in quality and individual moral conduct, and fails to develop beneficial supply as well as distribution channels. Ultimately, the organization is faced with disastrous results and possibly extinction.

In declining or expanding profitable marketing opportunities, management has failed when its rivals begin to gain a competitive edge and start threatening the firm's sales, its market share(s), its market position(s) and capabilities, its market power—and eventually its financial strength and survival.

Specifically, management failure occurs in several areas such as financial, marketing, human-resource, manufacturing and operations, procurement and supply chain, distribution channels, information collection and management, legal and ethical, and business innovations and developmental areas. We can further classify and categorize management failures as follows so that they become easier to comprehend, identify, and resolve:

Product development failure: This becomes evident when a competitor comes up with an innovative and superior product or service, abruptly changing the competitive position in the marketplace, gaining immediate competitive advantage and pausing threats. The corporate leaders are not prepared for such unexpected competitive moves. This situation results largely from the failure to invest in R&D and develop innovative technologies and better products as competitive strengths for advantage in the marketplace, or when current products fail to meet the fast-changing market demands.

Market analysis and forecast failure: The product development failure highlights failures in other marketing areas, including market research, analysis, and forecast. Often this failure is reflective of management orientations and views regarding long-range planning and forecasting. When the focus is on immediate results, there is no effective use of available relevant information or data outside or inside the organization. Business decisions are made on personal judgments, intuitions, and hunches, not on sound and pertinent market information. There may be inadequate investment in information collection and management, and in case the relevant information is collected and available through market research and other means, the management tendency may be to ignore it, largely not depend on it. Sometimes, information collection and analysis efforts are skewed to gain research validation and corporate board support for management's preconceived notions and plans. The result: inappropriate market analysis and forecasting.

Marketing-mix (4Ps) failure: The careful forecasting and planning failure leads to ineffective decisions related to product and service offerings, place locations and channels for product and service distributions, advertising and sales promotional efforts, and competitive and profitable pricing.

Quality maintenance and enhancement failure: When management fails to develop effective organizational processes, state-of-the-art technologies, good work environments and incentive systems, and essential work skills, the quality of products and services suffers. When the company's products are inferior in quality in the marketplace, they lose their values in the marketplace and the ability to compete diminishes.

Cost-reduction failure: This becomes evident when a competitor gains competitive advantage in product or service values in relation to quality versus cost. Price reductions by competitors as a result of cost-savings from process improvements and reengineering can put uninventive leaders at a disadvantage. Superficial price-cuts and cost-reduction measures, aimed at quick results without long-term benefits, could jeopardize corporate future growth, profitability, and possibly survival.

Facilities-related failure: When management has failed to modernize plant and equipment, or improve manufacturing and service facilities, increased efficiency or productivity is sacrificed. Shortcomings in this area become apparent when competitors are cutting costs and gaining through facility modernization or improvements.

Human-resource-related failure: This becomes evident when the organization fails to attract, motivate, and retain well-qualified, experienced, hard-working, and capable men and women. This is a result of ineffective organizational policies, inadequate organization structure and procedures, and inappropriate incentive systems.

Sudden or massive loss of key and productive individuals: Poor human-resource management becomes evident when the firm experiences a sudden or massive departure of key staff or human resources—such as professional or knowledge workers, qualified and highly experienced executives and operational managers, financial backers—at one time or over a short period in time. The departure may be voluntary or involuntary. Lay-offs and firings, early retirement, and self-motivated separations could lead to inevitable organizational failure, accidents, and malicious acts. Unfair or inflexible policies could cause loss of key productive resources.

Labor-union-related failure: Poor human-resource management becomes evident when corporate leaders have labor unions as adversaries, and cannot recruit and retain them as allies and collaborators. It is indicative of poor labor-management relationship. Consequently, there are union contracts with inflexible and restrictive employment terms and practices tying management discretion and choices. Misuse of managerial power, inadequate or unjust compensation and incentive systems, ineffective human relations, and unsatisfied workforce are fertile grounds for countervailing union force and strong labor movements.

Supply-chain-related failure: This becomes evident when, unexpectedly, management loses a major supplier or suppliers and when the cost of supplies seems significantly higher on a comparative basis. Lack of competitive advantage from the supply chain perspectives is indicative of inadequate or failed relationship with suppliers.

Distribution-related failure: This is evident when there are inadequate distribution channels, when it is difficult to find and retain efficient and cooperative distributors, and/or the relative cost of distribution is high. Frequently, poor channel planning and management is evident when the online or new channel possibilities are ignored.

Failure related to communication and promotion: This is evident in inappropriate budget for advertising, sales force, and other promotional communications and efforts. Often communication efforts are ineffective, in spite of adequate budgeting.

Failure related to political and regulatory environment: This management failure is a result of sudden or unanticipated political and legal environment over which management has had very little or no control. Unpredictable changes in the legal and political climate could alter competitive positions, making entry of extremely strong competitors possible or easier; or they could entirely block access to specific market or markets. Inability of management to predict or influence political and regulatory forces could jeopardize the firm's success and growth.

Industry-wide failure: This management failure occurs when the entire industry is threatened, unprepared, and unable to compete against substitute technologies and products that are lower in price, higher in quality, and better in delivering customer satisfaction. Sudden and unanticipated changes in customer characteristics, needs, and desires could destroy a particular industry and its traditional market. Industry-wide unethical or criminal conduct can destroy a particular industry. This failure is indicative of industry-wide cooperation and collaboration to protect its vital interests.

Failure related to ethics and morality: The fast pursuit of self-interests and financial gains at the top in management is reflective of decay in individual ethics and morals. When corporate managers fail to carry out their fiduciary duties effectively, business eventually suffers. Unless certain fast outcomes are critical for corporate immediate financial security and survival, they are ethically and morally unjustifiable—especially when they overlook, jeopardize, or do not meet the long-term interests and expectations of key stakeholders.

Failure related to leadership personal traits styles: This management failure has to do with individual or personal qualities—such as beliefs, attitudes, values, expectations and motivations, knowledge and skills, education and training, experiences, leadership philosophies as well as approaches and styles, mental flexibility, curiosity and desire to learn, willingness to adapt and change, aversion to risk and uncertainty, creativity and inventiveness, self-esteem and confidence, openness to differing viewpoints and perspectives, decision-making skills and practices, acceptance of responsibility, professional integrity, and overall, exercise of personal authority and power.

Failure related to capital or financial planning and management: When there are inadequate management decisions and plans concerning capital acquisition, allocation, utilization, and controls, management has failed. When the cost of capital exceeds its return, there is a leadership failure. The absence of good accounting records and controls is an indication of serious failure. When budgetary controls are arbitrarily used, there is an evidence of failure. When the required funds cannot be obtained in timely fashion and at reasonable cost, it is a management failure. Management failure is apparent when the capital structure including equity and debt liability is costly and extremely risky. When cash flows are inadequate to meet the forthcoming cash obligations, business is in trouble. When management cannot find operational capital, the company's survival is threatened. When bankruptcy or takeover by other firms remains the only option, there is a very serious management failure in the financial and accounting area.

Corporate-board-related failure: When the corporate board largely ignores its fiscal obligations to the stockholders and the community at large, corporate managers become more assertive, self-centered, act irresponsibly, and pursue goals for fast personal goals and financial benefits.

Failure related to stockholder and speculator expectations: When stockholders and speculators have expectations of fast and high quarterly or annual returns on investments and expect immediate improvements in operational outcomes and stock price appreciations, pressures on management are enormous, and corporate managers may have limited choices. Changing expectations of stockholders and others have to be addressed. When both small and large investors expect quick returns on their investments, corporate managers may have to focus on short-term results, and ignore the development of corporate core competencies and capital investments for success in the long run.

Competition-related failure: Overall failure to understand the competitive strengths and moves of rivals and respond forcefully and effectively to competition, in timely fashion, in order to maintain and enhance the market share and position is a failure of management.

Many of these organizational and industry-wide failures have become clearly evident over the past decade or two. The recent disasters of certain real-estate lending practices and investment instruments suggest the management shortcomings of the financial institutions and capital markets worldwide. The competitive and financial problems facing the U.S. automobile companies highlight too many specific leadership failures at both the corporate and industry levels.

In the categories above, there is some apparent overlapping. One could certainly expand the list. The classification or categorization of management failures is intended to explain and clarify how or where corporate managers fail in different strategic areas. In the chapters to follow, we further examine certain leadership realities and business situations.

PART II

Role of Management Leadership: Realities and Myths

CHAPTER 3

Realities of Leadership Contribution

To understand where, how, and why the corporate leadership fails, it is important to look at the contribution of business administrators toward the corporate security, survival, and growth. We have to examine the quality of management performance in terms of what is expected of corporate leaders and what they actually deliver as their achievements in the dynamic, competitive, and global marketplace. If the corporate board of directors, CEOs, and other top managers do not effectively carry out their roles and meet the expectations, essentially they have failed, and they should be held accountable for their leadership shortcomings.

The extent of business failures and disasters in recent years clearly points out the quality of leadership performance. There is plenty of evidence that leaders in many big businesses and financial institutions are performing well below the expectations. Many corporate CEOs and other top executives have been convicted of wrongdoing, and several are under judicial investigations for legal and unethical violations. The magnitude of the U.S. government bailouts and other actions required for Bear Stearns, Merrill Lynch, Countrywide Financial, AIG, General Motors, and others is indicative of business management failure. The situation in some other countries is not much different. The corporate world is faced with a serious leadership crisis.

Leadership Responsibilities and Obligations

In light of the social and economic challenges facing the world today, it is imperative that corporate leaders effectively fulfill their fiduciary duties. All business leaders have certain moral and ethical responsibilities as well as obligations. All stakeholders expect their corporate managers to lead the organization toward its aspirations and accomplish the ultimate long-term goals and objectives. Thus, the most important responsibility of corporate managers is to lead the organization productively and profitably in order to ensure its survival and success over the years to come, and, preferably, satisfy the stakeholders beyond their expectations.

The leadership's primary obligation certainly is to satisfy the business owners (stockholders) and protect their capital and other long-term financial interests. In addition, though, corporate leaders have obligations to satisfy the needs and expectations of their customers, employees, creditors, suppliers, distributors, and the community at large. While fulfilling their duties, business leaders are expected furthermore to behave and act morally and ethically and, more importantly, lawfully. Good business conduct is expected in a free and democratic society in order to preserve the fair and uncorrupt judicial systems.

The roles and contributions of business leaders are important for the social welfare and well-being of society. When the business leadership fails, everyone suffers the consequences one way or another. The society at large expects all business leaders to perform well to the best of their abilities in everyone's interests.

In essence, thus, at least implicitly, corporate CEOs and other policy-makers do have certain fiduciary duties and obligations that require them to effectively acquire and manage the precious and scarce economic resources to meet a variety of social and economic needs. It is the leaders' moral responsibility to enhance the productivity of limited physical and human resources, to serve not only their own personal interests but also the broader interests of their stakeholders. Corporate managers must utilize and develop efficient and effective business processes, technologies, and facilities; beneficial social and financial relationships; and productive and cooperative human or individual efforts to serve different interests.

To lead the organization right, corporate leaders have to utilize a variety of sound business strategies, policies, and practices to accomplish the set objectives and keep the organization profitable and moving forward. They have to acquire or develop, and use essential human skills to carry out the required tasks. They need and must have skilled, qualified, and highly motivated people. Effective management of human resources is indispensable within the organization, as well as throughout the associated or allied entities, including the distribution and supply chains.

In order to manage and improve the economic efficiency and effectiveness of scarce economic resources, business leaders have obligations specifically to undertake good conduct, make the right decisions, and facilitate the productivity and profitability. The following list highlights some key leadership features, responsibilities, and obligations:

1. Corporate board directors and executives first represent the stockholders, who have given them appropriate discretionary authority and power to acquire and utilize necessary resources to reach the desired long-term business results.
2. The primary obligation of business administrators or managers is to preserve the organization's capital and ensure its survival. After that come long-term profitability and growth. Corporate management must effectively balance business security and prosperity and satisfy the interests of all stakeholders.
3. Organizational interests must supersede all other interests—including individual or personal interests.

4. Corporate managers must remain competitive and successful in the long run by developing organizational core strengths and advantages—meaning competencies—that would enable the business to maintain and enhance sales revenues and market shares with the right products and services at the right prices. While short-term profits are desirable, they cannot and should not endanger the corporate security and competitive vitality.

5. Corporate activities have to be lawful, fair, moral, and ethical. Leaders have the responsibilities to undertake good and socially justifiable business conduct reflective of the society's overall economic, social, and cultural values.

6. The corporate board of directors represents and speaks for the owners or shareholders, who elect the directors. The board has the ultimate authority, power, and responsibility to protect the corporate long-term interests. The board's main responsibility is to guide the corporate CEO and other executives and provide adequate supervision and control over them to ensure good executive performance and conduct.

7. The corporate system considers the board's role and its contribution very vital for business survival and success. Not unlike corporate executives, the board has the fiduciary duties and obligations. Together with the corporate executives, the directors bear the leadership responsibilities for any business shortcomings and failures.

Realities of Leadership Performance

As reported in various business newspapers, television broadcasts, and magazines, there are countless business problems and disasters. What is expected of corporate managers is not delivered. This is a reality in many major business firms and industries. The management performance toward business survival and success has been very disappointing over the past several years. Failures to effectively compete are evident in almost all strategic business areas. It is not uncommon to observe that most long-range business objectives are not being met profitably, and resource potentials are not being realized. More often than not, corporate administrators are not fulfilling the expectations of most of their stakeholders.

Over the past decade or two, the level of stakeholders' satisfaction with corporate management has been steadily declining. There have been huge numbers of business bankruptcies, takeovers, permanent door-closings, and income and job losses—not to mention the scandals of political corruption, illegal leadership conduct, and imprisonment. The subprime crisis, dot-com bubble, Enron, large bank and S&L failures, stock market losses, and government bailouts underscore the quality of leadership performance. What takes place in the marketplace is less than sound or ethical management decision-making.

All the contemporary problems are the results of the corporate managers' efforts toward maximizing corporate profits quickly in any possible way, legal or not. CEOs and their lieutenants choose imprudent shortcuts for fast operational gains under the "watchful" eyes and with approvals of their board directors.

Because the tactics are usually not aligned with any long-term competitive goals, strategies, plans, and policies, corporate managers put their firms in peril.

Evidently, there is not much strategic or long-term leadership thinking. Can you imagine the big financial institutions trying to justify their recent disastrous real estate lending practices or investment instruments on the strategic grounds, or General Motors (GM) and Chrysler defending their past neglect in investments for fuel-efficient auto engine research and technologies? It is clear that there was very little or no thought or concern about the long-term consequences of their actions (or lack of them) at the highest management level.

The unfortunate reality is that instead of developing competitive strengths and advantages for the future, corporate managers weaken their organization's capabilities in fast pursuit of their revenue enhancements and cost-cutting measures. They put their firms on the path of business disasters. The short-term leadership focus and behavior are not healthy for the corporate well-being in the years to come. Any temporary gains in sales, cost reductions, cash flows, and profits cannot be construed as beneficial if the quick fixes have prevented the firm from offering the desired products and services at the right prices in the marketplace later on, if the operational actions have compromised most stakeholders' long-term interests and expectations, and/or if the results are accomplished through some immoral or unlawful business conduct.

There is apparent disregard or lack of serious management concern for the long-term consequences of such actions as cuts in R&D, employee layoff, reduction in operational budgets, cuts in capital investments for production and service facilities, application of inferior supplies and materials, neglect of equipment maintenance and repairs, freezing of employee salaries, elimination of employee merit raises, offering of fewer or inappropriate products and services, and reduction in product and market developmental efforts.

The deteriorating corporate financial and market situations are evident in the prevailing dissatisfaction with the corporate management policies and practices. Workers are unhappy with the work environment created by the management's operational cost-cutting moves. Labor-management problems are at a very high level in years. Employees do not seem to perform to their full potentials, because of lack of financial incentives. Work-related accidents and improper work behaviors are high. Customers too are dissatisfied with the rising prices, product defects, and declining quality. The business need for government assistance and bailouts has angered the public at large. The approval of executive conduct is almost at an all-time low. The disappointment with corporate leaders is all around us, a reality reflective of management performance.

The management tendency for quick fixes to improve profitability fast has been stronger than the corporate leadership would prefer to admit.

Underlying Motivations

The short-oriented leadership behavior is not difficult to comprehend. It is driven by the management's self-serving motivations—desires for personal financial gains. Most corporate managers strive to maximize their own financial gains through the fast-result-based actions in their corporate operations. Their salaries, bonuses, severance packages, and other benefits are very closely tied to immediate corporate accomplishments in sales revenues and cost reductions. Executive compensations are strong motivators and drivers. Basically, corporate managers have no personal reasons or desires to think of or focus on the distant future. Because of their own personal financial interests and job security, corporate managers do not mind disregarding the impact of their policies and practices for their business in the future.

In 2009, because of the level of serious financial problems in major corporations and financial institutions, executive compensation was front-page business news and headlines several times, and the unreasonable compensation amounts in the millions came under closer public scrutiny.

The reality is that most corporate executives earn high compensations. The compensation systems and practices encourage decisions-makers to remain short term in outlook and orientation. The current corporate merit-based systems reward corporate CEOs, board directors, and others at the top largely for quick fixes in business operation without any regard for their consequences in the future; there is no consideration as to what if these gains later on turn out to be temporary, unsustainable, and even dangerous to the corporate competitive capability in the marketplace—and thus to corporate security and growth over a longer time period. Clearly, the performance-measurement criteria for executive compensation are not appropriate and aligned to the executive fiduciary duties and obligations and to the interests and expectations of all other stakeholders.

Most corporate compensation systems use operational outcomes as performance measures to hire, retain, reward, and fire corporate leaders. Operational or current corporate results are widely used measures to evaluate the quality of leadership performance. So, in reality, executives are rewarded or fired on the basis of their immediate results, while they are expected to contribute significantly toward the development of organization's competitive products and better technical and human skills and competencies. In other words, the performance measures or criteria discourage corporate decision-makers to look beyond the current year or two.

In retrospect, the huge rewards to the former U.S. auto leaders indeed look unjustifiable. These individuals weakened their companies by their neglect; they failed to invest in energy-efficient technologies. Their lack of strategic decisions in the past is now threatening the very survival of their firms. At present, many corporations are faced with similar predicaments, due to their management's past failures. The executives who put their organization in jeopardy are long gone, taking with them their big financial rewards at the time for cutting corners.

The unfortunate fact is, in spite of the lessons of the past economic crises and business disasters, the executive compensation systems have not changed much. As a result, the leadership tendency has not changed much over the years. When President Obama suggested restraints on executive compensation and, particularly, when his administration imposed certain compensation restrictions on some government–bailed out firms, there was considerable resistance and protest at the corporate headquarters. In recent years, it seems that the management tendency for quick business fixes by any means for personal gains has strengthened.

The primary reason for unsatisfactory leadership performance undoubtedly is executive greed. The sad fact is, we pay corporate leaders primarily on the short-term basis to accomplish long-term results. The leadership role importance and expected contribution are not truly reflected in or tied to the appropriate compensation criteria.

This is briefly why and what corporate leaders deliver in terms of business success and failure. What they contribute are momentary but unsustainable operation results and profits—and, in the process, they weaken their organization and its competitive capabilities in the marketplace for years to come. We will further examine this problem of compensation in Chapter 5.

Question of Changing Stockholders' Expectations

One may attempt to justify the short-term focus on the ground that stockholders today are different from their predecessors, and that they want fast corporate results so that their stock prices would quickly rise. This may appear to be a good reason—at least on the surface. But it is not largely true.

Many of today's shareholders, large and small, indeed are short-term investors and speculators. They are much more interested in daily, weekly, and quarterly stock price increases than in a long and steady stream of dividend incomes year after year. These young and professional individuals are not worried about their old age. Confident in their abilities, they believe that they can manage their own money, savings, and retirement funds much better than the professional financial managers. Not averse to risk, these shareholders prefer to move impatiently fast on the track to riches. Oblivious to the lessons of the dot-com bubble and the S&L scandal, they are speculators at best and gamblers at worst. The subprime bubble may have been a costly lesson for them and a waking call; the situation may turn around the tide and cool the speculative fever. In any case, the number of shareholders who are interested in the immediate corporate results is extremely small.

Most other shareholders are unlike this minority of speculators with short-time framework. The vast majority would prefer fast improvements in corporate profits, but not at the expense of corporate long-time financial well-being and growth. There are millions of stockholders who prefer satisfactory returns over a long period of time. Their time frame is years in length. As long as the organization is secure, continues to show a steady and "reasonable" growth in corporate profitability, and remains competitive, these long-term investors are content. Instead of uncertainty and unpredictability of the volatile stock prices, they would rather choose dependable annual dividend incomes, slow stock price appreciations, and fair returns on their investment over the years.

Almost all institutional stock investors (insurance companies, retirement fund managers, etc.), corporate founders and their families with considerable ownership interests, large individual long-term investors, employees and managers with company stock ownership, millions of middle-aged and older shareholders, as well as others who are averse to risk, and countless other small investors are not preoccupied with quick returns. They prefer and expect corporate managers to perform well to enhance their long-term financial interests and other objectives.

Not unlike venture capitalists, some managers of institutional shareholders aim for fast personal financial gains. These individuals may exert pressure and sometimes even collaborate with corporate managers for self-enrichment. Such self-serving behavior is contrary to the institutional basic investment objectives; it can be viewed as in violation of the investing manager's fiduciary duties and obligations unless the funds are being managed specifically for the speculative returns.

While large shareholders could affect the corporate management behavior in some way, millions of small stockholders have very little or no influence. As a result, small investors remain unrepresented in top management. In many large corporations with a huge number of small shareholders worldwide, there is nobody to represent these small investors and their interests forcefully. Most corporate board directors and managers tend to disregard the millions of small shareholders, and they act as if they are accountable to no one except to one another; they have zero interest in the firm, except using the firm for self-enrichment. For their own financial gains, these corporate leaders pursue their own agenda, become collaborators, and overlook the best interests and expectations of their corporate shareholders, employees, customers, and other stakeholders.

In his 2009 inaugural address, U.S. President Barrack Obama identified executive greed, irresponsibility, and unwillingness to make and live by hard decisions as a major business problem. His presidency may have slowed down the self-serving, golden era of the professional manager. But, if the past is any guide, that does not mean the end of money-grabbing by the people in position of power at the top in corporations. Executive greed may bring in another crisis, much sooner than later.

Internal Cooperation and Collaboration

While corporate leaders continue to strive for self-enrichment, they ignore the needs and expectations of other individuals at different levels in the organization. They fail to create conducive working conditions that generate effective and productive efforts and contribution from the entire organization, from everyone starting at the top and then down the management hierarchy.

For business growth and success over time, the organization needs a cooperative and collaborative spirit as well as efforts at all levels. In reality, though, it does not get it because of the quality of organizational leadership. The security of business depends upon the success-oriented motivation and performance everywhere throughout the organization; it takes the collaboration and cooperation of almost everyone at all levels for business success. When the leadership under-takes layoffs, carrot-and-stick approaches, threatening tactics and pressures, disproportionate reward-sharing schemes (many for leaders and relatively few for others), and other maneuvers for fast and better operational profits, ultimately there emerges a serious worker morale problem.

When corporate leaders cause the work environment to deteriorate, people below become disenchanted and less committed to organizational success. Their creativity and productivity diminish. Process and operational inventiveness and improvements are fewer in numbers, and work efficiency is far below its potential. Productivity gains become far from reality. The desired results become almost impossible to achieve. The low morale could even threaten the organization, its future survival and success. The leadership emphasis on quick fixes turns out to be nothing but the management contribution toward the possibility of eventual business failure.

Strategic Decision-Making

Sound strategic business decisions are important for the organization's long-term competitive strengths and overall health. When corporate leaders make their decisions on the basis of careful environmental scanning and audit of business strengths and limitations, they tend to raise the productivity of the firm's human and physical resources. Effective strategic decisions improve the organization's working environment and conditions, employee morale and performance, cost structure, product and service quality, sales revenues and market shares, cash flows, profitability and security, incomes and fringe benefits for employees and managers, cash dividends, and stock prices. In contrast, inappropriate decision-making affects almost everything adversely.

The absence of good strategic decisions is evident in hundreds of recently reported business cases and events. U.S. automobile firms and financial institutions are not odd examples or unusual cases. Just look at other U.S. industries and their rapidly declining global competitive vitality! Professional business managers talk about strategic management, but they do not practice it. They play a self-serving game, endangering their organizations with their narrow focus and risky behavior. In reality, they obstruct and hamper the competitive effort and progress with their decisions and choices, and deliver much less than what is possible.

Although sound decisions are hard to make and not easy to implement, professional corporate managers should be able to do their job effectively. They have the adequate education, experience, and training. They do have requisite qualifications and skills to meet their obligations. Nonetheless, corporate CEOs and other top managers do not excel in their leadership roles, because of their fast pursuit of what they evidently believe are their entitlements. Their self-serving motivations prevent them from formulating and implementing effective strategic plans. This is the root cause of business difficulties.

Besides personal factors, the availability of information and other extraneous factors affect the quality of strategic business decisions and plans. Almost the same factors are encountered in the marketplace by the competitors and others, both within and outside a specific industry, who manage to remain strong and prosper over a long period of time with their strategic commitment and decision-making. More than anything else, the lack of long-term thinking and orientation impedes the process of strategic management.

For management decision-making, information available in the organization is usually fragmentary and often distorted. Sources of information or channels of communications may filter, block, or affect the quality of essential information in some way. Sometimes information is overly abundant, causing confusion and delays. Nevertheless, if the adequate information is available to the decision-maker, it does not guarantee that the right motivations would be there to make the correct decisions.

In addition to the relevant, accurate, and timely information, every decision depends upon the individual decision-maker—specifically, his/her decision-making skills, motivations, and values. Individual psychological, social, and cultural characteristics would affect personal perspectives and judgments.

Conflicts may or do exist between organizational and individual interests, and they do lead to the suboptimization of decisions. From the business perspectives, if the values of the decision-maker are not compatible or aligned with the needs of his or her organization and with its technical, human, and financial capabilities, decisions would tend to be irrational, suboptimal, and not in the best interests of the organization. If workers are not part of the decision-making process, or if they are not content with the existing work incentives and conditions, they may withhold vital information necessary for sound decisions. Disgruntled workers may even sabotage the leadership efforts. Imagine what financial harm a frustrated medical technologist could do to a hospital, in liability terms, with his/her intentional medical errors causing patient fatalities!

The organization suffers in case the ability and judgment of the individual making the decisions are affected by his/her lack of proper motivation, education, training, and experience. When the CEO or another executive employs unqualified relatives and friends for important corporate positions, the organization pays the price. When the "loyal" management consultants, financial advisors, and certified public accountants are retained simply as "rubber stamp" for support and approval of management actions and no other reasons, strategic decisions and plans are less than optimal, and the business firm suffers.

Failure of decision-makers occurs in many different personal ways. Selfish individual interests distort judgments, create conflicts, and fail to serve the organization with the most ideal strategic decisions and approaches. The organization's performance is dependent on its management's motivations and capabilities. Since management is an organizational phenomenon, its failure would be reflected in its organizational performance. The failure would show up gradually and in a creeping way, deteriorating the organization's ability to compete and its ability to serve the interests of its shareowners, customers, employees, and other stakeholders. The inability or unwillingness of management to formulate and implement the right business strategies and practices is largely a personal or individual phenomenon.

Many factors could contribute to business success and failure that may not be within the leadership's control. But the uncontrollable situations should not dissuade executives from sincerely and carefully anticipating and preparing for the future. With proactive behavior and genuine motivations, corporate leaders could avert the competitive pressures and take advantage of the business opportunities and overcome the problems. All it takes is the "right" desire. After that the "right" thinking, drive, planning, and decision-making will follow.

The development of current executive compensation systems and practices should be viewed as decay in the corporate world. It breeds personal greed in business leadership and saps the individual integrity and judgment at the highest corporate level. Selfish personal reasons are detrimental to the organization's long-term business progress. For personal financial gains, capable and knowledgeable corporate policy-makers degrade themselves and short-change their organizations. Their personal reasons cloud their good intentions. Their moral and fiduciary failure shows up in business disasters.

Corporate leaders are very clever and careful in enhancing their own personal interests and management credibility. In collusion with others in positions of influence and power, they create a false impression or illusion of confidence, success, and indestructibility. In reality, though, they irreversibly weaken the pillars of marketplace strengths inside the organization. There is plenty of evidence around. Otherwise, there would not be so many business problems and failures.

As the business realities suggest, the leadership contribution is viewed, measured, and rewarded on the basis of wrong premises or assumptions. The false premises propagate the myths about the importance of corporate leadership. Basically, corporate managers are self-serving professionals—and nothing else. Their contributions are not noteworthy. Most of them are not exceptional leaders. Nor are they worthy of high compensations. The fact is, the corporate leadership is solely responsible for most business problems and failures because of the risky management decisions and behaviors. While everyone else pays the price of management failures, the responsible leaders remain financially protected. When a corporation fails, the CEO and other managers walk away with lucrative severance packages and benefits. Their failures get rewarded in some way.

What corporate managers have is a win-win situation. They win because they use their corporate positions and powers to appoint the "right" individuals at the "right" posts. Afterwards, along with others, they keep securing and enhancing their mutual financial interests. Corporate board directors, for instance, get nominated by the CEO or one of his/her executive team members. Because the board election is heavily influenced by the corporate managers, the quality of governance by the board gets compromised. Not unlike corporate executives, the board directors get heavily compensated and earn good money for their few hours of part-time work. There is no reason for the board director to dissatisfy the executive(s) who nominated him or her. Cross-memberships on the corporate boards are a modern-day phenomenon. Such practices perhaps have evolved to ensure support and collaboration both inside and outside the organization. Together, as college fraternity brothers and sisters or management club members, they could enhance mutual benefits.

When a corporate CEO or other top manager eventually is forced to leave as the price of serious business shortcomings, he or she walks away with huge separation financial and other benefits, and the individual has no problems in finding another high management position elsewhere if so desired. There are plenty of powerful friends ready to help out. This is all part of the contemporary win-win game.

To cure this economic "disease," it is important to find the "right" remedies. Otherwise, the competitive vitality, strength, and creativity of business will continue to be compromised—mainly because of executive greed. The fact is that, in pursuit of their own high financial compensation rewards, corporate managers waste our scarce economic resources and fail to solve our serious economic and social problems. This is the sad reality of leadership contribution!

Summarized below are some key features of corporate leadership and its contribution:

1. The quality of corporate leadership over the past several years is evident in the numbers of business bankruptcies, consolidations, forced sell-outs, investment and capital write-downs, permanent closings of business doors, governmental bailouts of corporations and banks, and other reported business events in the United States and elsewhere.

2. The leadership contribution problem is rooted in the way the corporate leaders are nominated, elected, hired, retained, compensated, promoted, and/or fired.

3. Because corporate executive compensations (salaries, fringe benefits, performance bonus, severance payments, and other rewards) and job security depend on the firm's immediate operational results, they affect the leadership orientations, focuses, and actions. The shortsighted behavior is the result of corporate management performance measures.

4. For their own personal financial gains, corporate leaders tend to focus on current business operational problems and aim to quickly improve corporate sales revenues and cut costs. Their operational preoccupation ignores the future competitive challenges of the dynamic global marketplace, overlooks the development of products and markets, underemphasizes investments in technology and human competencies, and overall threatens corporate security and successful growth.

5. The neglect in the formulation and implementation of strategic plans to stay ahead of competition is a failure of management's fiduciary responsibilities and obligations.

6. Even though corporate board directors and top executives are capable individuals, they lack personal long-term financial motivations to think of years ahead, plan carefully, and fulfill their fiduciary obligations and duties effectively.

7. From the long-term corporate perspectives, the business practice of executive compensation and retention is incompatible with what is expected of executive contribution.

8. Management shortcomings creep up and develop slowly over a period of time, and emerge as serious business inadequacies. The surfaced problems are confronting a different set of leaders who had nothing to do with them.

9. Lack of long-term management concern is simply the result of the fact that professional corporate managers have no major stock ownership or stake in the corporate welfare and well-being in the years beyond their tenures.

10. The average corporate CEO's tenure tends to be shorter, less than a decade on average. Even a slight drop in the corporate profitability over a year or two could jeopardize the position of the CEO and his/her associates. To protect their positions, corporate leaders tend to focus on and implement business tactics and tricks for quick operational improvements that may turn out to be disastrous for the organization in the long run.

11. There are numerous misconceptions concerning the role and contribution of corporate leadership. Prevailing perceptions and beliefs about organizational leadership do not reflect the realities of the business world.

In the next chapter, we will briefly look at some myths about leadership.

In conclusion, corporate leaders are not performing well in meeting their organization's serious market challenges. In not-for-profit organizations, too, management failure is evident in various forms. Government is not immune from the leadership failure. Self-serving motivations of political leaders, hospital administrators, school administrators, and other institutional heads are evident all around us.

The failure of organizational leaders is no longer based on lack of knowledge or capability. Rather, it is a result of personal greed. Self-serving motivations of leadership weaken the social fibers, erode the moral foundations, and waste the scarce and precious economic resources. Today, what we have is an unhealthy organizational leadership phenomenon. Selfish interests corrupt personal values and philosophies, perceptions and beliefs, orientations and focuses, attitudes and decisions, and good moral conduct. Business leadership motivations affect the corporate goals and strategies, plans and policies, practices and actions, and overall accomplishments for the stakeholders.

As leaders fail, the most ideal and enlightened competitive response in the marketplace remains far from reality—essentially inadequate, absent, or blocked. The recent economic crises in the United States are the contribution of business leaders. This is the corporate world reality!

CHAPTER 4

Leadership Myths

When the actual or real contribution of business leaders is examined closely, it becomes clear that contrary to most widely held beliefs, the CEO and other top managers contribute little to justify their exuberant compensations. Corporate success depends on human motivations and efforts all across the organization, not on just one or few individuals at the top. On the other hand, an unhealthy environment, created by the self-serving leadership policies and practices, affects productivity and leads to serious competitive problems in the marketplace. So when business encounters a threatening situation or complete failure, it is usually a management creation. This reality is not widely recognized. This nonrealization creates a multitude of myths about leadership.

Propagation of Myths

In countless leadership studies, the principal focus is on successful businesses and their leaders—especially their CEOs. The researchers analyze specific personal attributes of CEOs, such as religious belief or work habits, and based on the study's limited scope and sample, they suggest the importance of some traits for business success. Dozens of books similarly magnify personal attributes of corporate managers for business security, profitability, and growths in market shares and stock values. Some writers go further and imply that some well-known leaders are absolutely indispensable; without them, their organizations could not continue to prosper or survive.

These assertions are far from the truth. The business realities suggest that it takes an entire organization, a "village," to accomplish the aimed results. As pointed out by management guru Peter Drucker a long time ago, management is getting things done through people. His message is simple. No organization can flourish without the collaboration and cooperation throughout. Corporate CEOs and other leaders can plan for and influence the outcomes, but they are not the sole determinants of achievements. Leadership visions, policies, and practices can guide and provide essential resources. However, unless the people below have the desire to put forward their best productive efforts, satisfactory results become highly improbable. We discussed some of these points in the preceding pages.

In the literature, frequently, there is mention of visionary business leaders. A personal vision at the top could lead and contribute to business success. However, the vision's eventual success depends on the quality of organizational resources and efforts. We do not read enough that perhaps somebody else in the organization had the vision and shared it, and that the corporate head served only as a facilitator but took all the undeserved credit and millions in executive compensation. Business publications do not seem anxious to acknowledge the reality that it takes more than leadership to reach the corporate goals and desired destiny.

Leadership Self-Interest in "Untruths"

Most corporate boardrooms know the truth about their "real" importance and worth. They understand the fallacy of research premises and popular misconceptions. It is not in their best interest to let the truth be known. They have no desire to shatter the prevailing management "delusion." There is no need to crush the myths that serve them well. Their vested interest lies in furthering one myth after another, advancing the importance of their contribution at the top. As long as they can maintain the illusion regarding their worthiness, they can continue to earn high retention and performance rewards. How else can they justify their relatively outstanding salaries, money, or stock bonuses and huge severance packages—such as widely publicized Exxon Mobil Chief's $350 million plus in personal benefit in the year 2006?

In many large corporations, "professional" managers earn over 500 times as much in compensation as the average individual earns in his/her organizations. These managers are rewarded even when their corporate profits are way down or their business survival is uncertain due to the financial losses from their ineffective and poor management policies.

In 2008, for instance, corporate stocks were in downfall, losing billions and billions for their investors. Nonetheless, there was no slump in CEO compensations. Fortune's top 20 of 500 corporate executives were paid twice their 2006 earnings. In 2007, Sovereign Bancorp Inc.'s CEO received a 285 percent increase in his compensations; just a year later, his company lost more than 55 percent of its stock value. Not unlike him, most corporate executives continued to receive millions in compensation at the time many families were losing their homes in mortgage foreclosures and bank loans were turning sour.

Separating Myths from Realities

The fact is, corporate leaders do not deserve to be paid much more than anybody else in the organization. Corporate success does not directly depend on its leaders unless they are entrepreneurs or inventors, in the true sense of these terms, risking their lifetime savings and expending their creative energy, time, and effort 24/7, day in and out for years, with no guarantee of financial rewards. Although most management professionals have made no major contribution toward the corporate results, they earn high, undeserved compensation, claiming or believing that they are indispensable for success.

It would be wrong to say that most corporate leaders do not deserve some credit for their organizational success. Indeed, they do, not because they do something outstanding, but because of what they do *not* do. Many managers do not guide their organization toward the path of business disasters. They do not make wrong decisions concerning such areas as R&D, employee retention and wages, product or service elimination, product quality, sales promotions and advertising, and facility maintenance. They may not competitively advance their firms, but they do not at least harm them by their selfish cost maneuvers.

What we tend to identify as desired leadership attributes, and for which we reward the leaders accordingly, may be the seeds of corporate disasters in the making in one year, five years, or ten years' time. These so-called attributes are the myths. Contrary to many leadership misconceptions, most corporate leaders are no entrepreneurs. They are not innovators, and most of them never started any business or created anything worthwhile. The truth is this: most corporate leaders are nothing like Henry Ford (Ford Motors), Arthur Sloan (General Motors), Bill Gates (Microsoft), Sam Walton (Wal-Mart), Steve Jobs (Apple), Larry Page (Google), Sergey Brin (Google), or Jeff Bezos (Amazon.com).

No doubt, conceptually, entrepreneurship and corporate leadership are not alike and should not be used interchangeably. There are questions as to whether the traits of entrepreneurship and leadership are innate or they are acquired in the classroom or on the job. The question becomes moot, though, when an individual is successful as leader in one organization but badly fails in another firm—like a former GE executive who did not succeed at Home Depot and failed to meet expectations. Many organizational phenomena are related to multiple factors. The organizational culture evolved over time, the quality of people, and other corporate resources are as important to the firm as corporate managers.

Most successful and recognition-deserving individuals, such as Steve Jobs and Henry Ford, started their organizations and/or changed them significantly over many years through their ingenuity and hard work. Their positive contribution toward the success of their organizations and the enhancement of lives of millions worldwide is unquestionable. They contributed significantly over a long period, or continue to contribute, by developing core business competencies that paved the road to sustainable and durable growth and success. They could not think of compromising the corporate well-being for quick personal gains.

Unlike most current corporate professional managers, almost all of the individuals mentioned above have earned their fame, honors, and financial rewards. They suffered the pain of their business growth. They were not given the reins of a well-established and running organization. They had the vision(s), creativity, and patience to plan and toil for and monitor growth, and later enjoy the fruits of their labor. They did not expect or earn huge rewards immediately. Over the years they laid a strong foundation to secure the corporate survival and growth. They were not running with a motto "Profit, Now!" They were the true pioneers—not self-serving, business-school-trained money-grabbers.

"Professional" care or management is essential, but it is not the sole or major determinant of business success and growth. When a firm grows, the nature of its leadership changes from creativity and innovation and informality to "professional" approaches taught in business schools. As the business founders and creators become unable to remain in charge as the organization crosses over from its "small" size, the operations are turned over to professional managers. As the owners remain distant and lose their direct influence and control, the future success or growth of the business is highly compromised. This organizational phenomenon alters the success formula.

Numerous entrepreneurs and business start-ups provide plenty of evidence as to why they are successful, and, in spite of their size and limited capital and human resources, why they are able to grow fast. Their successes shed light on some success determinants—such as individual inventiveness, creativity, flexibility and adaptability, motivation, and perseverance. When small enterprises change and become large, their institutional character or culture changes with different business processes, policies, procedures, and practices. Many organizational features get altered as management "professionals" start taking over operational and strategic policy matters. Communication networks get modified. Work conditions, relationships, and motivations change. Employee morale and drive, "intrapreneurship" or empowerment, supply and distribution chain relationships, and several other unique business traits may take different shapes and meanings with growth in size. Synergy with growth is not easier to accomplish without the productive motivation, creativity, and efforts all across the organization.

Here is a reality of large business: Success is a collective endeavor! Failure, in contrast, is a leadership or individual phenomenon.

Recent business crises or events provide considerable evidence to this fact. The nature of business problems in big firms suggests the quality of contribution of professional leaders in the already well-established businesses. Their short-term corporate accomplishments get overblown, but later on they turn out to be unjustifiable. A few "cosmetic" changes cannot assure long-term competitive market security and success. In most large firms, particularly, the incoming CEO acquires the existing institutional core strengths that were acquired or developed in the past; these competencies continue to exist as long as the working environment remains conducive and motivating. But often this is not the case. When the leadership implements unreasonable practices for fast personal gains, the productive conditions get compromised and the available resources become mismanaged.

"Professional" leadership contribution is thus an illusion, a myth. Its importance is overblown by the news media, business books and periodicals, and corporate public relations efforts. Corporate leaders know how to blow their own horns successfully to convince the general public about their importance and financial worthiness. They take the credit for their organizational success but never accept any responsibilities for their personal failures. More often than not, they guide their organizations in the wrong direction and lead them toward the path of bankruptcies and failures. This reality becomes apparent in the disappearance of large, well-known corporations via mergers, acquisitions, government bailouts, and permanent business door-closings. In reality, most corporate managers are far from being "real" or "true" business leaders.

Leadership and Corporate Results

Because corporate leaders are in positions of power and influence, they someway affect the corporate results over a long period of time. The leadership's "positive" contribution toward business security and growth over many years may be (1) very minimal (indirect), (2) some, but not noteworthy, or (3) "exceptional." On the other hand, serious but reversible business problems may be the result of management "neglect," "incompetence," or some "inconceivable" factors (e.g., the end of the Soviet Union) beyond corporate control. Irreversible business disasters and failures are usually the outcomes of major management shortcomings. Thus, corporate CEOs and top managers bear (1) some or (2) sole responsibility for "normal" or exceptional competition problems and business disasters, or a responsibility (3) greater than other stakeholders.

The extremely high level of executive compensation falsely presupposes the availability of "exceptional" individual talent at the beginning of his/her tenure and a very high probability of "exceptional" management contribution thereafter during the tenure toward corporate success for years to come in the future. The reality of poor management achievements all around us reflects this fallacy. Nonetheless, unlike others in the organization, executives continue to receive high compensations even in abnormal times or during times of self-created problems, compounding the difficulties. The inadequacy of needed business innovation and growth to overcome our social and economic problems underscores the myths about leadership contribution and importance.

It is a myth that corporate CEOs and their deputies are *solely* capable of meeting business challenges and, thus, they should be handsomely compensated because the society depends on them; no one else could solve the problems otherwise. This is nothing but a delusion.

The fact is, in spite of their CEOs or other leaders, some organizations could continue to exist and move forward in the right direction. Frequently, people at lower levels overcome leadership shortcomings through their commitment, inventiveness, and creativity. As long as the leadership provides minimal resource support, leaves other people alone, does not interfere, and does not do any major harm with the "demotivating" or "dissatisfying" organizational policies and practices, people would rise up and do their best under the circumstance. Their productive instincts and moral values would take over.

But when the appropriate resources are not provided or when there are organization-based "dissatisfiers" (demotivators), the business suffers from the flaws and fumbles of its leadership. Motivated people prefer to use their capabilities, fulfill their work obligations, and try to excel. It is management or executives and their policies and practices that lay down barriers, hamper business progress, and lead toward the failure.

In other words, individually or collectively as a management team or "club," corporate management professionals contribute significantly to business problems and disasters. They are *solely* responsible for business failures with their reckless policies, such as real estate lending to clearly unqualified individuals for high immediate corporate profits and personal gains. Instead of accepting their responsibility for mistakes, they either cover them up or find scapegoats to blame. Almost all business competitive problems have their roots in management. Yet, rarely do corporate managers accept or acknowledge their personal responsibilities for business failures.

Instead, they create a myth that without them holding the reins of authority, the situation could have been worse. The CEOs of some major banks and some other major firms indeed bragged about their success in performance during the subprime by claiming that their companies lost only a few billions, not hundreds of billions like some other firms in the industry or in the world. In other words, failures of different shades are described as "success," worthy of high compensation rewards.

Corporate leaders are too quick to take full credit for success, but not for failure. Usually, those deserving most credit and financial rewards are employees, capital providers, suppliers, distributors, marketing researchers and promoters, financial advisors, and management consultants—just to name a few. Even some of these individuals do not deserve credit for success if they have neglected their fiduciary duties and moral obligations by serving as management collaborators or "club" members in collusion with corporate management, for fast personal gains.

Some Specific Myths

At best, the following are some misconceived popular notions or leadership myths:

- Corporate leaders are the sole determinant of business success. (It takes people across the organization to succeed.)
- Business cannot succeed without its corporate leaders. (Often, in spite of its CEO and other top managers, business succeeds.)
- Corporate managers are not solely responsible for business failures. (Most businesses fail mostly because of their CEOs or people at the top and their decisions and actions—not because of their people at lower levels.)
- External factors beyond management control mostly affect business success or failure. (Business problems and failures are largely company-based or internal, with root causes deeply related to self-serving leadership motivations.)
- Business failures cannot be avoided. (Business failures are avoidable even under the most adverse business conditions. It takes skilled, competent management and the right leadership motivations to develop and be prepared with contingency plans and actions.)

- Most financial or market analyses and research studies are objective and accurate. (Management bias leaning toward specific decisions or course of business actions, either obvious or specifically conveyed, tends to influence "objectivity" of the data collection and analytical efforts. Often management studies are carried out to support management decisions, not to make them. Preconceived notions make corporate managers basically incapable of formulating and implementing the most appropriate competitive strategies and plans.)
- Professional corporate managers deserve their high compensations. (In relative terms, most CEOs and other leaders do not contribute to business success in any major way. Others in the organization contribute as much as or more than corporate leaders.)
- Business failures are never planned or intended. (What may appear to be a management failure is not necessarily a failure of management's purposeful actions. For personal gains, a careful plan may have been carried out to earn immediate and high corporate profits that would make the firm a good takeover target. The takeover may not be in the best long-term interest of the acquired firm and its stakeholders. For details, refer to Chapter 2.)
- Board directors, management consultants, financial advisors and investment bankers, public accountants and market researchers, and other associates of corporate managers—both inside and outside the organization—are most valuable and indispensable corporate resources. (They are indeed valuable as long as they do not serve as collaborators with the corporate managers for selfish reasons. The reality is, often they are there to back up management's preconceived notions and plans. When they compromise their professional integrity for personal financial gains and act as management "team players" or "club members," they become worthless. They cannot provide critical and honest guidance, advice, or approval.)

Most readers could think of some additional myths based on their own organizational situation, personal experience, and observation.

Corporate leaders use a lot of buzzwords, such as "team efforts" and "team players," but rarely do they share the available financial rewards equitably or fairly. When money is filtered down as compensation for good corporate or individual performance, there is not much in relative terms. In lieu of financial rewards, corporate leaders pass out certificates of outstanding performance to people below. The fairness of the compensation systems within the firm is a myth underlying most corporate entities. Unjust and unfair performance rewards lead to low morale at all levels below the top, and this situation becomes evident in the exponentially growing human errors and in people performing below their full potential. Barely meeting the minimum performance standards or management expectations becomes the norm. Superficial achievements are realized and claimed; they get stressed and overblown, and they do get recognized, ensuring corporate demise sooner or later.

A multitude of right decisions and right tasks are essential to succeed. By virtue of his/her position, all a corporate leader can hope to contribute for success is to guide and facilitate his/her group or team efforts. The teamwork that dictates the productivity of corporate resources—human, capital, technological, and so forth—actually is responsible for the results. When the team effort remains essentially unrewarded in financial term, the level of productivity is likely to be less than ideal.

Once again, the simple facts are these:

1. A corporation rarely succeeds solely because of its leadership at the top.
2. Corporations do succeed, more often than we realize, despite the quality of their leaders.
3. Corporate failures are directly related to their leaders, whose decisions and policies, whose values, whose behaviors and management styles adversely affect the ability and quality of performance at all management levels directly or indirectly.

The above facts are clearly evident in the hundreds of examples that describe the rise and fall of corporations. Because there are so many interrelated variables and success determinants, it is not easy to pinpoint one or a few major factors without making certain assumptions or premises that may or may not be valid.

What we have is a system that does not hold management accountable for corporate results beyond a year or two. For quick improvements in corporate sales and costs, the corporate board rewards the CEO with big salary increases, bonuses, stock options, and other benefits. His/her severance package is reevaluated and repackaged upward with additional financial benefits, guarantees, and fringe awards. The CEO, in turn, rewards his/her immediate deputies fairly well—subject, of course, to the corporate board's approval—for their support and "loyalty."

The corporate board does not hesitate to compensate its executives well, because some board members may have been recommended or nominated for board appointments by the CEO or one of his/her "loyal" supporters. The board members make a fair sum of money for a few hours of work on the board. So it is payback time.

It is a win-win situation for the board members as well as professional executives. The whole scenario is based on wrong premises, simply on myths that are widely held in the corporate world. These myths are responsible for our perpetual problems with management failure that surfaces every few years.

Leadership myths have been propagated over the past few decades by management gurus, whose lucrative consulting assignments too depend on our professional leaders. Business school professors pass them on through their classrooms and academic writings. The myths justify the institutional existence and growth of business schools. Wanting to emphasize the professional training and its importance for success, corporate leaders encourage and support business education. Executive MBA and doctoral programs have become "cash cows" for many business professors and institutions. To these can be added consulting projects for business faculty and funding of various academic programs by businesses.

Such incentives, offered by professional corporate leaders to back up their wishes and decisions, are too enticing to pass for the business school administrators and their faculty members. Once again, it's a win-win situation—at least for professional business leaders and academic institutions. It is a good arrangement to promote leadership myths. It is like a fraternity, a management club—one for all and all for one.

As myths get popularized under the guise of academic integrity, it becomes easier to push the importance of the people at the top who hold the economic decision-making powers. In the process, those people below who really deserve the credit get stepped over, overlooked, and unappreciated.

So what we often identify as desired leadership attributes are no more than myths or society's delusion. The contribution of corporate leaders toward their organizational success is a factor, not completely without value. But it is not the determinant of success, though it can certainly be the root cause of business failure.

By virtue of his/her position, all a corporate leader can hope to do to contribute for success is to guide, facilitate, and directly or indirectly influence his/her corporate efforts throughout. It is easier for the corporate leaders to take their organizations to their demise than to keep them moving forward as successful ongoing entities. Shortcuts to success are the seeds of business failures!

PART III

Underlying Causes of Management Failure

CHAPTER 5

Executive Compensation—Unsound and Unjustifiable Practice: A Driving Force behind Short-Sightedness

Compensation Basics

Basically, a good compensation system is fair and equitable, and it motivates people to perform well to the best of their abilities. Ideally, people should be compensated appropriately in relation to their qualifications (education, training, skills, experience, etc.), authorities, and responsibilities.

At the time of hiring, salary, severance package, fringe benefits, and other incentives should be based on what the individual brings to the organization in personal strengths and what he/she is expected to contribute to the organization immediately as well as in the long run. The organizational and job market realities should dictate the overall starting compensation package.

The retention, promotion, and separation (retirement and firing) compensation policies should reflect the application of fair, equitable, and objective performance-measurement criteria that accurately measure the individual contribution for the financial and nonfinancial merit considerations. The periodic evaluations for merit raises and promotions have to be prompt and realistic, and they should provide adequate incentives and motivations to excel at work. Not only must the compensation policies and practices facilitate the human productive efforts, but they must also relate to the individual contribution toward the achievement of the organization's specific objectives in the past as well as in the future.

Leadership Compensation: Individual Responsibilities Versus Contribution

To understand the effectiveness of executive compensation practices, let us review once again the corporate management's fiduciary duty and contribution toward the firm's overall business success and failure as an ongoing entity. (See chapters 3 and 4 for details.)

The corporate CEO and other top managers have the fiduciary responsibilities and obligations to preserve the organization's financial well-being and promote its long-term business interests. These highly educated and experienced corporate "professional" managers are expected to ensure and secure the organization's survival and growth through careful strategic planning and management. The shareholders expect their corporate managers to provide a reasonable return year after year on their investments while not jeopardizing their capital investments and financial interests; any managerial accomplishments better than or as good as the rest in the industry or elsewhere are preferred in the long run. Other corporate stakeholders—customers, employees, suppliers, distributors, creditors, and the community at large—also expect corporate managers to perform well to enhance everyone's best interests and well-being.

The authority and discretionary power given to the corporate managers empower them to acquire and develop the corporate resources (capital, technology, plant, equipment, facilities, human, etc.). These resources are to be deployed to enhance the firm's long-term security, profitability, and growth. Thus, the corporate CEO and his/her top lieutenants have obligations to use their best knowledge and skills in managing these resources. They have to formulate and implement effective business strategies, policies, and plans. Their decisions and actions should be aimed toward the accomplishment of the organization's goals and objectives that would benefit the shareholders and other stakeholders one way or another in the long run. In return, the corporate managers should be compensated fairly and appropriately.

Executive compensations should depend on the management's real contribution toward the firm's progress on the long path to its ultimate destined goals. For their specific achievements in fulfilling the stakeholders' long-term expectations, the CEO and other individuals at the top receive compensations in the form of basic salaries, bonuses, fringe benefits and perks, and severance payments. As long as the people at the top perform effectively, their positions should remain secured and they should be rewarded in both financial and nonfinancial terms. Their compensations should be in line with and justifiable in relation to others in the organization and elsewhere, in terms of each individual's actual importance and contribution toward the firm's competitive success and progress in the very dynamic global marketplace.

Corporate managers continue to work, lead, and run the organization at the pleasure of their organization's owners, the stockholders who are represented by the corporate board of directors. The corporate directors speak for the shareholders and other stakeholders.

The board of directors, elected periodically by the corporate shareholders, supervises and guides the corporate top managers. It is the board's primary responsibility to provide effective governance to ensure that the organization continues to move forward toward its destined goals through very careful management policies, strategies, and practices. The board has to provide watchful eyes in the formulation and implementation of corporate policies by its corporate administrators.

For their positions on the corporate board, board members are nominated and elected periodically by the stockholders. The nominations may be initiated by anyone. Often some top corporate executives do nominate certain individuals for board election, and they may carefully manipulate the election process. In addition to the elected members, there may be nonvoting members on the board. Most board members are compensated for their part-time service on the board. Because most large corporations have thousands of small investors worldwide, corporate managers are in position to easily influence the election process as well as the board members' financial compensations and other perks. (See Chapter 6 on corporate governance by the board.)

Such corporate features or arrangements, on the surface, seem very appropriate, useful, and fairly effective. In reality, though, there are several serious inherent problems, such as conflicts of interest. Many such problems prevent many corporate boards from fulfilling their fiduciary obligations effectively.

As many recent business problems and failures suggest, our corporate leaders (corporate board members and corporate executives/managers) do not seem to be fulfilling their long-term fiduciary duties effectively. The main culprit: their personal-compensation-based motivations and actions. Our corporate leaders are compensated on the basis of performance criteria that do not correctly take into account the leadership's fiduciary responsibilities and obligations. In pursuit of their own individual financial interests, our corporate leaders tend to accomplish the results that are detrimental to the business in the long run.

Performance Measurement Criteria

The effectiveness of executive compensation depends very much on the quality of the criteria used for the decisions concerning top management positions (hiring, retention, promotion, and separation) and their compensations (salaries, bonuses, perks, fringe benefits, and retirement and severance payments).

While the seniority or length of tenure is very precise and objective, the performance-based criteria differentiate and encourage individual initiative and creativity, productive efforts, and overall accomplishments or contributions toward the organization's goals and objectives. The main problem in the merit-based compensation policy or practice is that the leadership performance (accomplishments) is difficult to measure in precise terms. Because many management decisions and actions—in addition to a variety of external factors in the marketplace—could impact the organization's profitability for some time, it is not easy to precisely measure the management contribution toward corporate success. As many recent examples of business troubles point out, simply measuring current or only a few operational results is not an effective way to conclude or call the management accomplishments "good" or "outstanding" and reward executive compensations accordingly. Merit-based criteria indeed are imprecise and difficult to formulate and implement, and they could produce undesirable consequences if used with bias—and, specifically, for personal financial gains and other benefits by those in the positions of power and authority.

In large corporations, most CEOs and other senior executives and staff members are compensated on the basis of the firm's current or immediate profitability. Operational incomes (sales revenue minus operational costs) over the past few quarters are used as indicators of the quality of management performance. The firm's recent stock price reductions or appreciations too are used as market perceptions regarding the quality of top management team and its performance. Such widely used executive performance measures for compensation are quantifiable but not very useful or appropriate criteria, especially from the perspectives of management's long-term fiduciary duties and responsibilities.

Because the impact of management decisions or of its current policies and practices on the results in the distant future is very difficult to predict, there is a business tendency to use and apply the measurable "operational" dimensions for executive compensation purposes. Current or immediate sales revenue gains, cost-cuttings, recent improvements in corporate profitability and stock prices, and/or some other "objective" criteria are widely utilized for decisions concerning executive hiring, retention, firing, and compensation. But such practices are not in the corporate best interests.

Instead of providing the right incentives for the corporate leaders to fulfill their fiduciary obligations, they entice the individuals at the top to pay closer attention to immediate sales revenue enhancements and cost-cuttings. To improve their own personal financial gains fast, the corporate leaders race to improve the business' operational profitability while overlooking the long-term consequences of their actions for the company's long-term competitive strengths and market advantages. To increase the current operational profits and cash flows, the corporate managers overlook resource allocations altogether or underemphasize appropriate investments for product and market developments for the future. The use of "operational" dimensions for management performance evaluation, in other words, could and do adversely affect the corporate survival, success, and growth in the future.

Sometimes highly "sophisticated" financial theories and models are applied with the use of "advanced" or "high-powered" computer programs and machines to determine the corporate market value at present in terms of future cash flows or returns that may result from the management strategic decisions and practices. On the basis of this computation, the quality of executive contribution is measured. The problem, however, is that all sophisticated approaches suffer from many inherent problems of their underlying assumptions. Consequently, ambiguous and imprecise financial models and their results are "speculative" or "educated guesses" at best. They are not very good indicators of the future. Nor can they effectively measure the quality of executive contribution toward the corporate future success or growth.

Given the limitations of most performance measures, the operational measures are easy to apply and justify. Most executives prefer them because, in order to maximize their own personal compensation packages right away, they could easily influence and manipulate their company's immediate sales and cost-cuttings.

So instead of serving as useful tools, the "operational" performance-based measures tend to encourage and produce the executive behavior that is counter-productive for the organization.

Compensation-Driven Motivation and Behavior and Their Consequences

As pointed out earlier, many recent business events suggest that the practice of executive compensation is extremely ineffective. It is important to emphasize again that the practice suffers from some serious flaws and drawbacks. The number of big corporate disasters only in a few years is unimaginable and highlights the fact that the way we compensate corporate "professional" leaders is based on false premises. It reflects our "management delusion." Instead of ensuring and producing corporate success, the practice tends to produce wrong leadership motivation and behavior.

Once again, the major problem is that the "operational" performance-based compensation criteria encourage the corporate CEOs and top executives to focus on immediate corporate gains and ignore the development of products and markets for the future. From the organizational long-term perspectives, the self-serving management tendency for quick corporate profitability is risky and dangerous. The leadership short-term orientation undermines the importance of planning and executing effective long-term strategies for security, profits, and growth.

The operational-gain-based salaries, money bonuses, vested stock options, financial fringe benefits and other perks, and severance packages lead to self-serving motivations, inappropriate management focus, and preoccupation. Almost all of CEOs and top leaders at the time of hiring negotiate for, and usually secure, good compensations packages. Subsequently, after good quarterly or annual corporate financial results, they successfully renegotiate and get better packages. Each time, the corporate leaders aim for higher corporate operational profitability by using sales improvement tactics and gimmicks, and drastic cost-cuttings. In the long run, though, such compensation packages may turn out to be not in the best corporate interests, because they induce executives to take chances for huge and fast corporate profits.

Because the decision-makers come out ahead irrespective of their performance (long term or short term) in most cases, it is a win-win situation for them; they can afford to take unreasonable chances and be reckless in their managerial conduct. If the firm does poorly and some corporate leaders end up losing their jobs as a result, the lucrative severance packages still enable the fired executives to earn huge sums.

Many times, there is no relationship between the severance packages and the duration of the executive tenures. This fact entices many corporate leaders to undertake very risky decisions, which may threaten the firm's survival. High severance packages have a tendency to hasten executive separations—involuntary (firing) or voluntary (retirement). For most managers, there are better and more lucrative positions elsewhere. Even mergers and acquisitions provide for nice individual financial gains for many executives.

The amount of salaries, bonuses, and severance benefits recently earned at the top in management in numerous failed big firms is unimaginable. Obviously, the large sums are unjustifiable. In 2008, for instance, stocks were in downfall, losing billions and billions in investors' dollars. Nevertheless, there was no slump in executive compensations. More than 20 of Fortune 500 corporations' executives were paid twice their 2006 earnings. In 2007, Sovereign Bancorp Inc.'s CEO received a 285 percent increase in compensation while his company lost more than 55 percent of its stock value a year later. The median executive salary across the Fortune 500 companies was $8.4 million at the time many families were losing their homes in mortgage foreclosures and their corporations were downsizing. In just a few years, the top executive annual compensations in big corporations and financial institutions jumped from under 50 to over 500 times their average worker salaries.

There is plenty of evidence to suggest that the disastrous management policies and actions were pursued deliberately and voluntarily to maximize personal compensations as fast as possible. In many instances, the individual management conduct was unprofessional, dishonest, unethical, and perhaps illegal. Executive compensation seems to bring out the worst in corporate leaders.

Specifically, the executive compensation practices offer incentives for management to cut corners and not be strategically concerned about such important activities as R&D, employee skills maintenance and development, plant/equipment maintenance and modernization, customer relationship management, creation of productive and motivating work environment, supplier and distribution relationship management, product and service quality management, and public image. There is no self-serving motivation for the corporate managers to focus on the corporate core competencies that would maintain and develop markets and profitable customer base, and improve the corporate bottom line in the long run but add nothing immediately to the executives' own compensations. The fact is, any investments for the development of core competitive strengths could dampen the corporate current profitability and cash flows, and this may adversely affect the executive performance review and assessment. In essence, the corporate managers have no incentives to compete in the marketplace using long-term effective strategies.

Instead of competing in the marketplace, corporate managers prefer to use other means to protect their individual and corporate interests. Individually, or in collaboration with other leaders in the industry, they tend to depend on political corruption or lobbying influence to secure favorable regulatory protection and protect themselves from foreign competition. They readily seek out public assistance programs and resources (government-sponsored research, bailout money) as part of their major survival and growth strategy. They use aggressive public relations campaigns to justify their leadership importance as well as their high executive compensations. Furthermore, they do not hesitate to repackage their former disastrous policies for self-serving purposes.

For instance, within the months after the subprime crisis and government bailouts, and under the watchful eyes of regulators in late 2009, some financial institutions (banks and insurers) repackaged their bonds; these "re-remics" were designed mainly to make the bad securities look better and to superficially improve the institution's financial positions. It is interesting to note that in the United States, the United Kingdom, and elsewhere, the governments had to make concessions while negotiating executive compensations and some pay restrictions with the top executives of certain businesses and financial institutions that were bailed out by the taxpayers and are, thus in essence, partially or fully owned by the public. How many of these reluctant executives were responsible for their firms' disaster, and still expected to remain highly compensated even after the bailouts? Unbelievable! There seems to be no end to executive or personal greed.

What we have observed, and continue to do so, is that in pursuit of personal financial gains, many professional management practitioners are prepared to do anything. They do not hesitate to formulate and implement business strategies and tactics that are unsustainable for too long. We have observed countless incidents of unsound leadership conduct in the real estate, automobile, banking and insurance, capital, and other industries worldwide.

The main reason for such a short-term profit-driven orientation is fairly simple to understand. When the firm is profitable, its executives are well compensated. On the other hand, if the firm is not profitable or expectations are not met, some executives may lose their lucrative positions.

Most U.S. corporate leaders are highly paid. Many earn millions of dollars annually—well above what everyone else earns in the organization. Invariably, they enjoy considerably high salaries, top fringe benefits, and excellent severance packages that often provide lifetime personal financial security. Frequently, people at the top receive high rewards in disproportionate amounts while others in the organization receive meager financial rewards but very high praises, some certificates of outstanding performance, and many other "worthless" trophies of recognition.

On the surface, the executive compensation systems may appear to be fair, commensurate with the leadership responsibilities. But when measured against the relative leadership contribution in the long run, it is hard to justify these systems.

Flaws of Compensation Practice

The existing executive compensation practice has flaws in two areas. First, the corporate CEOs and top leaders receive much, much higher compensations relative to what other individuals in the organization are paid on the basis of their contribution. The higher levels of executive authority and responsibility do not necessarily justify the high disparity in compensation within the organization.

As was pointed out in the earlier chapters, contrary to what leaders may believe, it takes joint efforts within the organization to succeed. No doubt the top leaders are making worthy contributions. But the same is true for everyone else in the organization. Business success and failure depend on the commitment, cooperation, and collaboration at all levels of the organization, on all people across the organization and throughout the supply and distribution chains. Without the appropriate and adequate inputs and productive efforts from the researchers and scientists, sales and marketing people, production workers, motivated suppliers and distributors, creditors and others, no corporate leadership plans and policies could succeed on their own. Corporate leaders do their jobs as others do theirs. Everyone is there for specific reasons. When people fulfill their individual responsibilities satisfactorily, there should be no doubt why the business should not prosper.

It is true that competent leadership knowledge and skills are more important than some other qualifications, and that they are not readily available in the marketplace. This is, however, much more true for many other specialized areas such as scientific and research, technical and production, marketing/sales, and financial. Besides, differences are already recognized in basic wage and salary structures in relation to differences in job description. It is wrong to assume that the top leaders contribute much more toward success than others in the organization. The profitability of business in the long run is a result of collective productive efforts; it does not solely depend on one individual or a group of individuals at the top in management hierarchy.

In contrast, though, business disasters are because of poor and ineffective management decisions, policies, and actions. The truth of the matter is that business failure can be directly attributed to management, but not business success.

Do top leaders deserve much higher salaries and other rewards year after year? Do they really deserve when they had nothing to do with the organizational origin, or with the core strengths and other good characteristics that existed prior to their arrivals in the organization?

The fact is that many top leaders arrive at their organizations when the organizations are already well established and have been relatively successful with their core strengths and other resources. The corporate rein is not very difficult to handle. The new leaders ride on the back of the ongoing strengths.

The typical leadership tenure in corporate America is under ten years. Some leaders arrive with the intention of voluntarily departing in a very short time after superficial achievements and high rewards. Frequently, they undeservedly derive substantial benefits from the contribution of others.

In many instances, during their short tenures, professional managers may become too aggressive or myopic, too competitive for fast gains or very reactive and defensive for status quo. In either case, their behaviors and business tactics lead the firm toward its downfall in the marketplace. Nonetheless, these managers continue to receive exceptional rewards including exceptional severance benefits.

Imagine when an employee comes up with a simple idea that saves the company millions in manufacturing cost. Guess what the employee receives for his/her creative and profitable contribution! Yes, some intangible recognition or honor, and a little increase in the paycheck. Who gets a big chunk of that cost-saving as merit performance? Guess! You are absolutely right; of course, the people at the top.

Can you imagine any organization enjoying success or making profits without the contribution of other people in the organization?

The only reason the rewards for corporate executives are much higher is that they have the power to secure their own rewards. They use their position and power to exploit the situation.

The second flaw or fallacy of the executive compensation practice lies in the fact that while their main responsibilities are in strategic management areas that require long-term thinking and careful long-term planning and implementation, their compensations are tied to recent or short-term operational performance.

In essence, the corporate leaders are not compensated on the basis of their long-term responsibilities and the stakeholders' long-term expectations for accomplishments. Corporate managers are expected to effectively navigate the enterprise in its long journey safely and profitably; however, their performance is evaluated for compensation on their recent accomplishments—not in terms of the actual contribution but in terms of unmeasurable contribution up to that moment. Executive compensations should realistically reflect on the actual contribution.

In reality, what the current executive compensation practice does is to reward the top leaders on the illusion of some worthy contribution, on the performance whose outcome is unknown at the moment and nobody would know with any certainty until sometime in the future. Years later, when the effects of the executive decisions are felt throughout the organization, the individuals who made the decisions are no longer there either to enjoy the rewards or to suffer the consequences and pay the price of their costly mistakes. Their positions are occupied by different leaders who have to then bear the responsibilities of the conduct of their predecessors.

A Few Specific Case Examples

We must not forget the price the U.S. automobile industry has been paying for years for the failure of its past leadership's strategic mistakes and failures. Since the early 1970s, GM, Chrysler, and Ford have been aware of their energy and foreign competitive challenges. Nonetheless, for years their executives ignored the challenges for immediate high corporate profits and personal compensations. It is not difficult to understand why American automobile industry leaders have resisted investing in fuel-efficient or alternate energy technologies. The leaders who should have invested in such technologies decades earlier are long gone. They each made millions in rewards by avoiding investments in essential technologies, investments that could have helped their corporations maintain their worldwide market dominance.

The auto executives were smart enough to know what they should do for success in the long run. Needless to say, they did not do what was essential. They were fully aware of the consequences of their decisions and clearly understood the strategic implications of the energy crisis in the early 1970s and the emerging foreign competition in the 1980s. Had they appropriately responded to the threats of the external environmental factors and invested then in the right technologies, years later their companies would not be in a serious predicament and fighting for their survival. The fact is, GM had the "hybrid" technology almost at the same time that Toyota did, but it decided against making a huge capital commitment; in contrast, Toyota acquired the technology, took a chance, and showed its commitment. By investing and proactively adopting new efficient production techniques, Toyota improved its image as innovator and quality producer. Just a few years later, Toyota acquired an enviable competitive advantage and success.

The subprime mortgage crisis that finally surfaced and became clearly and fully visible worldwide starting in late 2007, causing massive financial destruction and global economic slowdown, provides the perfect example of CEO and corporate failures. The downfall of Bear Stearns, Countrywide Financial, AIG, Merrill Lynch—among others worldwide—is the result of extreme management greed, recklessness, irresponsibility, arrogance, pride, overoptimism, and blind wishful thinking for personal financial gains at any cost to other stakeholders. This crisis sheds light on our delusion about the executive importance and contribution toward success.

The compensation practice and its underlying assumptions are flawed. They inherently encourage business leaders to think short term for quick gains while not paying much attention to the long-term implications, especially for business disasters.

In 2006, the CEOs of both Citigroup and Merrill Lynch each received in excess of $25 million and $48 millions respectively on the basis of their company's profit performance. In less than two years later, the firms were forced to write down billions of dollars in losses and hundreds of their people lost their jobs. One wonders how such huge amounts of compensation can be justified given the gross misjudgments, unsound financial decisions, and policies of the CEOs. Their greed-driven actions threatened the survival of their institutions. Not only have such leadership missteps shaken these giant institutions, but they have also uprooted the public confidence in the ability and the soundness of the entire global financial system.

Many big companies in other industries are faced with similar leadership crises.

Compensation and Corporate Boards

What enabled these CEOs and others to earn such obscene amounts of money while their firms suffered miserably under their leadership? As we will see in greater detail in a later chapter, their corporate board directors, of course, who failed to scrutinize their executive compensations, and management decisions, strategic plans, and actions. Corporate directors have done a poor job in providing adequate "checks and balances." Like many other corporate boards, the Citigroup and Merrill Lynch boards have miserably failed to fulfill their fiduciary responsibilities.

The reasons for the corporate board failures are not difficult to understand. There are several serious issues: the role or influence of corporate managers in board elections and in compensations of board directors themselves, cross-board memberships, lack of allocated time and effort by the boards, and other conflicts of interest at the top levels.

It is not unusual that board members are nominated by the CEO or other administrators, who would be under their board supervision and guidance after the election. For their few hours of work occasionally, board members receive a fairly decent stipend, renumeration or compensation. In addition, for board members, there are several fringe benefits and perks, such as travel allowances and board meetings at exotic places. The Citigroup reportedly paid each board member a minimum of $225,000 while Merrill Lynch paid $260,000. Not bad at all for a part-time position! Nobody in his/her mind would want to jeopardize such a position by questioning or opposing the actions of the person who was initially responsible for his/her appointment to the corporate board!

The corporate systems have become self-serving in recent years. There are apparent conflicts of interest; many incentives are built in to support one another instead of to ensure that obligations are carried out honestly and ethically. For personal gains, it is best to join the "club" rather than to do the job "right." There is no need to shake the boat.

No wonder that in collusion, the professional corporate managers and board members rip off their corporations. When the leaders make wrong decisions, they could certainly destroy their organizations one way or another. But others pay the price while the corporate leaders walk off with huge financial rewards.

It is a win-win situation for all of them. For management failures, while everyone else pays the costly price, such as layoff or cuts in salary or healthcare insurance, as Allan Sloan puts it in his *Fortune* article (Nov. 26, 2007, p.77), the CEOs "still get to laugh all the way to the bank."

To sum up, the recent practice of leadership compensations has not been good for the corporate welfare and its well-being. Before certain proposals are outlined, it is better to clearly list why the practice leads to individual greed and unsound leadership behavior for business in several important ways.

- Corporate leaders earn much more in compensations than what they actually deserve in relation to their overall contribution toward business success. Others in their organization perform important tasks but do not earn as much in relative terms.
- Current performance-based executive compensation systems entice the CEO and other top managers to focus on the short-term gains for personal gains without much regard for the implications of their decisions on the firm in the years to come.
- Current compensation systems encourage the corporate managers to under-take risky and less prudent business strategies.

CEO tenures are fairly brief. Some last no more than 18 months. The average CEO tenure seems to be on decline from 9.5 years in 1995 to 7.6 years in recent years. When CEOs leave, other top corporate executives and staff members leave, too, voluntarily or involuntarily. Even when an executive loses his/her job because of strategic failures, he/she is financially secured because of the lucrative severance packages.

By the time executives are forced to leave or they decide to leave, most of them have earned much more than most other workers make in their entire work life.

Potential Solutions

To prevent the abuse of management authority for self-gains, we have to change the current practice of executive compensation. We have to ensure the long-run business success and prevent business failures. The present-day executive compensation systems need a major overhaul.

In essence, the incentive systems should force the corporate leaders to use their best judgments and capabilities in making their strategic decisions keeping in mind the impact of such decisions on the organization in the long run. The CEO and other top leaders should be motivated by their individual benefits in the years to come, not by what they could get immediately. Executive compensation payments should be for their long-term contribution, and these payments should reflect whether an executive led his/her enterprise on a path of success or disaster.

Tying merit benefits to actual outcomes in the future would discourage the individual from reaching for quick fixes and short-term "cosmetic" changes. Otherwise, there would be many cost-cutting and revenue-enhancing measures, which could harm the organization in the long run. To improve immediate profitability, it is not in the best corporate interest to have the executive undertake certain actions—such as staff layoffs, cuts in R&D budgets, reduction in customer services or product quality, neglect in plant and equipment maintenance and repairs, heavy promotions, and perhaps even unethical sales tactics or illegal business conduct.

Here are some potential solutions or proposals that managements could consider.

- Pay initially a salary and fringe benefits that are equitable externally, in line with what is normal for a specific industry, recognizing market conditions and existing conditions within the organization.
- Be careful of high severance packages at the time of executive hiring. Severance packages must provide incentives for "real" and worthy executive contribution toward long-term corporate success. No individual is worth an extremely high severance package for his/her short tenure. Involuntary or forced separation may be worthy of say premium of 10 percent within the first year, 7 percent during the second or third year, 5 percent during the fourth or fifth year, and none thereafter—compared to the benefits under the voluntary departure.

The following simple formula may be useful to determine the total voluntary severance benefits in money and/or stock options: Total benefits = (monthly salary × length of tenure in months, up to and including 24), in immediate cash plus stock options (@ the current market share price at the time of separation, vesting in small amounts annually each year after separation for many years in the future. The same number of company shares, adjusted for stock splits and stock dividends, would be vested each year. The annual vesting would continue for the total number of years that equals the length of individual tenure in years. After that there would be no more vesting of stock options. So if the individual was with the firm for four years, there would be four annual vestings after the separation, starting from the date of departure.)

We must be careful. Simply to recruit a qualified person from outside, a compensation package that is internally inequitable, out of line in a significant way, should not be offered. (A wide internal gap or disparity in compensations creates a serious and unbearable morale problem, resulting in the policy of bringing outside talent doing more harm than good)

In the early years of the executive tenure, huge merit rewards in cash bonuses or stock/stock options should not be paid out immediately.

Executive money bonuses, stocks, stock options, and other performance-based incentives should be tied to the strategic decisions and actions, and should be paid in relation to their "actual" outcomes in the future—not to some "illusory" or uncertain results in the years to come. Current or recent corporate profitability should not determine how much merit raises the CEO and other top corporate managers should get today, or would get next year, in extra salary increases, stock options, or something else.

Incentive payments over many years in the future, like an annuity, could be guaranteed. Such payments should depend on the quality of performance as determined by future results, the length of individual tenure, and some other measurable criteria. Only after the results of the past executive actions become visible with a great degree of certainty—perhaps in five years, seven years, ten years, or longer—and are reflected in corporate competitive strength, financial well-being, market shares, cash flows, profitability, and stock or market valuations should the top leaders become entitled to financial benefits. All merit raises should be deferred and vested in the decision-makers till results become more clear and evident.

Stock options as merit benefits, for instance, may be vested after the individual's voluntary or involuntary departure or separation, over many years, at a given price, adjusted for inflation and other extraneous factors that could have affected the stock price appreciation over the years. In other words, there should be some formula (see above example) that accurately relates the executive decisions with the actual corporate gains in the future.

Merit salary increases and bonuses should not be out of proportion; they should relate to the raises in salaries and benefits for others in the organization on average in absolute amounts and on a percentage basis. Widening compensation disparities within the organization would result in serious and harmful morale problems. Periodic increases in compensation across the organizations should be perceived as fair and reasonable, and should not unreasonably favor executives over others in the organization.

Like merit benefits, the executive severance packages should be designed to reflect the long-term individual commitment and loyalty. Benefits should be in proportion to the individual's direct contribution toward the corporate "actual" or measurable success over the years. There should be no individual incentive for quick turnover or departure, voluntary or not. Severance payments should not create incentives for quick departures, nor should they make risky decisions attractive or appealing for the corporate managers. (Refer to some proposals above.)

Executive compensations should not be set or approved by the corporate board, whose members are nominated by the CEOs or some other corporate managers.

Compensations for the members of the board of directors also need to be reexamined. Questions should be raised as to why some board members are paid hundreds of thousands in compensation for just a few hours of work per year. Cross-memberships on corporate boards should be carefully scrutinized and discouraged. The way the board members are at present selected and paid underscores nepotism and major conflicts of interest.

Stockholders must take charge and decide on executive compensations. All executive compensations should be subject to approval by the simple majority of stockholders.

Small stockholders must unite to protect their own long-term investment interests. They should not let an individual or a small group of large speculative investors compromise their nonspeculative objectives, such as long streams of cash and stock dividends and "reasonable" stock price appreciations over the years. The small stockholders' active involvement in corporate affairs—including executive and board director compensations—should minimize the abuse of power at the top in management hierarchy for personal financial gains.

If necessary, the stockholders could set up a special "compensation" committee to appraise and determine each executive compensation package. No corporate board directors should serve on such a committee. The committee should be composed of individuals outside the organization and not associated directly with the organization. Other major stakeholders, such as bondholders and bankers, could be invited to serve on such a committee as long as there are no conflicts of interest.

To prevent self-serving compensation decisions, the executives should not be able to influence or determine the compensation of the individuals who are responsible for the executive appraisals, management salaries and benefits, and management hiring-and-firing. Again, the stockholders should take charge and make decisions on board members' compensations, benefits, and perks. Incentives should be designed and incorporated so that each board member would become greatly engaged in corporate affairs and guide the enterprise effectively. Where board members are not paid adequately, or in line with what they are expected to do in terms of time and effort, it is in corporate interest to raise their benefits. Each board member should be compensated fairly; and, in return, however, each should be held accountable for his/her performance. None of the board members should be rewarded for too long if he/she fails to effectively carry out the tasks and cannot be trusted for the individual's integrity or sincerity. Those who are rewarded generously or overcompensated must be carefully watched for their bias and objectivity, and those who are not really qualified (such as celebrities like professional ballplayers) to fulfill their responsibilities should be removed and not continued to be rewarded.

A group of impartial "outsiders" may be involved in the nomination of board directors for election and appointment. This group too could determine compensations for directors on the basis of their qualifications and performance expectations, and it should periodically undertake individual director's actual performance appraisal and evaluation for any needed changes in the future.

Term limits—of say three years—should be set for board of directors, subject to early termination by the simple majority of the stockholders. Fixed compensations could be set during this period.

All major management contracts for outside professional advice and certification activities related to consultants, public accountants, public relations, marketing researchers, lobbyists, lawyers, and other similar services for management—especially on a retainer basis for long term—should be closely scrutinized for costs and conflicts of financial interests.

Government needs to control "unjustifiable" executive compensations through regulations and closer scrutiny on a regular basis. From the regulatory and taxation perspectives, corporate executive "unreasonably" high salaries, money and stock bonuses, and severance payments should be made subject to the "regulatory" supervision and control, and they should be taxed at very high income tax rates if paid out over very short time—say within seven years after entitlements; excessive bonus payments received beyond the seven-year-period should be made subject to low tax rates comparable to "long-term capital gain" taxes.

Our present-day leadership compensation systems have become problematic over the years, and their adverse consequences are far-reaching. Self-serving executive behaviors driven by individual compensation and other immediate gains are not conducive to corporate or overall economic welfare. The systems are inherently flawed, making our well-intentioned leaders greedy and selfish—and, to some extent, uncaring as to what happens to others. Their reckless business decisions and actions for personal gains are dangers to business and its stakeholders. We need to be on guard, watch the symptoms of potential pending disasters, and act to prevent the disasters if possible.

Listed below are some symptoms or warning signs.

Key Symptoms Or Warning Signs of Pending Business Disasters

- The CEO, and/or his/her immediate family, without a substantial long-term stock ownership or without any other long-term financial commitments or interests (The same applies in case of other top corporate managers. History of job-hopping by the CEO and/or other corporate managers. Departure of several ("mass") key technical and managerial staff members with the arrival of new CEO or shortly thereafter.)

- Inflow of several new individuals (executives, management consultants, public accountants, etc.) in the top management either as staff or as advisors shortly after the arrival of the new CEO or of some other key top executives
- High activity in leadership stock selling in the market
- Unusually high "recent" corporate profitability based on operational maneuvers rather than good and sustainable developments
- Lucrative executive salaries and benefits based on current or recent corporate operating profits
- Lucrative severance packages for executives
- Compensations that relate much more with individual reputation or celebrity status, in contrast to other essential qualifications
- Immediate vesting of interests in stocks and other benefits upon separation (Exception: those executives who have served the same organization admirably for years.)
- No restrictions on the disposal of vested stock bonuses and options for cash
- Aggressive and assertive CEOs or other top executives
- Passive board of directors
- Considerable cross-corporate board memberships
- Top leadership largely composed of relatives and friends
- Absence of regulatory watch and supervision
- Expanding markets and/or growing economy that could disguise actual executive performance

Conclusion

In conclusion, when executives have very little or no vested long-term interest in the organization, they aim for short-term gains and tend to manipulate company earnings through shortcuts. Such behavior compromises the company's long-term competitive position. In some desperate situations, executives may even attempt to falsify company records and exaggerate income.

Unethical or illegal tendency would be higher particularly among newcomers in the organization, in contrast to those executives who have been with the organization much longer. In order to maximize their personal wealth and to prove their personal worth, new or young leaders would tend to be more aggressive; besides, they have very little to lose as their high severance pay may provide them a sense of financial security. In the process, however, they may have put the organization dangerously at risk.

Finally, executive financial rewards must be fair and justifiable. They should reflect the individual's actual contribution toward the overall well-being of the company—its security, profitability, and growth in the long run.

CHAPTER 6

Corporate Board Governance—Fiduciary Neglect: Inadequate Oversight over Management Plans, Policies, and Practices

Board Structure

The structure of corporate board of directors has evolved over the years to manage the corporation and its business affairs on behalf of its owners indirectly. The primary obligation of the board is to protect the shareholders' ownership interests by providing adequate oversight over the corporate managers and their business policies and practices. The board directors are nominated and, subsequently, elected by the shareholders in accordance with the corporate charter and its bylaws. Board members may include stockholders, creditors, corporate managers, and other individuals from both inside and outside, who may have some vested interests in the corporate welfare and well-being. Almost all of the elected board directors receive some compensation for their services. Most outside board members usually have major business responsibilities and financial interests elsewhere. The directorship is essentially a part-time position or involvement unless, of course, an individual is on a full-time basis either as paid administrator or as investor. The board may have both voting and nonvoting members.

The voting members of the board have the ultimate decision-making authority and power on all business matters. They officially represent the stockholders and speak for them. In theory, the stockholders collectively have the ultimate power to overcome any board decisions, policies, plans, and practices. As owners, they could replace any or all of the board members at any time.

Director Obligations and Duties

Directly or indirectly the board is in charge of providing an oversight over corporate resources and ensuring that these resources are properly developed and deployed by the managers. It is the board's responsibility and obligation to move the organization effectively forward toward its desired future goals and destiny. In the competitive marketplace, the directors have to provide good oversight to protect the corporate survival, profitable growth, and overall success in order to enhance the ownership interests. In addition, the board has an implicit obligation to look after the interests of nonshareholders—namely, employees, suppliers, distributors, creditors, and the community at large. The board is expected to exercise its power to make sure that all corporate affairs are conducted in ethical and legal manner, and it is expected to deal immediately with any management conduct that cannot be morally justified. Periodically, the directors are expected to review various executive actions, accomplishments, and proposals for the future, and when essential, they must provide careful and necessary supervision and guidance.

To fulfill their obligations, the board directors have to attend a few scheduled meetings, discuss business matters, deliberate on pending issues, and eventually approve the management's overall corporate strategies, plans, and policies. One of the most important tasks facing the board is the selection, appraisal, and retention of corporate managers, especially the corporate CEO. The directors have obligations to recruit, hire, compensate, evaluate performance, and decide on the retention and separation of key people. The extent of the board's critical deliberations on important issues and the quality of its decisions reflect on the effectiveness of board performance as guardians of corporate resources.

As the organization grows, it needs more capital. The equity financing becomes the most ideal choice for the corporation to sustain growth and implement further expansion. With growing capital need, the firm is forced to share and expand its stockownership base. This takes the organization away from the concentration of stockownership in a single family or a small group of owners to multitudes of small stockowners—often across the globe. There comes a time when no one individual is able to maintain a controlling ownership or powerful force in corporate management. As a result, it is not uncommon to find a corporate board that becomes dominated more and more by "professionals." In most cases, these professional board members do not own stocks in a significant way for long-term investment purposes, nor do they have any other major financial stakes or interests in the firm concerned. In large corporations, in reality, the board has no direct stockholders' representation. This makes the board's effective supervision indispensable for the preservation and enhancement of shareholder ownership interests. The survival and success depends basically on the corporate managers and their board directors.

Reality of Board Governance

As the recent business events show, many corporate boards are not effectively looking after the welfare of the stockholders whom they represent. They are not providing the needed supervision, direction, and control. Over the past few years, the growing number of major business failures, the ever-rising and exuberant executive compensations (salaries, money and stock bonuses, severance packages, and other perks), countless unethical and illegal executive acts, regulatory and political corruption through forceful lobbying and huge campaign contributions, increasing business requirements for taxpayer bailouts, and many unimaginable bad corporate investment and other business decisions by highly educated experienced "professional" corporate managers offer considerable evidence to the fact that corporate directors have not fulfilled either their responsibilities or their obligations. They do not seem to meet the expectations of the stockholders or the society at large. As the facts show, there is a major failure of the corporate boards across the business world. There is some evidence to suggest that some board members may be willing collaborators and facilitators of executive greed. (See Chapter 8, "Management Club.")

For instance, the fact that the millions in bonuses handed out at Merrill Lynch, Bear Stearns, and Countrywide Financial—among others—while these businesses were on the verge of bankruptcy and financial disasters raises a serious question: What were their board directors doing or thinking while their firms were being looted by their managers? One also wonders where the boards were when General Motors (GM), Ford, and Chrysler were rapidly losing their market shares and their market dominance to Toyota and other foreign competitors. Were the directors of these car companies unaware of the approaching energy crisis over the years? Why did they not question their corporate managers' preoccupation with the big gas-guzzlers? How could they continue to reward their corporate CEOs and other top managers with millions in executive compensation? These firms certainly had not been doing well before their demise.

In relative terms of individual contribution, how could board directors justify high compensations of their executives? At Exxon for example, how could the board justify paying its CEO almost $400 million in retirement package in 2006? What entitles this executive to earn such an amount, compared to other Exxon managers and employees and their individual contributions? Would Exxon have succeeded without others in the organization and throughout its supply and distribution chains—or without rising oil prices—during the executive's 12-year leadership tenure? It is not surprising why this huge package raised a lot of public anger across the nation and resulted in congressional hearing. From the perspectives of the industry practice, the figure was considered unjustifiable; it was five times higher than at Chevron.

The neglect of board governance seems to have reached a crisis level in the past few decades. Many board directors play some part in business failures, and they must bear responsibilities for executive greed and bad management policies and practices. The reality is that leaders at the highest level in the corporate world are not doing a good job.

Reasons for Ineffective Governance

There are a number of reasons why the corporate board governance does not seem to work effectively. One major reason is that most board members have very narrow vested interest in the corporation they supervise. Their only personal financial interest may be in their high compensation for their occasional, few hours/days of service. In some large corporations, a board director is paid in excess of $200,000 in annual compensation plus numerous other perks. Often board members are there not for their expertise; they are there because of their celebrity status, and they receive high compensation for public relation reasons. Another fact is that many individuals serve on several corporate boards; this makes it impossible for them to devote their full attention to business matters. Cross-board memberships, a common occurrence, could lead to conflicts of interest. Sometimes an executive from a financial institution, such as bank, may be on the board specifically to protect his/her institution's interest (huge loan amount to the corporation). Even though no board members would want their firm to fail, they do not have any reason to be genuinely concerned about the organization's long-run success, because there is no significant self-financial commitment or interest beyond some specific personal reason.

Many corporate boards meet periodically several times during the year. Each of the meetings lasts for a couple of days, often at exotic places where they are lavishly wined and dined. Board members know very little about the company for which they have the decision-making power and responsibility. They are supposed to formulate or deliberate on policies and plans on important issues, on the basis of their limited knowledge. Information for the board decisions is invariably provided by the corporate CEO and his/her close staff members. Many times the board members receive certain pertinent key or complex information just a few minutes before the decision has to be made. So it is not difficult to imagine the quality of information or time that the board receives. Frequently, the available information may have been filtered in such a way that the approval becomes easier to get without closer scrutiny or critical questions.

There is also a problem with the management influence in the election of board directors. It is not uncommon for the CEO or other corporate managers to nominate or suggest the names of individuals whom they personally know, socially or otherwise. Reciprocal arrangements in the selection or elections of corporate boards are not rare, and they affect individual performance as director.

The influence of corporate managers in the board governance is a result of widespread ownerships of corporate stocks across the nation or globally. As pointed out earlier, as the number of shareholders grows and the individual shareholder's proportional financial interest lessens, the individual shareholder's desire and ability to directly get involved in the corporate affairs diminish. With the rising number of smaller and smaller fractional individual stockownership, the power to nominate and elect the board directors becomes insignificant on an individual basis. Since late 1990s, with the increasing adoption and utilization of the Internet, the corporate stockownership has become a mainstream. More and more small investors, with middle and lower income levels, own some stocks.

This recent phenomenon of diminishing shareholder interest, power, and control has transferred significant authority to nonowners, particularly the professional corporate managers. These professionals have access to the corporate resources to nominate the candidates of their choice and influence the elections. By influencing the election, these corporate managers are able to put the "friendly" and "sympathetic" directors on the board. This way, the managers secure collaboration rather than opposition or conflicts for their management decisions. Mutual interests get served.

The reality is that most corporate board members tend not to be as critical or diligent as their other corporate stakeholders expect. Instead of closely scrutinizing the corporate managers' achievements and future plans, the board members avoid serious questions related to the critical business issues. They become very accommodating to management wishes and desires. They do not "shake the boat." Economic, social, and peer pressures on the board members are enormous in favor of corporate executives.

In essence, the corporate board has evolved over the years to become a self-serving comradery, characterized by cross-nominations and rubber-stampings of the administrative plans and proposals with approvals. There is a growing indifference toward the stakeholders' vital interests and concerns, as well as toward the rising executive compensations. There is no one within to question leadership actions or high compensations of corporate managers and directors. It is a win-win situation for them.

Merrill Lynch and the Citigroup, for instance, reportedly paid somewhere around $250,000 to each board member. Not bad for a few hours of work and fun! While the board members and their executives earned large sums, their firms lost billions in the subprime crisis. Their boards failed to scrutinize their managers' unsound business policies and practices with greater concern and care; they could—and should—have easily foreseen the financial disasters and avoided the risk of extinction to their firms.

Consequences of Poor Governance

The current structure and processes of the corporate board prevent the directors from functioning effectively and fulfilling their fiduciary obligations. The board structure creates a self-serving environment that is not in the best corporate interest or its security and successful survival. There has been a common failure of the board members to ask pertinent questions, seek the useful and pertinent information from its managers, deliberate carefully before making important decisions, and hold executives accountable for their poor decisions and job performance. The system has become a threat to corporate future. The board shortcomings enable corporate managers to be dangerously reckless and aggressive in pursuit of high and fast corporate profits, which result in enormous executive compensations and other personal benefits. This fact has become extremely clear in several business disasters over the past few years.

The reality is that the corporate board system is not functioning well. The board evidently is not very attentive and on guard until the organization is in terrible trouble and facing problems of survival and growth. By then, the situation may have become nonreversible; it may be too late to save the organization. For example, GM and Chrysler may be beyond the point of no return!

Some Contemporary Characteristics

Listed below are some contemporary features of corporate board governance and their impact on business success and failure:

- A corporate failure is directly linked to the failure of its board of directors to effectively fulfill its responsibilities.
- The whole corporate board structure has become inherently weak with the rise in insignificant fractional corporate ownerships because this development has transferred significant power over to the professional corporate leaders without much "real" accountability.
- The nomination or appointment of most board members by the corporate executives creates conflicts of interest, making the appraisal of executive plans, policies, and practices extremely biased and self-serving.
- The part-time work nature of the corporate board makes it impossible for the majority of the board to have detailed and informed knowledge about the corporate facts and realities, in relation to the competitive global marketplace and the environmental trends.

When the corporate board does not adequately and carefully supervise and guide its managers in the formulation and implementation of corporate strategies and plans, it essentially does not serve the interests of the nonexecutive stakeholders. In essence, the board fails to protect the interests of its long-term small investors, creditors, employees, suppliers, distributors, and the public at large.

Legislative and Governmental Efforts

The U.S. government has tried to address the situation by trying to make the corporate management more apparent. The Sarbanese-Oxley Act created the Public Company Accounting Oversight Board to monitor corporations' disclosure of pertinent information to the public.

Seemingly, corporate executives and board directors do not like any government rules and regulations. So they have tried, and continue to try, to use lobbying efforts and some illegal means to subvert the legal and political processes. None of our professional corporate leaders wants any rules and changes that would improve corporate governance and thus performance. (More details in the next chapter.)

After a lengthy study recently, the Organization for Economic Cooperation and Development (OECD) has outlined some principles of good corporate governance. The OECD does not dispute the importance of good incentives for the corporate board and management. Nonetheless, this international organization wants greater objectivity in leadership decisions primarily for the welfare of the company and its shareholders. To discourage self-serving and bad leadership behavior, the OECD suggests a number of specific requirements for information disclosure, leadership behavior, and organizational structures and processes. The lengthy OECD guidelines are useful tools to improve the leadership performance at the top.

When the organization lacks adequate tools for checks and balances, the corporate governors fail. When the corporate directors and executives unite together in collusion and collaborate to further their own selfish interests, they have violated their public trust. When the board overlooks the illegal or unethical or socially irresponsible executive behaviors and practices, because of either personal greed or indifference, it becomes an accomplice in planting the seeds of organizational failure in the months or years to come. When the corporate administrators have no personal financial stake in business or its long-term well-being, the leadership compensation becomes the driving self-serving force, which is very detrimental to business success unless there are some personal accountability and serious financial consequences for bad management decisions and actions. When the board structure itself is inherently flawed because of widespread corporate ownerships, it is time to critically evaluate the practice and corporate governance and improve it. And change we must! No legislative efforts or governmental guidelines alone could solve the problems facing the corporate world.

Proposals to Improve Board Governance

The following are some proposals that may help to overcome some of the problems and improve the supervision and guidance of corporate managers by the board:

- All stockholders, large and small, domestic and foreign, need to become proactive and more involved in the business affairs.
- Outside committees should be selected by the shareholders to elect and compensate the top corporate leaders, both executives and board directors.
- Director tenures should be limited to one term not exceeding three years. Directors may be able to serve on the board again, in any paid or elected position, only three years after their each term expires.
- Like any elected position, any paid position on the board should be subject to approval by the stockholders' majority.
- All compensations for board directors and top managers should be subject to the approval of the majority of stockholders. They should not be out of line—in relation to others in the organization and across the industry. They should not disproportionately increase year after year, irrespective of corporate operational profitability or other current results. They should be tied to some actual long-term organizational situations and accomplishments.
- Executives and top corporate staff members should not be allowed to nominate any elected board member, nor should they be allowed to influence the election process.

- Cross-memberships on the board should be eliminated, possibly made illegal by the legislators.
- Celebrity nominations should be eliminated and avoided in favor of qualified individuals.
- Conflicts of interest in leadership selection, supervision, and compensations should be carefully monitored and publicized.
- Any violation of laws by the corporate top leaders should be dealt with promptly and with the full force of the law.
- Corporate stakeholders—particularly the shareholders, employees, and the community at large—must become proactive in monitoring the abuse of corporate leadership power and authority.

Ideally, there should be a member on the board representing each major constituency—besides stockholders, such as labor, suppliers, distributors, creditors, customers, and the society at large.

In the next chapter we will look at the contributions of regulators, legislators, and politicians toward creating a climate of deregulation over the past many years that encourages irresponsible business behavior.

CHAPTER 7

Regulatory Climate—Power of Money: Contribution of Regulators, Legislators, and Politicians

Toward Deregulation

Over the past few decades we have observed a global trend toward deregulation of business. The marketplace began to experience some major deregulation world-wide starting in the 1980s. In the mid-1990s, deregulation picked up speed at a faster pace to attract foreign capital and gain access to world markets. The pace has somewhat slowed down recently because of some political and economic events. The subprime crisis has crystallized some opposition. The critics are putting pressure on the legislators to reverse the trend and prevent another crisis of wild business management behavior.

The subprime crisis was possibly the result of the political and regulatory climate under the Bush administration. Not only was the Bush administration ideologically committed to the free-market principles, but it had also adopted several deregulating policies and ignored enforcement, favoring unrestricted market-based, profit-driven business activities. Essentially, what the Bush administration did was to move forward toward greater deregulation that had actually become a major government economic policy since President Reagan took office and that continued thereafter. The probusiness government in the United States became a facilitator across the world, creating an environment that is considerably free from government rules and regulations and that enables business to pursue profits in anyway possible—even with unconventional or unsound management strategies, policies, and practices.

The emergence of greatly deregulated and lax marketplace with the beginning of the twenty-first century specifically may have precipitated the incidents of big business failures and, subsequently, worldwide crisis.

This, however, is not the sole cause. Several factors have contributed toward management failure vis-à-vis business disasters. As discussed in the preceding chapters, the executive-compensation-based greed and the corporate board governance are among many contributing causes. Not least is the ineffective or tempting deregulatory climate for market power and quick financial gains.

Business Pressures, Government Response, and Consequences

With the politicians and regulators listening to the business community, the business has learned to push harder for greater legislative and regulatory concessions. Forceful business lobbying and huge financial contributions to support political causes and campaigns have become indispensable business strategies and practices simply for the purposes of influencing politicians, legislators, regulators, and law enforcers. Such business leadership behavior to manipulate the law and its enforcement seems to have become much more important than competing effectively and ethically in the marketplace.

One of the primary obligations and responsibilities of government is supposedly to protect the society from irrational and unsound business practices and speculation. The government is supposed to provide economic stability as well as steady and good economic growth for employment and income. Instead, though, in recent years, in the United States and in some other regions, the government has been following policies and practices that are producing quite the opposite results.

The political and legal climate in the United States has enabled the corporate management to increasingly pursue self-serving motivations freely and without any fear of regulatory actions by the government. Under the Bush administration, the U.S. Department of Justice published a new set of guidelines essentially protecting business monopolies from antitrust actions. For instance, under these guidelines, a proof of actual harm from big business actions was required before any accusations could be made and legal actions pursued. In other words, big business was given a tacit approval to exercise monopolistic power in the marketplace and eliminate competition for higher gains without better products/services and lower costs.

Instead of government encouraging businesses to develop sustainable long-term competitive advantages through creativity, innovations, product- and service-quality enhancements, product development, and improvements in business processes, it may have provided many deregulatory incentives to implement shortcuts for fast and higher profits.

Unintentionally, by deregulating in response to heavy "lobbying," the government may have even created a business mind-set that it could assume unbearable risk and count on government bailout in case of serious financial problems. What has happened is the emergence of unprecedented dependence on political and legal protection, in lieu of effective long-term business strategies and practices. This phenomenon is not limited to one or two specific firms. There are instances of major firms within an entire industry uniting and collectively seeking political, regulatory, and financial support from the government on economic and national security grounds. American automobile and banking industries are just recent examples.

Lobbying and financial contributions by business have been part of our political processes for years. What is new is the extent to which the business community in the United States has used such tactics and been successful over the past several years.

Evidently, especially in large corporations, most business leaders have been extremely proactive in openly soliciting political and regulatory support. The extent of money and effort spent by the healthcare organizations in the United States, particularly by the healthcare insurers, has become clear in recent years. Lobbying in Washington, D.C., has become a major industry. In the U.S. Capitol, the ratio of lobbyists to legislators—20 to 1—is higher than it is anywhere else in the world. The amount of money spent by the business community to influence the legislative processes is enormous, in billions of dollars annually. In contrast, imagine what businesses could accomplish if they were to spend that amount on R&D, market research, and other really worthwhile economic activities for product and market developments!

Social critics believe that the business community has corrupted the political environment in the United States and threatened not just its capitalist, competition-based marketplace economy but also its democratic way of life. The public too is concerned about the business necessity for huge taxpayer bailouts and government supporting (or perhaps collaborating with) greedy business leaders.

Self-Serving Politicians, Legislators, Policy Makers, and Regulators

When not actively pursued by the business leaders and their hired lobbyists, the politicians seek them out for financial contributions and other support for a variety of personal motivations and causes—including election campaigns. Because the presidential campaigns cost in excess of one billion dollars and congressional elections in multimillion dollars, it is not inconceivable why the politicians have become dependent on financial support from business and the public at large. In the process, they have become "accomplices" or willing collaborators with business leaders.

In essence, intentionally or unintentionally, the self-serving public leaders in government have become part of the recent economic problems. Some individuals become part of the government mainly for the purpose of enriching themselves, like one state senator in Texas who was able to insert a minor clause in a law and get it through unnoticed, to secure exemption for his own personal property—to enhance its financial value. There are hundreds of similar cases.

The interdependence between business and government is compromising the integrity of our democracy as well as our capitalistic, free-market systems. The growing dependency of each sector on the other may eventually corrupt the integrity of the legislative, regulatory, political, and economic processes. What has become evident in the past few years is that the government has allowed the corporate leaders to fail in the long run. When big businesses are faced with difficulties because of their bad management decisions and their willingness to gamble, they rush to seek out government assistance and bailouts, and the government listens for self-serving personal reasons and motivations.

Essentially, the individual needs of the people at the highest legislative, regulatory, and administrative levels in government have created a very probusiness and supportive regulatory environment for leaders of business and government to pursue their own financial gains and other personal agenda. Their personal interests have become a social burden.

Government financial bailouts, legislative maneuvers, and other actions underscore the social and economic crises. They are the result of leadership shortcomings at the highest places in the society.

Reality of Corporate World

The reality of the corporate world is that the government assistance in some form is safely assumed by big business in the accommodating regulatory and economic government policies. In the absence of the readily available government concessionary actions, many business leaders in large corporations would not undertake certain strategies that reflect unjustifiable or unreasonable potential financial risks and business failure. Instead, these business leaders would be adopting prudent and very competitive strategic policies and practices.

The problem is, in pursuit of self-serving personal financial interests, professional corporate managers seem to have adopted the "socialist" mentality for their businesses, pressuring for more and more government support while advocating "free enterprise" in the marketplace and earning huge personal compensation rewards. Personal greed and the self-serving behavior at the highest levels have weakened our economic, political, and social fibers.

Individually or collectively, our politicians and regulators may be among the contributing forces of business disasters and bankruptcies. Not unlike corporate directors, they have become collaborators and drive our businesses in the wrong direction toward the path of failures in the long run. Like business executives and corporate directors, our government leaders are failing badly in fulfilling their fiduciary responsibilities and moral duties in the manner in which all of the stakeholders expect and demand. Anything less than effective ethical leadership behavior in business and government is an indication of failure in our so-called capitalist democracy.

Recommendations

To prevent "socialist or elite capitalism," for which the United States has a cultural distaste, the time has come in the United States and elsewhere for political, regulatory, and economic reforms. As free citizens of the world, we must expect and demand the best from our leaders. We must prevent the concentration of wealth and power at the top in the hands of a few people.

It is time to start the reform movements and pressures at the grassroot levels, and progress upward proactively. As we move forward, we must modify and adapt so that ultimately we get the desired changes in our corporate and political policies, processes, institutional structures, and leadership decision-making.

Above all, we must discourage business lobbying and political contribution. Ideally, if possible, we must eliminate the interdependence between our business and government, which tends to corrupt the political and regulatory environment.

The regulatory reforms over the past few decades evidently have gone so far that they seem to do more harm than good. Here are some simple proposals that we need to consider carefully:

- Review the existing laws concerning business lobbying and political contributions and modify or refine them, one by one, eliminating loopholes and other flaws. Campaign-financing laws and political fund-raising regulations must reflect the realities of the political, technological, campaign-financing variable.
- Eliminate unnecessary regulations and requirements that are impractical, confusing, ambiguous, complex, conflicting, unenforceable, and/or without much economic value in contribution.
- Eliminate government bailouts of business. Let free market forces work. When social assistance is necessary to create jobs and income and for basic personal and family needs in times of high unemployment, provide financial assistance directly to workers and consumers in the forms of tax cuts and direct payments—but no immediate financial bailouts or guarantees.
- Eliminate or curtail leadership flows across business and government in relation to subsequent or future cross-sector "employment" or "consultation" opportunities and other career or professional moves and advancements. After appointments to key government positions and after the completion of important regulatory and enforcement tasks, closely monitor and supervise cross-sector movements for several years for any legal or ethical violations. Unlawful or immoral conduct should be handled promptly and forcefully within the scope of legal and professional standards.
- Stabilize financial institutions and minimize economic domination by any single organization or a few financial institutions or businesses. Legislate how far a financial institution could grow in size and market share.
- Expose all improper actions by the business or political leaders promptly and deal with them forcefully and without delay.

Our business leaders must stop using "government as a strategically available financial resource in case of corporate disaster. Government should not be part of the corporate contingency plan. During the formulation and implementation of competitive business plans and policies, business must develop market-based "real" long-term competitive strategic strengths for success.

CHAPTER 8

The Management Club—Collusive Team-Playing and Players

What Corporate Leaders Expect from Workers and Associates

Anyone who has talked to a headhunter or recruiter in recent years for an entry level or higher management position knows that most employers look for "team" players. Company representatives make it very clear from the beginning, during the interviewing process, that the firm wants someone who is a willing and cooperating member of the management team—or, the "club," so to speak. The importance of being a team player is invariably stressed. The organization prefers everyone at all levels of management to follow the "rules," like a football player, taking orders from the head coach. The coach, directly or indirectly, calls the shots and guides his/her players, along with some serving as assistant coach, team captain, quarterback, and so forth. Each player accordingly plays the tune under the direction of the maestro, in coordination and harmony, like in a musical concert.

The corporation is no different. Each individual is viewed as a team player and is expected to join the management "club" or "fraternity" and play by the club's or fraternal rules or codes of conduct. Whether explicit (formulated, written, spoken, clearly conveyed) or not, whether team opponents follow them or not, the "rules" have to be understood and honored by each player as part of the team culture, with each individual's primary mission being to contribute toward the main goal of "winning," to excel in playing so that the team becomes number one in the arena and continues to be at the top.

Winning Is Everything Today

At the top of the hierarchy, collectively and individually, scoring at any cost to win is of utmost importance to the coach, his/her superiors, and his/her immediate lieutenants below. Whether the club owners and others prefer and ultimately want trophies, psychic satisfaction, and/or financial gains is secondary. To win for the coach and others at the top, the players and associates should be prepared to work hard, take chances, bend rules when necessary, overlook violations by peers or someone else higher up, adhere to implicit cultural codes of conduct, show no open dissent, express no opposite views openly unless invited or encouraged clearly in subtle ways, provide support, and above all, play the game, and be good "club members" and "team players," ultimately to win.

Rewards

One quickly learns that it is important to play right, willingly participate in the game, and cooperate. The coach and his/her followers look after each trustworthy team member, both inside and outside the organization, as long as the individual does not betray. The willing, cooperating, and contributing members beyond the call are very much appreciated and heavily rewarded.

Untrustworthy or nonconforming members, on the other hand, are perceived as nonteam players and troublemakers, and they become very dispensable players. As soon as the individual in position of power finds an opportunity, troublemakers are sacrificed. Or they are ignored within the club. Troublemakers remain part of the team—but without much recognition, self-esteem, chances for merit promotions and career progression, and good financial rewards.

It is easy for an individual to get on the wrong side of management, because of competitive work environment and "dirty" organizational politics. Although one is expected to be a trustworthy team player, it is not in the best interest of anyone to blindly trust others at work and in business—peers, subordinates, bosses, and business associates. Self-interest underscores each individual motive and action in the business organization during the working hours and beyond.

For one's survival and financial well-being in a large organization, it is better and easier to join the club for mutual interests. Cooperation is better than conflict; otherwise, the weaker one has no chance of surviving and succeeding in corporate backstabbing, superficiality, and game playing. Team-playing with the superior and those in positions of power is a key to advancing financial and career interests.

In large corporations and elsewhere, those in the positions of power do not hesitate to give themselves disproportionate personal salaries, bonuses, and other rewards. Periodically, too, they hand out "reasonable" rewards to their team players, both inside and outside the organizations—such as business consultants, advisors, operational managers, and workers—aiming to prevent damaging discontent, opposition, operational sabotage, or dysfunctional environment.

These leaders protect themselves and their loyal team players with the individual performance evaluation systems, based on mostly "vague" and imprecise performance measures. They utilize "merit" rewards for performance and give raises, bonuses, promotions, contracts, and recognition or achievement certificates to keep the club members playing by the "rules" to win.

Above all, they keep adding team players to build up team support from top to bottom by recruiting and developing confidants, acquaintances, and other collaborators.

Loyal and Collaborating Club Members

Among team players within the organization are major or powerful stockholders, board directors, the CEO, other top executives and managers, divisional and operational managers, project leaders, various committee members, knowledgeable or professional staff members, and a variety of key workers. Many report or have direct access to the CEO or some other individuals at the top.

Outside team players may include management consultants and market researchers, public accounting firms and other certifiers, rating agencies, investment bankers, commercial banks and other major financial institutions, politicians and legislators, regulators and enforcers like Securities and Exchange Commission (SEC), community leaders, lobbyists, key suppliers and distributors, contractors and other service business firms, major customers with mutually beneficial financial interests at personal levels, other firms' CEOs and executives, business associates, close and powerful friends and acquaintances, industry leaders, and trade and professional association officers.

Usually, the leaders of major corporate stakeholders join the club to preserve and enhance essentially their own individual interests one way or another. Sooner or later, they look after one another through employment, business, or financing "cross-border" opportunities at the present or in the future.

Almost all of team players have some vested financial interests and aim to build up networks and relationships. They do understand, or learn quickly, how the game is played, and they all wish to protect or enhance mutual interests. They all want to belong to the management club, simply for their individual financial, career, or social upward interests. They do not mind compromising their integrity or ethical standards to secure their positions.

Some professional service providers, particularly, ignore their trade's codes of conduct, and sometimes, in order to protect their own business interest, knowingly manipulate findings or unlawfully certify false data to fulfill their management client's specific wishes and needs. The outsiders often justify their "club membership" or participation as team player in the name of "community" service or for greater good. Politicians join the club to seek financial support for their campaigns and other interests; that's one of the reasons why lobbyists are so successful in influencing the regulatory and election processes (details in Chapter 7, "Regulatory Climate").

How Team-Playing Begins

Often a team-playing and capable team-building CEO or top executive is searched for and preferred and hired. In many organizations, the roots of unhealthy situation go back all the way to the practice of executive hiring and compensation.

For the candidate chosen for a top management position, it is not uncommon to negotiate at the time when the job is offered that he/she could bring in or have his/her own team at work (assistants, advisors, consultants, etc.). More often than not, the corporate CEO gets his/her request or demand met as part of the initial employment package offer.

While this may seem to be reasonable, it raises several key questions:

- Why does the candidate want to bring his/her team from outside? Why would the people he/she wants to bring in want to leave their current positions to work with the candidate? Do they all want to bail out before the business problems that they have already created elsewhere become evident? Are they all hopping from one firm to another together as a team for their own personal gains?
- How could the firm avoid the potential problems of "loyalty," or "yes-man" (or woman)? Would the leadership welcome or crush constructive opposite/alternative views for the good of the institution?
- Would the management evaluations and reward systems be fair and equitable? How could the organization minimize the problems of employee morale resulting from the positions being filled from outside while some qualified people inside the organization are awaiting and expecting the promotion, opportunities, and challenges?

As soon as an executive brings his/her own acquaintance or team from outside, there is a potential problem that could lead to unhealthy working conditions, or organizational "dissatisfiers." There are serious consequences when an executive brings his/her own team players and opposing views are not encouraged, heard, or considered. Internally, also, individuals begin to undertake actions to be accepted as team player with the potentially incoming new leadership. Let's not forget the Bush administration, its demand for "loyalty," its motto emphasizing that "if you're not with us you're against us" (not exact words or quote); we understand the consequences of such loyalty premises.

Implications of Team-Playing

On the surface it may seem that cooperation and collaboration are essential aspects of the team "effort." Without harmony and coordination across the organization, winning may not seem possible. To accomplish the specific goals and reach ultimately the long-desired destiny, team-playing, both inside and outside the organization, becomes utmost important for integration and synergy of collective efforts.

But, as recent events clearly point out, team-playing can be extremely detrimental to the organization's well-being if its leaders are preoccupied with their own financial interests and use the collective efforts and organizational resources for personal enrichment. They show how team-playing or collaboration, in pursuit of mutual self-interests only, without any regard or concern for the needs or expectations of other stakeholders, leads to crises.

The subprime problems—and other economic crises before them—highlight what team-playing means when it is used by those in positions of power for selfish personal reasons. Then, team-playing has a different meaning. It stands for using people dishonestly and disingenuously, coercing others to compromise their high moral and ethical standards, committing crimes and enticing others to violate laws, forcing professional people to falsify records or misuse pertinent information, corrupting the judicial and political processes—and above all, using professional education, training, and experience to plan and implement unsound business policies and tactics for personal gains while sacrificing the long-term interests of most stockholders, employees, suppliers, distributors, creditors, customers, and the community at large.

The self-serving leaders coerce others into believing that once in a while, for greater good, it is okay to bend or ignore the rule, not to follow the formalized or sanctioned policies and practices. They convince the people under their guidance that it is everyone's responsibility to do whatever is required to "win." The team player may be led to believe that he/she must survive and succeed for one's own self and the family; each team player has to play in any way necessary even though there may be some rule violations or the action may not be right ethically, morally, or legally. The justification for doing is that the opponents do the same, not playing by the rule; that is how the game is played to win. The team "culture" evolves to the point that every member believes winning at any cost is in everybody's interests.

The reality is that team-playing has become a self-serving game. The "club" members have joined together to pursue mutual self-interests. While the individuals in the positions of power enrich themselves by coercing and rewarding collaborating members, others pay the heavy price. The game may be won, but winning may be illusory. Everybody may be suffering from "management delusion." There may not be glory if winning benefits only the few and the large majority of stakeholders lose. It is not a win-win situation for everyone. It is a win-lose situation. The bystanders and minor players pay the heavy price at the end.

While the corporate managers enrich themselves through high salaries, financial bonuses, good stock options, and lucrative severance packages through their shortcuts and unsound management practices, others struggle economically to protect their jobs, incomes, homes and health care benefits; provide education for their children; and meet their few other necessities.

Business is not a game, played simply for fun or only for personal glory and financial well-being. Many lives depend on its survival and success, on the fairness of the game playing in the long run. Team-playing can be a win-win situation if it is conducted with honesty and integrity, without deception. Indeed, the success or failure of business depends on the quality of group efforts. Team-playing does produce harmony, coordination, integration, and synergy in collective efforts— provided it has a sincere underlying mission for greater good in the long run.

Temporary and unsustainable current gains may provide long-term benefits for some self-serving individuals in positions of power, but in the long run such gains turn out to be illusory for everyone else. Our past three crises show how even well-intentioned individuals compromise their values in the name of team-playing and team loyalty.

Concluding Remarks

Why the contemporary self-serving professional corporate managers prefer team players is not difficult to comprehend. To maximize their own personal gains, they want workers and business associates who would collaborate, go along, enhance their gains, not question or hinder their plans for self-enrichment. The professional managers do not want independent and conscientious managers, employees, creditors, consultants and advisors, public accountants and certifiers, regulators and legislators, or anyone else to spoil the plans. They would rather bribe and corrupt, cut corners, and reward those who could enhance their personal benefits rather than work hard and honestly to earn the desired benefits in the long run. They do not prefer to play the game by the rule, by letting people do their job diligently and to the best of their capability. They do not want workers and business associates who are not able to take orders without questioning, who are not afraid to ask tough questions, who like to speak their mind and express their honest disagreement on the basis of logic and convictions. Corporate leaders do not want overtly righteous individuals, who are committed to fulfill their responsibilities "right" with honesty and integrity, and without compromising their work ethics.

Corporate managers surround themselves with "team players," "yes men and women." They reward the loyalist while crushing the opposition or overly ambitious. They create a consensual and conforming culture. From the top they essentially hand down management plans, policies, and key decisions while creating an illusion of "participative management." They invite operational inputs, proposals, goals, and budgets from below, but approve only those that are in line with the management wishes at the top and those that are capable of achieving the desired results fast. When needed, these professional leaders are not hesitant to take control, dictate, take action, and micromanage.

These professionals use the process of building teams or networks with individuals who can be team players, presumably for common corporate good. Yet, the players are retained and deployed for the leadership's fast personal gains, often putting the institution at a disadvantage in the long run. The team membership discourages constructive opposite views and suggestions, diminishes creativity and flexibility, disenfranchises independent thinkers, demotivates productive workers, and overall creates unhealthy working conditions that adversely affect corporate long-term strategic strengths and well-being.

Because of the desire to minimize opposition, the top management maintains strategically and operationally useful decision-making powers at the top and utilizes its position and individual authority to formulate and enforce the "rules" of the game. The vested authority is exercised from above. The pressure for team-playing is exerted in proportion with the desired results. Loyalists become more powerful by receiving greater authority and power. Free-spirited and talented people lose out and, in some way, are encouraged from above to leave. All across the organization, personal safety and individual rewards become more important than the organization's welfare.

While the corporate managers carry out the game plan for fast and higher corporate profitability, the organization bleeds internally. Recent business crises prove this fact. Team players seemingly are collaborators on the path of disasters. There is sufficient evidence of business failures and serious troubles from team-playing inside and outside over the past few years for mutual personal gains.

An unhealthy environment exists when people are afraid to express their views openly, or when they are not allowed to try alternative approaches to fulfill their duties, or when performance evaluations are perceived as biased, unfair, and inequitable by individuals below, or when promotions and raises are handed out to "team players" arbitrarily as favors in reciprocity for loyalty and for playing by the club rules.

Whenever a demotivating work condition is created and the situation continues to persist, creative and talented people leave. Skilled and knowledgeable people do not perform well under unfavorable working conditions or undue pressures. When people are not able to utilize their talents, they become discouraged and discontent; they find their jobs unsatisfying. Either they quit or they become less productive. The organization suffers from the lack of creativity, lack of new ideas and ways of thinking, and lack of different but better strategic approaches and practices.

The same situation emerges elsewhere when competitors become industry-wide collaborators and team players. Productivity suffers.

The self-serving, game-playing leadership company-wide or industry-wide—or across the world—becomes self-defeating in the long run. The worldwide crises highlight this truth and reality. Most stakeholders, even many team players, eventually pay the price one way or another. Many pay more heavily than others. Some team leaders and their law-violating lieutenants end up in prison! Enron, Merrill Lynch, Bear Stearns, and the AIG represent the worst of self-serving team-playing at the top.

PART IV

Failure of Strategic Management

CHAPTER 9

Absence of Strategic Thinking and Outlook: Missing Long-Range Orientation, Focus, and Approach

Any business school graduate knows how important it is to have strategic thinking and outlook for long-term corporate survival, growth, and prosperity. To fulfill the corporate vision and reach its desired destiny, the corporate leaders must think strategically, have a long-range outlook, and focus on looking forward beyond just a year or two. They must manage the organization beyond day-to-day operations, and not be preoccupied simply with the immediate corporate profitability.

Strategic management basically includes the formulation and implementation of long-range plans, followed by the periodic measurements of actual results or outcomes. Planning decisions and actions are guided by the leadership's strategic thinking and outlook, as well as by the strategic orientation and focus. Also, included in strategic management are the postperformance adjustments. The whole process continues with the necessary postmeasurement adaptations and modifications in the operational and strategic directions. There is constant scrutiny of requisite vital resources.

Components of Strategic Management

There are several important components of effective strategic management. Among them are the following:

- Long-term business outlook, orientation, focus, and direction over a period of many years—not just over a few days, weeks, months, a year, or two
- Careful assessments of a host of important factors—both external and organizational
- Formulation and selection of specific and realistic long-term goals or objectives to be accomplished in the years to come

- Formulation and selection of strategies, policies, and plans that underscore corporate differential advantage, its unique strengths and competencies (resources, skills, and capabilities) that could deliver customer benefits and exceed customer expectations for product and service quality as well as price
- Implementation of plans, or undertaking actions, in a timely fashion to ensure and achieve specific operational results and moving forward toward the desired long-run outcomes
- Periodic measurement of progress and actual results achieved
- Postevaluation adaptations, modifications, and corrective actions

The whole strategic management process revolves around the anticipation, acquisition, and use of essential resources for the desired long term. While it's important to keep the organization primarily afloat as an ongoing, productive, and profitable entity, the business leaders have to keep serving the broad interests of its stakeholders. The corporate stakeholders are not just its managers or shareholders; there are others as well including customers, creditors, employees, suppliers, distributors, and the community at large. For its long-term success, the firm cannot ignore all stakeholders' interests.

Effective corporate leaders acquire, develop, and manage vital resources profitably while fulfilling a variety of stakeholders' expectations and desires.

Importance of Broader Strategic Thinking

But to do so requires a long-term and broader outlook and a strategic approach. This is where professional corporate management practitioners fail. Their self-serving short-term objectives affect their performance. Their immediate operational-results-based outlook and approach do not serve their organization well.

Having originated from the Greek word "stratos" (army), the term "strategic" implies that the management orientation and focus ideally should be "long term" in nature, not short term or "operational." Managers should not be occupied primarily with the objectives for immediate corporate gains; they should not neglect the distant future. While operational, month-to-month or year-to-year results are important, they should be part of long-range strategic management and should lead the organization closer toward its prosperous future.

The business organization must not be led, guided, or dictated largely by what the organization aims to accomplish over the next year or two for quick profitability. Rather, current profitability could be pursued and should be aimed for as long as the development of long-term strategic advantages for the competitive marketplace is not compromised. The short-term operational pursuit should not replace management's long-term business thinking and outlook.

There should be actual or "real" commitment and allocation of resources all the time, on an ongoing basis, for developing organizational core advantages in profitable markets, such as better products, skills, lower prices, efficient distributors, and good after-purchase service centers. If a specific region or market is not the preferred battleground, the organization should not weaken its current position; the aimed advantages of the other markets could become useful when the time comes.

Organizations have to make competitive decisions and take action proactively, planning ahead carefully and preparing for the future, staying ahead of competitors, being ready for market challenges as they emerge all the time and not waiting for surprises. There should be better products and services at reasonable prices to deliver satisfaction whenever and wherever there are customers with the ability to buy. The organization must be able to respond promptly and effectively to changing customer needs, desires, and economic capabilities. It must excel and nullify each and every competitor's move.

Consequences of Missing Broader Strategic Outlook

Instead, what we observe is the leadership's narrow outlook. The effective strategic approach is almost absent and invisible. There is a tendency to focus on and react to competitive pressures and challenges, with management struggling to increase current sales and cut costs with quick fixes.

Recent events prove this fact.

Corporate managers are so preoccupied with their immediate corporate needs that they have largely adopted the "short-term" outlook, ignoring the long-term market realities and implications of their current orientation, focus, and business approach.

When the business organization leadership does not possess, or fails to adopt, the appropriate strategic outlook, orientation, focus, and overall requisite approach, long-term plans suffer. The leadership thinking and short-term behavior affect the organization adversely, causing very serious harm in the years to come.

The absence of essential broad and long-term approach results in ineffective strategic management throughout the process. It impacts the organization's costs and revenues, its short- and long-term profitability, its ability to compete in the marketplace, its protection from takeover or acquisition by a stronger firm, and/or its actual survival as business.

The business crises in the past few years suggest the consequences of self-serving compensation-driven motivations, underscoring shortsighted operational outlooks and approaches, and preoccupation with immediate results.

For many business firms the cost has been enormous, ranging all the way to business acquisitions and extinctions. Examples of serious business problems with worldwide consequence are plenty in the United States; even as bystanders, many people and businesses have suffered badly from business leadership failures elsewhere.

The failure of strategic management in businesses is avoidable, because it is more personal in nature than anything else. It is a failure of leadership; organizational or external factors are not responsible in any major way.

Individual financial motivations and egoism affect the leadership outlook and corporate strategic approaches. Most operational-results-based individual compensations are adversely affecting leadership orientation, focus, and decision-making—in other words, the way the corporate leaders practice strategic management. Each component of strategic management is affected.

Here is what corporate leaders do:

- Instead of developing a broad, long-term outlook and thinking in terms of years in the future, U.S. corporate leaders largely think narrowly—often only a year or two ahead of time.
- Instead of planning and preparing for the next 5, 10, 15, 20, or more years, they are frequently preoccupied with plans for the coming year or two.
- Instead of being market- or customer-oriented or driven, the professional managers are company-oriented, looking inside out trying to overcome their firm's immediate problems.
- Instead of making strategic investments—such as those on developing R&D, new technologies, building or modernizing production and operation facilities, developing new markets, building customer relations, acquiring or developing human skills and knowledge through education and training, enhancing employee morale and productivity through fair and equitable compensation and reward systems—professional managers focus on immediate profitability through cuts in investments, employee layoffs, frozen wages, reduction in advertising and sales budgets, elimination of products and services, cuts in training programs, and other quick fixes or operational measures that could immediately reduce costs, improve operational profits, and increase cash inflow but may have serious long-term competitive implications.
- Instead of looking at their organization as a whole, corporate leaders overlook and ignore integration and coordination that could provide synergies, eliminate unproductive resources and unnecessary activities, improve processes and efficiency, improve productivity, improve quality of products and services, expand markets and sales, reduce costs, enhance customer satisfaction, and deliver benefits to customers beyond their expectations. They do not integrate and coordinate corporate resources (technologies, people, capital, plant and building facilities, suppliers, distributors, etc.). They do not build corporate strengths and capabilities, markets and customers. Instead of undertaking proactive competitive strategies, our corporate leaders react to competitive pressures and challenges as they emerge, struggling just to stay afloat.
- Instead of enhancing creativity, innovation, and flexibility within the organization, our leaders insist on company-wide conformity and adherence to corporate policies and bureaucratic procedures.
- Instead of rewarding actual contributions toward corporate productivity and profitability, the leaders hand out financial rewards and promotions on the basis of individual loyalty to the superior in charge in the management hierarchy.
- Instead of hiring experienced and qualified individuals for the available corporate positions and consulting assignments, corporate leaders make

offers, on the basis of personal loyalty, to relatives and acquaintances upon whom the management can rely and count on for support.

- Instead of making strategic decisions after considerable research and discussion throughout the organization, the leaders ensure that information-seeking, advice, and discussion are carefully led and influenced from the top, achieving consensus and support from below for the preconceived executive notions or decisions.

- Instead of showing "real" commitment to long-term strategic plans by allocating the needed resources, the top managers formulate and make them available on "paper" in writing, but support them only superficially in policies without any "actual" resource allocation. Strategic or long-term plans receive a lot of buzzwords and lip service but no adequate real financial support.

- Above all, instead of ensuring that the operational and strategic (if any) decisions, policies, and practices are guided by corporate long-term objectives, needs, and interests, the leaders allow these crucial issues to be dictated by individuals or by personal objectives.

The list is of course much longer.

All such actions or failures have consequences that range from insignificant to significant and life-threatening to the organization. Indications that a firm may have serious problems include a failure to generate enough profit or cash flow relative to comparable firms in the industry, substantial income or sales loss, the organization's exhausted cash reserves and credit lines, inadequacy of the liquid assets to cover the operational bills or to pay the maturing obligations or debts. The insolvency of the firm could force it into bankruptcy and out of existence.

Such circumstances are typically the results of past management's strategic business decisions and actions. Management failures impact the current as well as future outcomes.

"Intentional" Management Neglect

When the leaders are compensated and rewarded on the basis of their current operational results, their performance evaluation is measured on the false premises. We expect our corporate leaders to guide their organization successfully toward its distant future, but we evaluate their performance on their immediate accomplishments for merit and retention decisions.

When the performance evaluations or their underlying assumptions are invalid, the whole process becomes weak, and there tends to be ineffective strategic planning and implementation.

The measurement of discrepancy between the actual and the expected executive performance for the long term is flawed, regardless of how abstract, uncertain, or immeasurable leadership performance is.

In our current dynamic environment, strategic management is difficult and imprecise. The outcomes are uncertain. There is no such thing as certainty (except uncertainty, of course). Most planning therefore is not likely to be error free. All management can try to do is to avoid errors as much as possible.

However, when the corporate managers make serious errors, due to a lack of long-range orientations, and lead their organizations to disastrous results, we have to wonder and ask: Why? Why do they fail to think long term and have a broad strategic concern or approach? Why do they overlook or neglect their corporate competitive strengths for the years to come? Why don't they try to minimize their potential competitive problems in the marketplace?

We do know that most of our corporate management practitioners are well educated, highly trained, and have good management experience. So they do not lack strategic management skills or knowledge. They understand the importance of strategic thinking, outlook, and approach. There is no lack of competence in strategic planning and implementation. Even if a corporate leader does not have adequate knowledge about specific planning tools and techniques, he/she can utilize qualified technical staff and consultants. All corporate leaders have easy access to knowledge and qualified workers.

Their failure, in other words, is not "skill" or "knowledge" based. Rather it is "rule" based. Most corporate leaders know how they should manage. Yet, they violate the "rules" of strategic management. Everything they have learned in business schools, they tend to disregard. Their strategic mistakes are hardly "unintentional," due to lack of knowledge or skill. They do not intentionally follow the good practices of effective management.

The CEOs and other executives are well aware of the basic principles of corporate management for long-term security, survival, prosperity, and growth. Yet, they practice almost the opposite.

The underlying intentions of leadership actions are to improve the corporate profitability as much and as quickly as possible so that executives can maximize their personal financial compensations and other objectives.

The executive actions, to put in some borrowed words of one scholar, Reason, (see the suggested reading list in the appendix) are "deliberate." They are "deviations from safe operating procedures, standards, or rules." They are "routine violations," resulting in "cutting corners" and "shortcuts" in skilled tasks. Sometimes their violations may be "necessary" (unethical or illegal) to get the job done to accomplish the operational goals.

The neglect by management in strategic outlook and approach is indeed an intended act with serious consequences for the business firm and its stakeholders.

Another way to understand strategic failure is to analyze the extent to which each of the following is responsible and contributes to failure: (a) the individual; (b) together or collectively, the top management team or group; (c) the organization—its unique complexities and other features; and (d) the environment external to the organization.

The individual, especially the CEO, who is the top leader with the ultimate authority and responsibility and power, must bear the full responsibility for his/her organization failure. This top executive's decisions and actions are based on his/her own motivations and cognitive characteristics.

Forces Influencing Management Strategic Decision-Making

The CEO's self-centered motivations, financially driven and aimed at immediate benefits rather than at those that may come sometime in the future, are strong forces behind the intentional, short-term outlook and approach. Moreover, the complex and dynamic organizational and external variables add to the individual cognitive limitations, creating perceptual distortions and making strategic decisions extremely difficult, future outcomes highly improbable and unpredictable, and thus long-term strategic approaches less practical. Such factors provide incentives to think near term and ignore any concern for the broader outlook and approach toward the distant years.

The quality of management decisions—and thus the quality of subsequent managerial actions—is dependent upon the individual decision-maker's underlying motivations, his/her intentions, abilities, and willingness to make the right or appropriate decisions.

The complexity of decision-making is compounded when more than one individual is involved in the process and shares the decision-making responsibility and authority. When the decision-making power is distributed to a group of individuals, the quality of group decisions tends to be different—either better or worse in comparison with the individual decisions.

Corporate management decisions are often the result of team efforts and group consensus, depending upon whether the consensus is freely reached or coerced into in some way. Group efforts and decision-making processes too are influenced by many different elements.

The corporate CEO is in a position to exert a lot of pressure. He/she can be very persuasive. There are a number of persuasive measures and techniques—including financial incentives; job security; and employment hiring, firing, and promotions. Individual personalities and interrelations are also at work in influencing group efforts and task outcomes. How much time, energy, resources, and efforts the group expends on task-completion or decision-making would depend upon the risk and benefit as perceived individually and/or collectively. There is not much concern about strategic thinking, planning, implementation, and decision-making.

When the CEOs have no certain preferences for corporate plans, they do not attempt to influence the team effort. They depend on top team efforts to come up with the right plan of actions for the future.

In his book with regard to executive decision-making, R. C. Nutt (see the reading list in the appendix) suggests that often corporate CEOs and other executives do not clearly understand or follow the strategic management process or its steps in planning and implementation. Executive actions may not be based on a rational or ideal approach.

Most management decisions are not based on adequate analyses of the relevant factors. Not all the pertinent information is available or collected and considered through conscientious efforts. Most of the feasible strategic options or alternatives are typically not understood, identified, analyzed, sought for, or even anticipated.

There is a leadership tendency to assume that as long as adverse consequences of the chosen managerial decisions or courses of action are not foreseen or are likely to be minimized for some reason, these decisions and actions are then appropriate or correct.

It is not difficult to understand why our corporate leaders find it easy, expeditious, and beneficial to focus on operational outcomes rather than on more uncertain distant results through long-range strategic planning and implementation.

When faced with top management teams or groups, our executives and staff aim to secure their own corporate positions, financial well-being, and personal and family security. They may find comfort in their management's operational decisions and guidelines, which they may find safe and justifiable, even though they may not fully agree with or endorse or support these decisions and guidelines. It is wise not to deviate from the wishes of the superiors; neither is it in one's best interest to go against the wishes of the peers, groups, and/or subordinates.

The complexity within the organization as well as outside makes management or group decisions hard to reach. To make the appropriate decisions, the essential information has to be made available, and it has to be filtered through efficiently for planning and implementation purposes. When it is not possible to implement this process, or when motivations other than organizational interests persist, preconceived notions or other forces emerge and certain conclusions have to be drawn.

Sometimes management decisions and actions get distorted and are first reached before even the process begins. In order to justify them then, the search for the supporting evidence begins, or what is described by one scholar (see Nutt in suggested readings in the appendix) as the "idea-imposition process." Appropriate information and team support are actively sought. If necessary, the individual in a position of power could pacify or crush any opposing views. When a team or group is involved in the decision-making process, its effort and progress, and ultimately its outcome, are closely monitored, influenced, and skewed.

When individuals work as a team or a group, often individual values, preferences, and choices are replaced by the "group-thinking." This usually reflects the wishes of the superiors or those of the individuals with some special power and influence. When the external "imposition" plays are not present, there may emerge influences of dominant personalities from within the group to affect the group-thinking and outcomes.

As a group meets often and the members begin to spend more time together, people stop thinking as individuals. They succumb to strong and powerful pressures to conform. To preserve their safety and position, individuals begin to adapt. What takes place is the "deindividuation." (See Hart, suggested readings in the appendix.)

The collective efforts generate a group consensus, and when reached, there is an illusion of the decision being "right" or "correct. A false sense of "invulnerability" may prevail from the belief that the collective "rationalization" makes the group decision appropriate and much more justifiable.

When the group decision is proved to be correct on the basis of later results, the leader (CEO, for instance) takes the full credit; he/she is highly praised and rewarded.

But if the results are just the opposite, the responsibility falls heavily on the group. The blame gets spread around and is shared. No one individual specifically pays the price for the bad group decision.

With the deindividuation of the decision-making process and the emergence of the group consensus, no one person can be held accountable for the disastrous outcomes. When the whole group or team is considered responsible, it's not feasible or advisable to punish everyone.

This reality of the organization encourages risky—sometimes even unethical and illegal—management or staff behavior at the top.

Team or group participation, whether real or superficial, creates a shelter for personal security. There is overconfidence. The organizational risk-versus-reward concept tends to be disregarded in favor of maximizing personal financial rewards and preserving one's individual security and position within the organization. It's a win-win situation for each member of the team as an individual, irrespective of the outcomes. But for the business organization, the situation is different: it is win or lose, and the consequences of bad decisions may be extremely serious for the organization.

If each individual were to pay the price on the basis of adverse results, the quality of the group-thinking and actions would be much more analytical and economically rational.

The reality is that the individual leader generally does not pay the price. The CEO or some other top executives may lose their jobs. But, even then, their severance or separation packages are loaded with tremendous financial benefits. There is not much for our leaders to lose.

This encourages our corporate management professionals to ignore strategic, long-term thinking and approaches. They ignore future risks while pursuing immediate and fairly safe organizational operational goals and objectives.

The complexity of the external environment provides further justification for the preoccupation with the foreseeable outcome, regardless of the long-term competitive risks or consequences. Additionally, the dynamic marketplace offers a way out for the risky management behavior and its adverse aftereffects. The CEOs and other leaders could always use another scapegoat and blame their failures on the uncertain extraneous variables over which they had no control.

It is not only that wrong leadership decisions fail. Right or correct decisions or plans could fail, too, if they are unacceptable to the individuals who are in charge of implementation. Unacceptable management plans tend to be sabotaged or implemented halfheartedly. Unless an appropriate plan is endorsed across the organization, receives a major support down the hierarchy, and/or is closely monitored and supervised throughout its implementation, providing operational creativity and flexibility when needed, success is not guaranteed.

In short, leadership failure revolves around the management outlook and strategic approaches—strategic thinking, planning, and implementation. Furthermore, it does have adverse consequences ranging from inconsequential nuisance to dire consequences—such as business failure. Management failure is costly and an avoidable waste of resources.

Corporate management has the responsibility for strategic management, for long-term corporate survival and prosperity. When corporate executives cannot make and implement sound and essential business plans, they have failed to fulfill their obligations.

Executive failure is evident everywhere in our corporate world!

Summary

Corporate leaders tend to neglect a broad and essential strategic outlook and approach for long-term success. Their focus on the organization's day-to-day operations and immediate results, while essential to some extent, overlooks the importance of building long-term competitive strengths and advantages.

The absence of appropriate long-term orientation and approach is a failure of strategic management. It leads to ineffective planning and implementation, which could have serious implications for the firm in the years to come.

Although there may be strategically formulated plans, their implementation by corporate managers is usually not backed up with the vital resource support.

While essential tasks for the distant future get insignificant attention, near-term operations are carefully thought out and carried out in order to cut costs and raise sales and improve immediate profitability.

From the long-term perspectives, operational decisions ignoring the ability to compete in the marketplace in the future are risky and they are made deliberately by the CEO, his/her top management team, and staff.

Management decisions tend to be "collective" and "consensual" in efforts, irrespective of whether or not they were preconceived by an executive even before the decision-making process began.

Corporate management team decisions provide a "shell" and protect the top executives individually, in the event of adverse results of wrong management decisions and actions. Because the responsibility for the decision failure is collective and shared, the executive's personal financial interests and job security remain intact.

The individual's short-term operational-results-based compensations entice the executive to adopt an operational outlook and approach in place of an ideal, long-term, proactive, market-based, strategic orientation and focus.

This long-term strategic approach would incorporate current operational decisions as part of the organization's long-term plans without sacrificing or compromising the right decisions to take the advantage of the available and emerging profitable opportunities in the dynamic, competitive marketplace in the years to come.

Both the short- and long-term management decisions should be made and carried out, correctly utilizing the available, relevant, and reliable market information.

CHAPTER 10

Slanted Management Intelligence Acquisition: Self-Serving Collection and Usage

When management is focused on current operational matters in order to improve the company's profitability immediately, long-range planning is not a major priority. Not much attention is paid to the distant future in terms of market opportunities and potential problems. The company's long-range competitive strengths and advantages for the dynamic global marketplace are not part of immediate concerns.

Because the available resources are being shuffled and reallocated to maximize the results over the next year or two or very near foreseeable future, anything beyond is out of consideration. The productivity of resources is evaluated in light of immediate benefits, not by their future benefits or returns that cannot be precisely predicted or measured and, moreover, most importantly, that cannot be justified relative to the individual executive's compensation plans.

In recent years many corporate leaders do not seem to be very much concerned about many important competitive issues or important strategic matters. They are not seriously searching for answers or insights into what the marketplace would be like in 5 years, 10 years, 15 years, or over a longer time period. Their time frame is narrow, now, as they are dealing with current problems.

Questions for Strategic Market Planning—Information Needs

At the present time, it does not seem to be important for the business executives to worry about specific strategic matters, such as the following:

- The profile of future customers of the organization—their needs, desires, and preferences; education and occupations; incomes; psychographics; behaviors; life-styles; etc.; whether domestic and/or foreign; geographical or national similarities and differences; how different will they be in comparison with the current customers; customers' expectations and their bargaining power—in other words, what will be the nature of market demand over the years

- The nature of competition—current and potential; competitors' strategies, practices, and capabilities; threats of competition—new entrants from within the industry and outside; quality of competing products and services; competitors' relative costs and prices; quality of competitors' advertising and sales efforts and their advertising and promotional budgets; degree of ease or complexity in entering or leaving the marketplace

- Availability and quality of substitute products and services and their prices and other marketing practices; the nature of "indirect" competition; characteristics of "indirect" competitors

- Supply chains—existing and potential; the nature and characteristics of supply chains; whether domestic or foreign; outsourcing alternatives and potentials; suppliers' quality, reliability, cost structures, capabilities, and bargaining power; feasibility for "backward" integration to achieve economic or cost efficiencies, coordination, quality control, reliability, or timely availability

- Distribution chains—existing and potential; the nature and characteristics of distribution chains; domestic and foreign; online versus offline; distributors' capabilities regarding quality of service, cost structures, bargaining powers, pricing, promotion, etc.; possibilities for "forward" integration to achieve economic or cost efficiencies, coordination, quality control, and higher support

- Current and emerging technologies that could affect the nature of demand as well as the rest of the marketplace; other environmental factors and developments—political, regulatory, economic/financial, social and religious, etc., with implications for the marketplace

- The current and future role of the company in meeting the dynamic needs of existing or potential customers in the future; how customer wishes or demands can be influenced or created in such a way that they are most appropriate for the company's current as well as potential corporate competencies, its competitive strengths and advantages, and its specific goals and capabilities; company's dependency on specific customers for success and survival; company's ability to respond promptly and effectively to existing and emerging competitive forces and assaults; company's financial, marketing, operational/production, human resources, and other needs for today, tomorrow as well as sometime in the future—in other words, what are the requirements for developing essential competitive strengths and advantages for the evolving and constantly changing markets here and abroad

These are among the many important issues for effective strategic planning and implementation. Yet, they seem to be ignored or not adequately addressed during strategic intelligence-gathering and planning.

Inappropriate Usage of Available Intelligence

Why are our professional management practitioners not concerned about such strategically significant issues?

The problem is not a lack or availability of timely and pertinent economic and market information. Nor is it the cost of information.

Ours is a generation facing an information explosion with an easy access, declining costs, and advancing technologies to rapidly process, search, and retrieve useful massive data in "real time." Over the past decade or so, an era of "petabytes" has emerged. Our rapidly changing information, communication, and computing technologies have made it possible for us to economically collect, store, and compute; statistically analyze; and retrieve, when needed, pertinent economic information for strategic management purposes.

For the necessary strategic decisions, both short and long term, there are data-mining technologies capable of digging through an unimaginable amount of data worldwide, and they could provide insights into the relationships between different market variables.

As Anderson wrote in his 2008 article in *Wired*, a highly regarded business magazine, the traditional scientific approach of hypothesizing and testing appears to be fairly "obsolete," as a result of our improved ability to search for corelationships between and among a multitude of factors. Corporate managers should find many wide varieties of relationships between economic factors sufficient for their strategic intelligence needs in terms of the present as well as the future.

The fact is that corporate executives use the available information resources (market research reports, management consultants, special projects, and other sources) not to make the appropriate or "right" decisions but to "support" their preconceived notions or decisions. They look for data to justify their short-term operational agenda. They do so not always but often. They spend a considerable amount of management time, effort, and money to find the useful marketing and financial information that would validate their decisions and actions with supporting data, corelationships, and inferences.

Often, corporate leaders do have the right marketing intelligence for the future, and they do know what decisions should be ideally made on the basis of such vital information. But they ignore the useful knowledge in favor of their immediate personal needs.

While both General Motors (GM) and Toyota understood the importance of the "hybrid" technology on the basis of available intelligence on the energy-related environment situation and trends, GM ignored the warning in spite of its access to the available technology because of its focus on immediate return and thus made itself extremely vulnerable in the marketplace in just a few years.

Indeed, the leadership's personal motivations and needs affect the management search for and utilization of objective, timely, and pertinent available economic data. The beneficial information sources are sought out, the data are manipulated, and the findings are skewed for personal reasons.

There has been a leadership tendency to ignore appropriate scientific methodologies and use research selectively for specific purposes.

This phenomenon is not just limited to business. There is sufficient evidence to suggest that even the Bush administration used the so-called scientific data in a selective way to formulate and support its policies on such issues as "absenteeism" (sex education), "science" education (evolution versus "intelligent design"), and "Iraq." For financial reasons, medical and legal professionals as well as university researchers and professors have tended recently to collect and use biased, nonobjective data claiming that these are "scientific" findings, without any concern about personal and professional ethics or integrity; more and more data are increasingly being manipulated for the company stock price appreciations, research grants, consulting assignments, or clients' defense in law suits in the court rooms.

As an advanced society, as we demand more and more scientific evidence for our decisions, policies, and actions, we're increasingly depending on collecting, storing, and using massive amount of data for personal reasons through advanced technologies and sophisticated techniques. Our massive data are being mined and manipulated for greed—financial or otherwise.

Tainted "Scientific" Inquiries for Decision Support

Personal greed has become the underlying characteristic of recent "scientific" inquiries for the sole purpose of influencing others for support on specific actions.

Sometimes even what "science" is gets blurred. A recent editorial in *Nature*, one of the leading scientific journals, admitted that popular or politically correct ideas do become scientific "truth" over time. Personal ideology can skew scientific research. Much more than we realize, there is a subtle acceptance in the scientific community that culture and extraneous variables do significantly affect science or what we refer to as scientific progress or advances. Studies on sex, race, global warming, genetics, and many other issues often suffer from bias caused by personal emotions, ideology, and motivations.

Indeed, the search for truth has become a rare phenomenon in recent years.

In corporate America, because of the inherent limitations of scientific methodologies or approaches in our dynamic environment, it has become easier for the business managers to ignore truth by not doing research or by guiding it and utilizing the available data in certain clever but biased ways.

Executive decisions are difficult to repudiate or criticize on scientific grounds. Economic outcomes are unpredictable as multitudes of variables affect the future results.

Need for Information Objectivity in Strategic Planning Decisions

Perhaps, at this point, we may want to ask: Is management decision-making a rational, objective, or "scientific" pursuit? Or should it be? Why should executives depend on research or available data for making decisions about the uncertain and unpredictable future? Why should executives *not* count on their "hunches," "personal gut-feelings," "intuition," "judgments," "experiences," "assumptions," "creativity," and "imagination"?

We may ask: What should be the best way to plan for and analyze and anticipate the future? Where should the analytical process begin? How should it be carried out and what should it include so that effective plans can be drawn up and implemented? If the executive decisions have already been made, should the search and analysis process be conducted or expected at all?

Answers to these questions are not too difficult to find.

Nothing in business is effective or correct unless and until the customer buys and pays for the product or service. Our corporate leaders know this reality of business. Almost all of our executives have studied "the marketing concept" in their business education; some of our business leaders are graduates of top business schools. Our leaders are management professionals with "professional" qualifications—education, training, and experience.

So we expect them to behave and perform like "professionals," methodically, following established sound management principles, approaches, and rules. We're a rational people, and we like to feel that our business leaders are driven by facts, not emotions, whims, or intuitions. We like to believe that rational or systematic approaches are used to analyze the economic and market factors to formulate organizational strategies and policies that could have a bearing on thousands of lives.

The business reality is that our corporate leaders do not want to behave like "professionals." They lack a serious commitment to scientific or rational methodologies to fact-findings. They do not prefer to do research before taking any actions.

However, not doing research is not an option. It is not professional or acceptable behavior; it wouldn't be tolerated.

Corporate managers cannot submit their plans and expect them to be approved by their superiors, like the directors, unless their proposals are supported by "systematic" research efforts based on evidence or by "truths," unless there have been analyses of the relevant market and organizational variables. Moreover, these managers cannot approach investors and creditors for financing of machineries, plants and buildings, or market expansion projects, or whatever else they need capital for, without backing up their plans and proposals with supporting research documents. (Let's not forget what happened to the auto executives in December 2008 when they went to Washington, D.C., asking the federal government for billions of dollars in bailout money without appropriate plans.)

Because the corporate managers are expected to do research in order to gain support for or approval of their strategies, policies, and plans of action, they have no choice about conducting research. They are forced to follow some "rules" and carry out information search and analyze external and internal variables. They have to do environmental scanning.

Meeting Objectivity Criteria

How this requirement is met is a different matter. Our executives have a lot of discretion to gather market intelligence and use whatever they prefer for decision support and approval. Numerous inherent flaws and limitations of scientific research methodologies or approaches enable them to guide the research and analytical efforts carefully for their specific needs and purposes.

They can lead and dictate the desired research findings, skew the efforts, and get away.

Nobody dares to question as long as some research studies are conducted and the findings are backed up with a lot of data. It does not matter whether or not the supporting data are valid and reliable, timely, objective, pertinent and accurate, or true and useful.

Neither the subordinates nor the board of directors would question the analytical approaches because most of these individuals are incapable of understanding scientific or analytical methodologies. Professional staff or management consultants (market researchers, financial analysts, scientists, etc.), who may be knowledgeable and perhaps understand and recognize "bias," usually have vested financial interests and, consequently, would not dare to raise questions or express "doubts." Some knowledgeable specialists, in fact, may have been accomplices in manipulating the fact-finding process and skewing the results.

Thus, the credibility of the leadership's search for "truth" is suspect.

Implications of Intelligence Gathering and Usage

Most research-based executive plans and actions have implications for executive compensations that are usually linked to current operations and not to results in some distant future. As a result, executive efforts toward information search and environmental scanning would be halfhearted and inclining toward bias, toward preconceived notions, toward findings that justify minimal strategic or long-term capital investment and actual resource commitment. Their information search further would be aimed in favor of specific operational decisions in terms of resource commitment and allocations for improving immediate corporate profitability.

For business planning purposes, it is not difficult for the corporate leaders and their hired researchers and analysts to use sophisticated ways to skew their findings in accordance with the management personal preferences. There are many different research definitions, many different samples and sampling ways, many different measurement techniques, and numerous other data gathering as well as analytical tools to effectively manipulate dozens of different economic variables that can produce the desired conclusions.

To some extent, the whole market intelligence process can be and is being skewed in our business world. Professional codes of conduct are being ignored by the corporate leaders, politicians, and legislators, lawyers and doctors, teachers, environmentalists, social advocates and critics, and others for personal causes and financial gains.

Lack of "real" personal commitment for greater good in environmental scanning and analysis may remain invisible for some time; in fact, the research efforts and findings, and the resulting individual decisions, may seem to be very productive for a while.

Later on, however, when a firm starts losing its competitive edge and the market shares start deteriorating, our corporate leaders begin to wonder why it has lost its competitiveness. Past research becomes the perfect scapegoat for bad management decisions, for the management failure in effective market intelligence gathering, strategic planning, and implementation.

Oh, it's a fault of our dynamic and unpredictable environment!

Summary

Because of their narrow, current-operations-based orientation and preoccupation, corporate managers are not very much committed to effective environmental scanning and gathering the relevant and useful marketing intelligence for effective strategic planning and implementation.

The sound market information search process tends to be absent. If a search is conducted, it tends to be halfhearted, without much commitment, and usually not aimed at finding the "truth" about the potential opportunities and problems.

To a large extent, marketing intelligence efforts are carried out to satisfy the corporate board directors, investors, and creditors who expect certain documents related to relevant organizational and external environmental analyses that support the executives' plans and proposals for the future.

Because of several underlying assumptions in various sampling and measurement techniques and tools, there are inherent limitations of "scientific" research and systematic intelligence gathering in our dynamic environment. As a result, it is easier for our corporate executives to manipulate the research process and skew the research findings, conclusions, and their business decision implications.

Corporate executives carefully guide or influence the research efforts and procedures through their budgets and the use of staff, management consultants, and research specialists.

Corporate staff, outside consultants, and researchers understand the executive "bias" leaning toward specific research findings, and scientifically, they could and often do produce the desired results. These individuals have vested financial interests in satisfying the executive expectations.

In order to maximize their current operating profits and cash flows, corporate executives use the "selected" market and financial data to justify their minimal capital commitment and allocation toward the development of long-term competitive strengths and advantages through investments in R&D, in plant and facility and equipment (technology) purchases and improvements, in employee education and training for skill development, and in other beneficial activities requiring major capital outlays.

CHAPTER 11

Lack of Marketplace Competitive Excellence: Reactive Strategies and Approaches

Market Forces

Over the past several decades, the global marketplace has become extremely competitive. Worldwide movements toward deregulation and toward political cooperation (in contrast to confrontation) and continuous technological advances have altered the nature of how the business firms compete.

Today there are small and large businesses competing globally for customers, products, services, natural resources, and for other resources—such as financial, human, and technological. No longer do big firms compete only with their large counterparts; almost all have to compete now with small businesses as well, at home and abroad.

The Internet has improved business capabilities to reach out beyond the local areas. Small enterprises have come up with a variety of business models to compete worldwide, in spite of their limited financial resources and other productive capabilities. Companies like Amazon emerged to challenge large and well-established book publishers and book distribution chains. With the evolution of the telecommunication and other related technologies, small firms within the industry and newcomers from outside have continued to challenge large firms with their entrepreneurship, creativity, flexibility, strong drive and motivations, and competitive spirit.

Many businesses compete because they have no choice while others proactively do so in search of profits. They use a variety of strategies and practices. Business collaborations of all sorts are taking place worldwide so that the firms are able to compete better and continue to survive and grow. Mergers and acquisitions have become common business events. Business owners find willing partners to collaborate and engage, on a contractual basis or as ownership partners, in mutually beneficial activities in areas such as financing, production, R&D, marketing, and purchasing.

In the contemporary competitive environment, in order to succeed beyond today and tomorrow, businesses must have strengths and advantages. If they do not have a market edge, they have to find it or develop essential capabilities. They need resources and skills to increase sales and cut costs. They have to carefully plan and implement effective strategies to find and retain customers.

Quality of Big Business Competitive Response

Many different market forces require business leaders to think strategically and have a long-term outlook, a market-based focus, a considerable amount of flexibility and adaptability, and other enabling features. In the absence of such traits, it would be very difficult for the corporate managers to maintain a competitive advantage for too long.

When a firm lacks competitiveness, it starts to lose customers. Its market share declines. The company's growth is affected, and it becomes harder and harder to remain profitable. Unless the situation is reversed, the business survival is at risk.

The growing number of business problems and failures suggests that large corporations have lost their competitive strengths. Many well-established, widely known big companies seem to have stumbled.

As businesses grow and become large, apparently they seem to become less and less competitive. They start losing their entrepreneurial and competitive spirit. Their customer focus begins to diminish, and they start ignoring market requirements for success.

While many of the CEOs and other top managers claim to be committed to their corporate long-term corporate destiny of building profitable markets and serving customers, their business strategies and approaches prove otherwise. Their preoccupation with maximizing immediate gains is clearly visible in the marketplace. As they shift corporate resources to meet immediate needs, the long-term corporate competitiveness suffers from the leadership neglect.

Because the customers have many choices for products and services to satisfy their varying needs and desires, a firm has to compete for sales with other business organizations in the marketplace. Also, in order to produce and offer products and services, a firm has to compete with other firms in the marketplace for capital, labor, technology, natural resources, and other scarce and costly but essential economic resources.

Determinants of Success in the Marketplace

A business' competitive success is measured in terms of market sales and costs of its resource acquisition and utilization. When a firm has an advantage in the marketplace, it does better in sales—compared to its rivals, that is, other competing firms. The firm's better sales performance depends on its low costs of products and services, compared to those of its rivals. The lower product/service costs depend on the productivity of the firm's economic resources—their efficiency (in terms of costs) and effectiveness (benefits/output) in relation to resource acquisition, allocation, utilization, and replacement, or disposal. Competitive market advantages are created through high resource efficiency and effectiveness.

When there are comparable advantages in the marketplace, a business remains competitive and it is able to offer and deliver customer satisfaction profitably. In contrast, when there is a lack of competitiveness for any reason, a firm suffers from weaknesses and loses sales. Inability to compete is a result of many factors, including the availability of resources and the quality of business leadership.

When customers are not satisfied and when their expectations are not met, they look for options in the marketplace for products and services. Customer purchase decisions and behaviors are influenced by many different market factors and forces. But, ultimately, it's the customers who determine whether or not a business firm is competitive and profitable.

A business firm could lose its competitiveness in a number of ways, because of its leaders' failure to consider and respond to all the marketplace forces adequately and effectively.

Several business scholars provide insights into numerous variables that could affect business' advantages and competitiveness in the marketplace. Among the most widely known are Michael Porter for his five forces of competition, and Gary Hamel and C. K. Prahalad for their concept of core competencies. (See suggested readings in the appendix.)

Porter refers to present competitors, potential competitors, buyer's bargaining power, supplier's bargaining power, and substitute products as major forces. In essence, he considers direct and indirect, current and emerging or likely competitors as potential problems in the marketplace. In other words, there is always a strategic competitive threat for business; a firm could face new entrants anytime from within and outside the "traditional" industries as well as from inside and beyond its domestic markets.

Indeed, technological innovations and political developments worldwide are part of competitive environmental factors or market realities, which continuously pose dangers and management challenges of having to face new types of customers, competitors, suppliers, distributors, mass communication media, and so forth—some even previously unimaginable.

This competitive market fact requires business leaders to be prepared. They have to plan on the basis of a critical and careful strategic thinking, a forward business outlook, and a careful analysis of all the pertinent factors. They have to formulate and implement appropriate long-term strategies and approaches to compete successfully.

In other words, what the corporate executives have to do is not stand still, not just focus on day-to-day operations. They have to look beyond and develop essential "core competencies" for the future, suggest Hamel and Prahalad. (See the suggested readings list.)

From the long-term competitive perspectives, the concept of "core competence" is important and very useful. Business leaders could use it to ensure the steady flow of desirable products at reasonable prices in the dynamic marketplace.

When businesses possess core competencies, they are in a position not just to deliver customer satisfaction but to exceed marketplace expectations too.

As Hamel and Prahalad point out, core competitive advantages represent profitable market opportunities because

- core competencies create potential in many different markets;
- they enable the firm to easily enter and compete in many different markets; and
- they could satisfy customers better than the competitors could do.

Almost all researchers and scholars highlight the importance of organizational culture that is proactive and forward looking. Creativity and innovation, flexibility and adaptability, knowledge and skills, and strong motivations are essential ingredients for success in the competitive marketplace. The organization has to be open to learning and has to evolve. Above all, it is important to have a business culture or a drive that enables the organization to remain competitive and excel in the long run, beyond just today and tomorrow.

When the corporate leaders fail to have or develop such a competitive attitude, there would be ineffective strategies, plans, and actions. There would be ineffective product or service offerings. Resource wastes and costs would be unjustifiably high and rising. Market pricing would be high, not in line with the quality and customer expectations—in other words, not competitive but detrimental to long-term business success.

Temporary competitive measures, like cutting costs through layoffs and use of poor service or inferior product materials, enable to lower price, raise sales, and improve profits. These maneuvers may appear to be appropriate for the time being. But they would not work for too long. They could affect the organization's capability for delivering customer satisfaction in the future. With such measures, the business firm cannot strengthen its ability or gain a competitive edge. To succeed, it has to stay one step ahead of its competitors; otherwise, the firm would become extremely vulnerable one way or another to competitive assaults.

Sometimes the management of a business firm becomes very content and feels secure, because of its current sales or its relative market share position in the industry. When a firm has the largest market share, it feels invincible and develops an attitude. There is a tendency to ignore emerging market forces. The firm may overlook better technologies, new management techniques and processes, changing political and economic climate, growing scarcity of nonrenewable resources, global warming, and changing customer behaviors and needs.

The current or past business successes may blind top management to the point that the firm's CEO and other executives refuse or are hesitant to acknowledge the apparent developments. They may discard the events or trends as insignificant. Consequently, it is not unusual that they act and plan in a denial mode.

Later on, when they are faced with new challenges or market opportunities, their organizations are completely unprepared. They are not capable of holding on to their customers or attracting new ones. They start losing customers to new competitors or existing rivals who are ready and better prepared to achieve customer satisfaction. For the formerly successful business managers, customers are now far away in sight.

Instead of being content and myopic, if the corporate executives could look at their immediate success as a starting point for building greater market strengths and advantages for the future, they would be more competitive and be able to avoid future disappointments and business disasters. If they could measure, evaluate, and use their present situations for better understanding of the changing competitive environment to identify their impending or potential problems, they could plan accordingly; they could direct and allocate organizational resources toward the maintenance and development of "core" competencies and future competitive advantages.

Effective Deployment of Resources

Vital resources could be planned for, acquired, or developed, allocated, and used to develop new or better products, new or better technologies and production facilities, and advanced human knowledge skills. Better use of resources could lengthen the life cycles of the maturing and declining products by finding different product uses that could offer new benefits to customers. As a result, the market rivals may find themselves lagging and at a disadvantage.

If certain products are likely to decline and may seem not revivable through alternate uses or modifications, or through promotional or pricing and/or distribution channel adaptations, these "dogs" could be dropped when the time comes. By planning and implementing a careful retrenchment strategy, the firm could minimize the problem of antagonizing its loyal customers, its good suppliers and distributors, and its investors and other stakeholders.

In other words, it is better to be proactive and avoid myopic, reactive, and passive management actions. Proactive leadership behaviors—analysis of competitive forces, decisions, and subsequent actions—could strengthen a business firm, even a successful one, and minimize future competitive threats and assaults.

But this is often difficult to comprehend for the corporate executives when they have been successful thus far enjoying a sizeable market share and a satisfying profitability.

Sometimes this problem is not limited to a specific firm. It may extend to the whole industry. All major players within the industry may feel secure and content with their status quo. They may all aim to maintain their immediate profitability and market share positions and just follow and imitate each other's moves. Together all big firms may display their total disregard of, or indifference to, any market happening beyond their industry's specific boundaries. American auto and electronics industries have experienced this reality. The persistence of this problem is evident in the most recent subprime financial crisis.

This market phenomenon represents an industry-wide or a collective attitude, a strategic management failure to plan for business challenges and new opportunities, a business or leadership neglect of building strategic capability to compete effectively.

This has serious consequences in the dynamic marketplace beyond the immediate present in terms of future competitive threats to sales, income, and growth, as well as to corporate survival. The current as well as the future marketplace could be enormously rewarding or brutally unforgiving.

It is important to understand the significance of planning for and building strategic advantages for the competitive marketplace.

All business achievements, past and present, have to be evaluated in terms of how well prepared strategically the organization is in meeting its future challenges, in taking advantage of the emerging opportunities or market potential.

The organizational core competitive strengths in relation to the marketplace should become the criteria for appraising the quality of managers' performance during their tenure. The major useful performance evaluation criterion should include contribution of management, actual or real, while in charge of corporate planning and policy formulation and implementation, toward (1) the organization's immediate financial results and, more importantly, (2) the organization's accomplishments in strengthening or enhancing the firm's competitiveness for the future and in enabling it to move forward toward its market potential and its corporate long-term destiny.

To simplify the concept of market-potential-based performance measurement for competitive planning and implementation, let us consider the following example:

Table 11.1 Market Shares Based on Different Market Perspectives

Industry	Total Sales	Current Market Share (Sales Realized & Percentage)	$500 Billion Market Potential (Percentage Realized ONLY)
	$100 billion	100%	20%
Company A	$40 billion	40%	8%
Company B	$30 billion	30%	6%
Company C	$25 billion	25%	5%
Other companies	$5 billion	5%	1%

As this example shows, 80 percent of the $500 billion potential or realizable sales are not realized. Such a huge gap between the realized and realizable sales is appealing to businesses, both inside and outside the industry at home and abroad. The lack of concern on the part of the three major players in the industry who are content with their current situation and are possibly behaving myopically and overlooking the potential is an open invitation to others to enter the market. Sooner or later someone else will enter the marketplace to take advantage of its growth, and the current players would be faced with a serious threat from one or more aggressive competitors.

We have seen time and time again how firms proactively seek realizable market sales with better products, better technologies, and better market strategies, often threatening the current dominant players. We have seen this competitive reality in countless industries worldwide over the years.

In terms of the production and distribution of "movies"—previously referred to as the "motion" picture industry, the nature of business has changed with the changes in the demand for entertainment. Technological developments (television, computer, the Internet, digital cameras, etc.) continue to affect the consumer demand for at-home and out-of-home entertainment desires and wishes, expanding market potentials not just for "movies" but for other forms of entertainment too.

In other words, creative and highly motivated individuals or businesses could perceive market potentials for a specific "basic" need, like entertainment, and with appropriate resources, they could take advantage of the prevailing or past products with new insights and ideas. As soon as the expanded market potentials are acknowledged, they could spot competitive weaknesses of current large players in particular. Subsequently, they could design better products and business models and enter the marketplace. Microsoft, Google, Dell, Genentech, and Amgen are among many leading technological firms that essentially entered and succeeded rapidly in the marketplace beyond imagination in such basic industries as information (communication) and medicine (health care), giving birth to "new" and narrowly defined "specific" markets and industries.

Usually, as history suggests, industrial innovations tend to come from outside a specific industry. Once innovative competitors are there with their aggressive and successful marketing strategies, the marketplace is no longer the same as before.

For businesses, the market conveys a simple message: those who stand still and react only for the moment with quick operational measures and fixes are destined to fail—sooner or later.

How Businesses Fail in the Marketplace

Many of the large corporations in United States have failed, or are failing, because their leaders have not listened to the market; they have failed to compete proactively. They have been oblivious to small and not-so-small businesses, both domestic and foreign, which have aggressively gone after the neglected markets, implementing long-term growth strategies and slowly eroding the positions of their rivals in the marketplace.

There are several ways corporate managers lose their competitiveness. Among them are the following:

- Insufficient allocation of capital resources for new product or market development efforts; superficial or nonexistent management commitment to R&D. Lack of research to understand alternate usages of current product offerings and intentions; not looking for different usage markets for the same products. Not staying abreast of competitors' (both direct and indirect) market moves and tactics and their long-term plans and strategies
- Poor product or service—noninnovative or inferior quality—relative to what competitors offer in the marketplace

- Too many old product offerings in the marketplace disguised under "new" or "improved" or under different brands and pushed aggressively without meeting the customer's expectations
- Chasing a wide variety of customers with one "standardized" product that cannot meet varying or specific needs and requirements. Or offering too many different products unnecessarily, keeping the costs and prices unjustifiably high
- High or unreasonable product prices relative to perceived quality or benefit and competitors' pricing policies. Or too low prices for "high" quality, prestige, "uniqueness," or "established brand" products
- Wrong prices for the selected distribution channel
- Distributors (retailers, dealers, wholesalers, etc.) not reaching the targeted customer groups; in other words, wrong distribution channel. Inadequate product or marketing support from distributors
- Inadequate sales and promotional strategies and efforts (funding, advertising, sales force, etc.). Sales people are not knowledgeable and/or motivated, and are unqualified and inadequately trained. Advertising and other promotional strategies (communication media, messages) are insufficient or inappropriate
- Lack of adequate presale and postsale customer service, support, and follow-ups
- Lack of market flexibilities and adaptability. Adhering to old technologies, manufacturing processes and facilities, and/or marketing practices.
- Abrupt dropping of unprofitable or declining products or markets, without proper planning, especially without warning, causing hardship and creating resentment to stakeholders—such as loyal customers, employees, distributors, suppliers, and other business associates (Improper retrenchment potentially could hurt other company products and future product offerings in the marketplace.)
- Absence of "bench-marking" and learning from competitors' best strategies and practices.
- Failure to develop a motivated and motivating, creative and driven, achieving and excelling competitive work environment and culture at all levels across and throughout the organization.

The list can go on and on. But the last one is the root cause of all other problems in the organization and, consequently, in the marketplace.

The failure of business leaders is imminent when they do not provide a conducive work environment through fair and equitable compensations and employment benefits; when their supervisory policies discourage decision-making and inventiveness; and when there is insufficient funding and support to move forward and to maintain and develop capabilities.

Today standing still is no longer an option in the marketplace. Aiming for the organizational growth for today, tomorrow, and a long time thereafter has become the prerequisite for survival and success. Corporate leaders who are preoccupied with improving only their immediate operational results and profitability are overlooking their organization's future needs. Because buyers have many alternate choices to satisfy their varying needs, it's not enough just to compete by copying and equally matching competing products and prices.

What customers prefer, want, and look for in the marketplace are better products, better services, and better prices. Always!

Forward-looking competitive growth strategies should be at the center of management's thinking and focus. Business leaders have to aggressively pursue customers and expand their markets for survival and profits. Current management decisions, business operations, and practices should further the organization's long-term goals, not hinder them.

The only way a business firm could meet the customer's wants and expectations is through effective business strategies and approaches that are indeed better than the competitors'. If a firm wants to keep its customers and provide some incentives for others to switch away from its competitors, it has to entice all of its present and potential customers.

Our environment is dynamic. Our environment is global. It is competitive, and it requires the business firm to excel and constantly improve its product and service quality. It also expects businesses to excel in operational processes and facilities in order to keep the cost down and prices low and competitive. Above all, it requires the leaders to stay abreast of changing customer demographics and psychographics so that they could formulate and implement effective customer-based competitive strategies and plans.

The importance of the right products, at the right place, at the right time, and at the right prices in the competitive marketplace cannot be overemphasized. Globally, business customers are everywhere, and the right product has to be produced most efficiently, cost-effectively wherever necessary, and offered wherever and whenever the customer wants at the price that the customer perceives reasonable.

Such are the realities of the contemporary global economic environment. To succeed, business has to play by the market rules.

Simple Competitive Ideas

The key ideas to compete successfully are fairly simple:

- Be committed to the marketplace with a genuine desire to excel in the long run and put in the best and conscientious efforts supported with the right resources.
- Become and remain customer-oriented and aim to exceed customer expectations—before, while, and after making decisions regarding purchasing. Don't ignore customer presale and postsale needs and requirements. Satisfying customers is an ongoing effort, in economic, ethical, and legal terms.
- Let customer satisfaction and demand serve as countervailing forces in the marketplace, as well as toward supplier and distributor powers.

- Excel and, when not possible, emulate the best in the business and aim to surpass.
- Pursue short-term gains without jeopardizing long-term strategic strengths and advantages. Operational decisions and actions related to resources, sales, and costs should address current weaknesses and strengthen the future.
- Maintain and develop better relationships with customers, suppliers, distributors, and other stakeholders.
- Seek inputs from all stakeholders concerned and overcome conflicting interests.
- Accomplish cost and marketing advantages through integration and synergy through the utilization of (a) most effective and efficient technologies, production processes, and facilities; (b) management policies and practices that provide creativity, encourage inventiveness, facilitate cross-communications, and provide flexibility and adaptability within the organization; and (c) productive relationship management within and outside the organization—including the available supply and distribution channels, advertising and mass communication media, investors, and creditors.
- Offer the best possible products and services at the most competitive pricing in the marketplace.

Conclusion

Despite their simplicity, these rules are often ignored by the corporate leaders—not because they are difficult to follow but because they may be someway in conflict with the leadership's personal, not corporate, interests. For the corporate executives, whose personal compensations and other immediate rewards depend on their operational performance and measurable achievements, it's easier and much more expedient to pursue the improvement of company's current sales and profits than to develop future "core competencies" for competitive strengths and capability and thus enhance market advantages. Improving immediate profitability for the firm is much easier for them; all they have to do is to implement cost-cutting measures, adhere to bureaucratic practices, maintain "centralized" management control, and use political lobbying—and, if and when necessary, even unethical or illegal business practices.

CHAPTER 12

Inadequate Product and Market Innovations: Unenthusiastic Commitment and Support

In this age of Internet, wireless, "nano" devices, telecommunications, instant messaging, and the rest of scientific and technological innovations, we are led to believe that we have become a highly creative, innovative, sophisticated, and advanced society. We use such term as "high tech" to underscore how far we have technologically risen.

Moreover, we assume that government and business leaders are very much committed to education and training, science and technology, as well as advances in our knowledge and understanding, and economic progress. Additionally, we commonly share a belief that to improve our economic processes and quality of life, and for us to have all desired products and services cost efficiently, the policy-makers back up their commitment with huge sums of money for research and development (R&D), innovations, and everything else necessary.

Globally, we have indeed made considerable progress in science and technology. We seem to be living longer than ever before. We cannot ignore the 24-hour news bombardments concerning countless scientific discoveries and claims in such areas as health care (biomedicine, biotechnologies, neuroscience, etc.), chemistry, physics, astronomy, engineering, computing sciences, and mathematics.

In the marketplace, too, we are continuously faced with highly priced products and services of different quality—including new and technologically advanced, fairly complex, and, often for most people, incomprehensible products.

The rising number of new products and services may suggest a high level of our product and market innovations based on research and effective business management. However, the available evidence suggests otherwise. We see a lot of leadership tendencies to resist market-imposed changes, resist product and market innovations, and resist creative and adaptive and perhaps radically different business growth strategies in favor of proven and status quo marketing practices.

Corporate World Realities

Over the past few years we have made the following observations:

- The percentage of money spent on education and R&D by government, relative to total government spending, has been declining.
- The percentage of money spent by business leaders on education, training, R&D, and "truly" new product and process developments has been declining, relative to their corporate total sales revenues and capabilities.
- While some specific industries—such as biotechnology and nanotechnology—spend more on education, research, and innovations, most well-established, older and large industries spend proportionally much less in percentage in relation to their total sales revenues.
- Most major product innovations and "commercial" or market developments come from outside the industry. Few recent examples: personal computers, online information search and store, Web advertising, telecommunications, and "nano" engineering.
- Compared to small and medium enterprises (SMEs), large corporations lack entrepreneurial spirit and tend to resist financial risk-taking, creativity and inventiveness, new technological and product developments, structural or procedural changes, and long-term capital spending investments with some uncertain returns on investments (ROI) and benefits. Their in-house efforts in product and market developments have been less than adequate, in spite of their size.
- Large corporations have better financial resources for R&D, but their commitment and allocations of financial resources relatively is less than enthusiastic. Only when they are faced with "real" competitive threats, they seem to act and are forced to follow a costly path of mergers and acquisitions (M&As). Sometimes they lag and are so far behind that their public image and reputation for innovations and leadership may be damaged for good and the situation may be irreversible. U.S. auto firms provide good case studies.

Corporate leaders, most of whom possess good education and advanced degrees such as MBA and business doctorate (regular/"executive") or other advanced degrees, would not be expected to resist scientific research, especially applied research, or resist the development of technologies and production capabilities that could create market advantages, and that could improve product and service offerings, improve productivity, and cut costs, and raise corporate profitability. The fact is, many of the management practitioners and decision-makers do show considerable resistance to required changes.

Reasons for Innovations from Outside the "Industry"

Let's ask: Why do actual research discoveries and innovations, major product and process improvements, and other creative achievements initially come from outside the established industries? Why are organizational and industrial changes imposed from outside frequently rather than from within?

This phenomenon related to industries and new products and processes has been observed over the history of scientific progress. But in light of the recent economic crises, it has become more evident and clear. The U.S. automobile industry provides a good example, given its current dilemma.

The emergence of new industries over the past decade or two underscores the market reality about industrial creativity, inventiveness, adaptability, product and market innovations, as well as different business thinking, strategic modeling, and unconventional approaches.

Industries such as personal computing, digital photography, telecommunications, wireless, nano-tech, and online retailing did not even exist only a few years ago.

The online consumer behavior was accelerating at the early stage of the Web development and its adoption, but business participation of the "brick and mortar" large firms was slow and reluctant—not necessarily cautionary; there was a denial as to this technological reality. Online buying, marketing, and conducting other business were eventually adopted as another way of doing business by the major "traditional" firms. After they realized that they had very little or no choice, the reluctant participants belatedly responded to the technologically changing marketplace.

Who would have imagined that companies like Polaroid, Kodak, and Wal-Mart would be laggards when it comes to product innovations and change from the digital revolution? Who would have imagined that shortly after their birth, Microsoft and Google would be larger in size by market capitalization than many established companies like General Motors (GM), Ford, and Bank of America—household names in the United States?

Relationship between Organizational Growth and Innovations

The fact is, as businesses grow, their leaders tend to spend less conscientious effort and money on scientific search for new discoveries or on the development of better technologies, production, and operational processes, and products and markets. Their commitment to creativity and inventiveness diminishes. They become less willing to change and adapt.

There is a growing leadership tendency to become more and more content with growth and show greater dependency on existing technologies and equipment, on existing other operational processes and facilities, on internally available human knowledge and skills, and on present products and markets. The leaders appear to give preference to continuity and stability over disruption and disorder.

The more internally focused the top leaders are, the more the scientific and market developments get ignored. Environmental trends, technological possibilities, potential business strategic opportunities, and threats are overlooked. Organizational future needs become neglected. Absent are corporate creativity, inventiveness, and adaptability.

With growth, the number of institutional policies and processes increases, creating procedures, rules, and protocols. Decision-making authority, responsibility, and accountability get clarified and specific, and flows of communication become more "formal." Growing inflexibility diminishes creativity and inventiveness, causing growing dissatisfaction and potential business difficulties. Inability to respond promptly and appropriately to varying market needs turns into a competitive disadvantage. Problems emerge, and management further tightens controls and decision-making. Deviations from the organizational "rules" are discouraged, even reprimanded by the book.

As processes and policies become institutionalized, flexibility gradually vanishes. It becomes more and more difficult for people across the organization to adapt, to create, to invent, and to change and respond appropriately to dynamic market challenges in relation to emerging strategic opportunities and problems.

Growth and past success, in other words, encourage management to become myopic and inflexible, focusing on the present while ignoring the future.

In his *Fortune* (December 8, 2008, p. 94) cover article, Alex Taylor, while evaluating GM's chances for survival, describes the company's age-old management problem of prior success—in other words, management being "comfortable, insular, self-referential, and too wedded to the status quo."

It is interesting to note and learn from how GM did not invest in the hybrid technology years ago when it had access, just like Toyota. GM lost its worldwide leadership in the industry and its number one position in annual sales or market capitalization around the globe. Its decline was the consequence of the policies of its corporate management. The former world giant has been struggling for survival and growth for years. Ford and Chrysler have been in a similar situation almost for the same reasons.

Not unlike some automotive companies, several drug companies are in trouble because of their management failure to maintain their market leadership. Their leaders did not adequately spend capital and invest on essential R&D, and as a result, their product pipeline is faced with a diminishing stream of product developments and drug inventions for future sales growth and profitability. Well-established companies in almost all industries encounter problems from past successes and present status quo management mentality. Their past growth and current market position make them content and myopic, and less enthusiastic for product and market innovations.

Status quo leadership behaviors tend to concentrate on addressing immediate competitive problems. Corporate managers aim to raise, perhaps "window-dress," operational profits to appear successful. They are not as much interested in investing for and building future core competencies and technology foresight for the organization. They tend to react rather than act proactively and aggressively for the maintenance and enhancement of competitive edge.

Consequences of Defensive and Reactive Strategies

From the perspectives of the corporate long-term strategic strengths and competitive advantages in the marketplace, reactive measures to respond to the actions of the competitors may turn out to be disastrous over a period of time even though they may help improve the immediate profitability. Current sales and profits may increase by cutting various costs and lowering profit margins, but that may not improve competitive capabilities or customer relationships. Why?

To improve inflow of cash quickly, corporate managers use numerous tactics. Among them are the following:

- Cancel, postpone, or cut R&D spending through reduction in scientific staff and activities.
- Outsource R&D function or eliminate it altogether.
- Cancel, postpone, or cut planned investment in operational technologies, equipment, and facilities upgrading and modernization.
- Outsource manufacturing and operations.
- When possible, terminate contractual obligations for plant and operational facility construction or renovation. Pay "acceptable" termination penalty if necessary.
- If possible, terminate all contractual obligations for purchases of capital equipment (production machineries, computers, and information or data management systems, etc.). Pay "acceptable" termination penalty if necessary.
- Delay plant and equipment maintenance, repair, and upgrading as long as possible. Perform maintenance and repair only when absolutely necessary.
- Freeze employee/staff hiring, and resort to layoff or "forced" retirement.
- Freeze promotion and salary/compensation, reduce or eliminate "merit" raises or payments, cut across the board "regular" or base wage and salary.
- Cut back in employee benefits such as healthcare, 401K employer contributions, travel and vacation, sick leave, education, and skill development.
- Eliminate managerial and nonmanagerial positions.
- Consolidate positions, activities, and functions.
- Increase staff responsibilities and workloads.
- Utilize greatly "temporary" and part-time workers.
- Renegotiate labor contract for lowering wages and benefits.
- Adopt production shortcuts, such as replacement of materials and parts with inferior or inexpensive substitutes.
- Ignore dependable, cooperative, and high quality suppliers and distributors in favor of low-quality, low-service, and lower-cost alternatives.
- Cut back quality control, inspections, and related measures.
- Cut back customer service or charge extra for items formerly complimentary.
- Reduce advertising and sales promotional budgets and efforts.
- Reduce and/or eliminate incentives and support for distribution channels.
- Raise or unbundle prices, if possible, to enhance sales revenues.
- Greatly centralize policy formulation and decision-making power and authority; implement micromanaging and top-down communications.
- Undertake careful and scrutinized financial planning and implementation.
- Introduce tight operational budgets and financial controls; monitor costs closely.

- Lower capital budgets and spending; cut spending on capital items such as office computers and other appliances, machineries, and other equipment.
- Lower projected spending on future investment projects, rearrange priorities for financing purposes.
- Greatly utilize low-cost sources of capital, regardless of dependability and long-term relationship building.
- Eliminate or cut dividends.
- Dispose of certain assets—account receivables, equipment, buildings, etc.

This list certainly is not all-inclusive. Management does not overlook any of the available quick-fix measures in order to enhance immediate sales, profits, and cash flows.

As capital-spending budgets get frozen and future spending remains on hold, all new product- and market-developmental efforts are essentially slowed down.

Thus, almost all strategically important activities for growth are adversely affected in the long run—R&D, updating and modernization of operational technologies and facilities, and acquisition and development of human resource skills and knowledge.

As operational cost-cutting tactics are endorsed and carried out, the working environment begins to get tensed and deteriorates, affecting human motivation and productivity. As financial rewards are reduced and position promotions become fewer and fewer, organizational creativity and desire to improve performance quality diminish. Work suffers, with tighter controls and less decision-making flexibility and adaptability. One-way, downward communications discourage feedback concerning new ideas, new ways of task and goal accomplishments, or anything concerning existing and potential marketing and operational problems or opportunities. Inventive, creative, and highly talented individuals, highly motivated and driven, quit because financial and psychological benefits are not available.

With productive people gone or leaving, essential capital spending in decline, and relationship with customers, distributors, and other business associates deteriorating, the firm's competitive position in the marketplace erodes with time. The firm's immediate financial situation may appear attractive, but potentially serious future problems await it. Over time, the situation may worsen and could become eventually irreversible.

There are companies facing such situations because of their leaders' unwillingness and failure to maintain and develop long-term strategic strengths. These firms have lacked in product and market innovations. Their managers have not spent needed capital for research and production facilities. There is a failure to practice effective employment policies. Their leadership has not shared organizational past gains fairly and equitably. Their work environment has not increased productivity, and their top management has neglected the development of human resources—people's skills, experience, and knowledge. There is a lack of drive for excellence and to compete successfully, and ultimately win. These firms have not been able to deal with and overcome the disrupting influence of technological and market innovations.

Approaches of Successful Firms

In contrast, there are firms, like IBM and Genentech, that have been successful in the dynamic marketplace through creativity, flexibility, and adaptability. There was a period when IBM was not very effective, due to some internal factors; but with the change in leadership at the top, it was able to revitalize its core strengths and regain its leadership in quality service and product offerings. Successful firms usually are in the forefront in R&D, product and market innovations, not reacting but being proactive and planning ahead and investing and spending capital, modernizing operational facilities, acquiring and developing knowledge and capable people, and above all, not standing still and being distracted and overwhelmed by current operational problems or temporary setbacks. They have not lost their sense of strategic priorities and ignored the needs for long-term competitive advantages.

Successful firms strive to be leaders in science and technology, in product and market innovations. They maintain a lead either through their own creativity and research efforts or, if necessary, they acquire and merge or actively collaborate with others for profitable innovations. Their strategic approaches focus on being the first in the marketplace. Their leaders take risk by investing in new technologies and products, and enter early to offer better or altogether different products and services—better substitutes; they attempt to go beyond customer expectations more effectively and with cost efficiency.

Sometimes they try to change the marketplace significantly by creating and offering totally new products that may or may not be somewhat related to existing market products. By so doing, they create new markets and aim to develop them by satisfying needs that have remained considerably unrecognized prior to their product development and prior to their market developmental informative and persuasive efforts.

Proactive firms take advantage of R&D, scientific and technological breakthroughs within their own fields of expertise or elsewhere, and they carry out careful environmental scanning and analysis of market forces. They do strategic thinking, develop foresight, plan ahead, and create appropriate strategies and approaches. They are committed to capital funding. They spend to create business advantages for better rewards and assume risk.

Their leaders, to be sure, take chances with their innovations in the marketplace with their "first-in" market strategy. But by being there first before everyone else—their competitors, current and potential, direct or indirect—they put their firms in an ideal position to realize huge market growth and financial rewards.

In case their firms are not successful in being the "first" in the market, the proactive leaders attempt actively to be at least among the early market leaders or entrants. These managers are not content to be latecomers, among the laggards, just by copying or imitating competitors. They strive for excellence.

When necessary, such striving leaders acquire, merge, or collaborate with other organizations that have a lead in scientific and technical research or are ahead in product or market development. When they're not ahead, they acquire production and marketing strengths, in the process swallowing their pride and incurring higher acquisition costs.

In the marketplace, such leaders are rare and very few. Most corporate leaders resist capital spending for the future.

Many firms, large and established, neglect investment and resource development until they have no choice any longer and are forced to act promptly. When they experience competitive disadvantage and are struggling with low sales and inefficient operations, they decide to move- spend investment capital. By then, their alternatives are few. They have to go for business acquisition at high financial costs in order to become more competitive.

If they do not have the financial capability for acquisition, they have even less desirable choices. From the weak bargaining position, they have to auction off their partial or full ownership and become acquired by other organizations. If the last option is not open, if there is no other firm with a merger or acquisition interest, ultimately the option of shutting down becomes clear.

Companies with deficiency in investment and in efforts for product and market developments are forced out of business. They have to decide eventually to go out of business forever. That's their ultimate cost of neglecting capital spending and failing to remain competitive.

Many firms try to avoid this fate with countless "superficial" product or promotional adaptations and exaggerated claims. This is evident in the fact that there have not been many "real" product or market innovations from old and established firms. The actual number is fairly small, and perhaps has declined. What we've found to be "new and innovative" is largely from the smaller and medium-sized, new and young and rapidly evolving enterprises—not from the "traditional" and household names.

In the past decade or two there has been a surge in new firms and emerging industries and their significant disrupting influence on the nature of competition. And the number continues to rise. These market entrants or newcomers have been successful in taking away market shares from big and previously "secured" business establishments. The technologically advanced products and innovative marketing approaches of these smaller and aggressive young and emerging firms are rapidly making many old or "traditional" products, services, technologies, industries, production and operational processes, and marketing practices "obsolete and dated"—and, basically, not competitive or desirable.

These market forces have made the "company-focused," "short-term-oriented" strategies and "approaches" of the established firms self-defeating in the long run.

Importance of R&D Resource Planning and Implementation

Forward-looking strategic management that aims at long-term growth has become a necessity for the organizational survival and success. Careful resource management has become essential.

Productive resources—human and physical, including technologically advanced— have to be planned, acquired, and allocated, and thereafter developed as necessary, utilized, and monitored effectively. They have to be economically managed for "profit maximization," for the accomplishment of organizational goals in the long run, and to fulfill the vision. Resource productivity should be maximized, not underutilized, and its potentials realized. When necessary, unproductive resources have to be replaced promptly, too, to keep the organization moving forward toward its goals.

Essential resources have to be productively managed constantly in order to gain and maintain core competencies and develop competitive advantages in the marketplace. Effective management of productive resources is indispensable for corporate survival, growth, and overall success. The technological, competitive, and dynamic environment requires it in order to meet the challenges of competitors as well as those of the continuously changing customer characteristics, desires, and market behaviors.

The Internet has made market information, resources, and customers accessible across the world to all sorts of businesses—young and old, small and large. The Internet too has empowered people around the globe.

To meet the growing demand and insatiable needs of Web-empowered customers for better and cheaper products, creative and entrepreneurial enterprises worldwide have been proactive and aggressive. They have begun to offer an increasing number of innovative products and market approaches. Many are technically savvy; some are not. Nonetheless, they are all hungry for fast growth and income, and they do not hesitate to use their knowledge, might, and determination to reach their goals—fast, "ASAP." They are using creative business models, strategies, and tactics. Their change-based, adaptive attitudes and innovative ways put them and their organizations at a very distinct competitive advantage—in contrast to their "traditional" rivals in the marketplace.

For many large and well-known household names, such as GM and Ford, executive failure to embrace and maintain leadership in technological innovations through research and/or capital investments in manufacturing and service facilities has been disastrous. They are experiencing the dramatic effects of their neglect in the past and paying a heavy price today. Their past decisions have adversely affected millions of lives. Their competitive ability has been seriously compromised by their failure to endorse and adopt creativity and innovation.

Undoubtedly, creativity and innovation have become a competitive, long-term-growth tool and one of the best strategic approaches or a way to succeed in the current marketplace.

Indeed, many different books on innovation (see Christensen, Hammer, Champy, and Schumpeter in the suggested readings list in the appendix) point out that creative and innovative products, as well as business models and approaches, are key to success. One of the scholars and pioneers in the field is Joseph Schumpeter, who is well-known for his work on "stages" of economic growth, several decades ago.

As the business literature continues to suggest and emphasize, product and market innovation should be part of organizational growth and renewable strategies in the competitive marketplace.

Today's marketplace is different. It has become quicker in pace, evolutionary, and much transitory. In it, as a business process, competition is no longer the same. New market entrants no longer compete with established businesses. Innovative entrants compete against older firms as well as with other innovative new market entrants, each one trying to outdo others fast with creative and better business models and business processes and products. While satisfying current needs, they usually aim to create new needs for future innovations.

Not only do proactive and aggressive business firms come up with products on the basis of new or recent scientific research and breakthroughs, they utilize not-so-new knowledge and economic resources more creatively, using their inventiveness and adaptability for competitive strengths and advantages and looking at market opportunities and potentials from different perspectives.

Creative and proactive leaders are different types of business competitors. They don't stand still for breakthroughs. They instigate change. They undertake and offer innovations by manipulating, combining or recombining, and repackaging "old" and "existing or current," and "developing or new"—products, technologies, business models, processes, and practices—in order to gain a competitive edge, in order to satisfy current or creatable customer needs and desires, and, essentially, above all, in order to beat competition and succeed by attempting to go beyond customer expectations.

They may compete as what Christensen calls "dominating regime" or "disruptive regime." They offer sustaining, incremental, or revolutionary technologies and products, replacing old and changing customers and markets. They also create and offer value with simple ideas and adaptations, making certain technical products and technologies less complex or sophisticated and more user-friendly at lower costs for wider markets.

In the marketplace, many incumbents lose out, not because of their incompetence or lack of knowledge ahead of time about various market trends and future competitive market requirements. They lose out, instead, because of their unwillingness to take risk, commit capital, and invest in order to develop better technologies, products, and markets. GM, Ford, and Chrysler have known for decades about the society's growing energy needs for fuel-efficient personal and public transportation. However, they failed to make the necessary investments in technology.

This business situation is not unique to the United States. There are numerous firms elsewhere facing similar strategic management orientation and problem. Many big and well-established firms outside the United States are known for their risk aversion. Despite their capability to effectively support in-house R&D and other developmental activities, they prefer a costly alternative of M&A. They seem to have distaste for investing in product and market developmental activities on a regular basis, presumably in order to improve their current operating profits for the year. Instead, they should be carefully planning and investing for product and market developments. Only when their market position is threatened do they act strategically and then they pay the heavy extra price for their past neglect.

In his study of some firms in the Philippines, Eduardo Garrovillas of Jose Rizal University finds such big and dominant firms as San Miguel Corporation, Unilab, Jollibee Food Corporation, SM Investments Corporation and JG Summit Holdings primarily using costly M&As or licensing for growth and expansion; he describes their commitment toward R&D capital investments as less than enthusiastic. Professor Garrovillas mentions his study in his review comments on a portion of this book to the author by e-mail. He writes:

> [T]here are a number of indigenous companies even from the developing countries of Asia that are guilty of or afflicted by the corporate viral disease described in the . . . [book], such as aversion to risk, lack of innovation and creativity, and who would rather take the easy route of acquisition and merger, than investing on R&D. . . . Among the five (mentioned above), only Unilab, a drug-manufacturing giant, took a different growth modality, that is in-licensing/partnership, which is dictated more by the uncertain and prohibitive R&D cost in the drug industry (i.e., R&D in the drug industry is like mining, one cannot tell whether you will hit gold or mud). Rather than investing on R&D, they would rather acquire or merge with existing companies to grow and penetrate other markets. Most of these companies are over 20 years . . . the oldest is a food and beverage titan, San Miguel Corporation, which has been in the market for over 100 years.

The contemporary new market entrants have competitive advantages in strategic thinking, technology, and cost. They first go after sophisticated or unique niche or niches—one at a time, aiming to share one small slice at a time while the established players remain unaware, unconcerned, and content. Many of the new marketers are well financed with venture capital so that, if they wish, they could go after a larger market or several niches from the beginning, threatening larger firms with established products and markets.

With their advantages over their established rivals in certain technical, business, and customer expectation areas, these creative and inventive newcomers are driven by financial well-being, self-actualization, and psychic benefits. They are not averse to risk.

They know too that once their larger and established rivals start experiencing sales and operational income declines, become aware of their competitive market situation, and subsequently recognize their inability to reverse it, they would be looking for a suitable business acquisition or two—possibly the entrants who have been taking away the market share. Being cognizant of this market possibility, some of the innovative entrants intend—and sometimes plan ahead—to be acquired by their rivals or other interested firms and become rich and financially secure instantly.

For the struggling market leader, acquisition and merger may seem to be the most appropriate route to instantly access better technologies and products in order to stop further decline. Possibly too, the acquisition may offer an option to replace or improve the inefficient operational equipment and facilities and revive the matured and dying products and lengthen their life cycles. The acquisition cost, to be sure, would be stiff but necessary for survival and growth.

Starting R&D collaboration with rival firms by sharing the cost and benefits is another option.

With foresight and careful strategic planning, many struggling large firms could have avoided their need for acquisition and their having to pay a high price. Had their leaders been proactive and innovation-oriented, they could have prevented declining profitability and growth. Had they developed what is referred to as "intrapreneurship" within their organizations, they would have their own, internal innovators and value creators; they would have been successful, if and when necessary, in reengineering, outsourcing, downsizing, and spinning off subsidiaries.

In other words, had the struggling business firms facilitated and let creativity and inventiveness flourish across the organization and below the top management level, and had they implemented appropriate incentives and employment policies, they would have been among the leaders in product and market innovations—not among the laggards. Their corporate managements instead hindered motivation, creativity, and participation, and thus put them in jeopardy.

Their short-term, executive-compensation-based leadership's preoccupation and focus with operational results discourage and prevent capital spending, slow down or stop product and market innovations, and eventually force them to bear very high and unjustifiable cost over a period of time.

Conclusion

In summary,

- Management must understand the competitive market dynamics.
- Corporate managers must recognize the market reality that corporate, industrial, product- or technology-based boundaries are not fixed, that market boundaries could shrink unless conscientiously expanded, and that all markets are open, unsecured, and can be invaded by anyone within or outside the market or industry with better or innovative products and technologies, with innovative business models, and with more cost-efficient and creative business processes.
- Product and market innovations strengthen the organization's competitive competencies and market advantages. Organizations with inadequacy in innovation efforts encounter serious difficulties later on.
- Because production and market innovations require appropriate financial commitment and investment, capital budgeting and spending have to be carefully planned and implemented.
- While R&D, technologies, and operations can be outsourced or acquired as needed, neither approach is cheaper in cost or better than an organization's own internal effort within its own bounds and management control. Internal innovations and developments are less costly and provide better protection of intellectual property rights and, in case of foreign operations,

better protection from potential political and legal problems. Furthermore, conscientious and appropriate product, technological, and market developmental efforts tend to be better, and they do guarantee steady flow in creative ideas, physical efforts, and products.

- For innovations, management must create an appropriate productive work environment and culture.
- To encourage and promote creativity and inventiveness across the organization and at all levels below, leaders must allow flexibility and adaptability. They must adequately delegate task-related responsibility and decision-making authority. Micromanaging and bureaucratic inflexibility are unproductive. Performance must be evaluated on the basis of task complexity and probability for expected outcome; on progress toward results accomplishment; on actual accomplishments over corporate policies, procedures, protocols, and prevailing politics inside the organization. Policies regarding ethical and legal conduct must be clear and must be promptly and equitably enforced.
- Intrapreneurialship or creative work behavior requires motivating incentives, fair and proportional financial rewards that are also internally and externally equitable, performance and merit promotions, job security, customary health care and retirement benefits, fair and justifiable managerial actions and staff treatments, safe and nonthreatening working conditions, and overall, appropriate job benefits and satisfaction.
- Finally, organizational profitability and growth are the by-product of "out-of-box" thinking, motivating, learning, flexible and adapting, innovating and creative, and productive culture.

The organization's survival and success are the creation of its owners and managers, its productive and motivating working conditions, and its knowledgeable, skillful, capable, learning, and motivated workforce.

Once again, it's advisable to keep in mind how so many companies fail to invest in efficient technologies and human capital and, consequently, find themselves in trouble.

We need to understand and remember how GM lost its global leadership by being myopic, while Toyota used the accessible and required technology to build up its reputation and image as innovator and became a successful world competitor and leader. We have to learn from the demise of other business giants.

Let's not forget the recent demise of some major financial institutions too, like Bear Stearns and Countrywide. Their failures suggest that it's not enough to be innovative in product and market developments. The organizational creative approaches must be ethical as well, and in line with customers' capabilities and realities, not just with their expectations and wishful desires. The business practices must be legal too to avoid the fate of so many business executives and politicians who were criminally convicted and put behind prison bars, dethroned from their social status and prestige.

Business history is full of management failure with examples of once innovative, successful, mighty companies and leaders. Their fate was determined when their leadership became content, myopic, assuming, and self-serving, ignoring their fiduciary, moral, and legal obligations, overlooking sound values and approaches, and taking unjustifiable chances and risks.

There are risks in being creative and unorthodox. Nonetheless, rewards of success are enormous. Useful innovations could present extremely profitable customers and markets. Business cannot afford to overlook opportunities and remain myopic in its strategic approaches and practices. Everyone understands and recognizes the importance of creativity, research, and innovations in the development of products and markets. But it is hard to commit funds for the uncertain future and far-distant rewards. It is expedient to focus on immediate outcomes and allocate resources accordingly. It is not easy, however, to move forward and achieve sustainable excellence to reach the corporate vision. There is no question that efficiency is important. It is difficult to balance organizational efficiency to control cost with creativity and inventiveness to gain strong competitive advance. But efficiency should not undermine any efforts toward product and market developments for the future.

Finally, corporate managers who give up or have given up on their commitment to market excellence for self-serving personal reasons are hastening the doomsday and collapse of their enterprises in the years to come!

CHAPTER 13

Unhealthy Work Environment: Inappropriate Employment Practices

Not unlike capital, not unlike land and basic materials, not unlike manufacturing and service equipment, and not unlike operational facilities and office buildings, in business it takes people to satisfy customer needs. Highly motivated and productive people enable the organization to gain an edge over competitors in the marketplace by satisfying customers beyond their expectations. If the firm is already ahead, it has to continue to retain and develop the "right" workers, who can continue to contribute excellence at work to maintain the competitive edge and, possibly, advance the organization's interests further.

To ensure cost efficiency and product/service quality, corporate managers need to create a productive working environment. They cannot afford to evolve work conditions that are not motivating or rewarding enough for employees and staff. The work environment has to be safe, healthy, and conducive to human efforts, and it should provide sufficient "economic" and "psychological" rewards for people. Financial rewards and promotions within the organization have to be fair and equitable to promote cost efficiency and to increase productivity.

Importance of Human Resource Management

As the scholar and pioneer in the field of management Peter Drucker suggested a long time ago, management is getting things done through people. Without people in the organization, nothing happens. People are a vital economic resource. In addition to physical resources, business needs people for the creation, production, and distribution of products and services.

The organization needs people who can provide ideas and technical skills for beneficial products and services. Besides capital and a variety of technologies (machines, equipment, computers, etc.), business requires human skills and actual physical efforts to produce, store, transport, distribute, sell, and ultimately make products and services available whenever and wherever customers want them for their use or consumption. It takes a whole village to carry out the essential tasks, accomplish the organizational mission, and reach the organizational vision.

In other words, business must have owners, investing partners, and creditors with financial resources. Business needs entrepreneurs, scientists and engineers, innovators and creative individuals, managers and supervisors, production/service workers, sales people, distributors, suppliers, and so forth for investments as well as for productive physical and mental efforts.

To deliver customer benefits profitably, the business firm should have motivated, capable, and qualified people both inside and outside the organization. Without them, business would not succeed and grow. In case the organization does not possess the essential human skills and efforts, it has to acquire or develop them.

Some business tasks could be outsourced. Other tasks, however, have to be carried out by the firm using its own human resources. How the organization acquires, develops, and deploys its human resources could determine its success or failure. The quality of people determines the business survival and growth.

This makes managing of people an important leadership function—especially for competitive reasons in the long run. From top to bottom, across and throughout the organization, people have to be made productive and capable of performing well so that the required tasks are accomplished as planned, or perhaps better than expected. "Right" human motivations and efforts have to be cultivated, developed, and accomplished to reach the desired goals in a timely manner, most "cost efficiently" and effectively.

To succeed, corporate management has to create a working environment that is motivating and productive. There has to evolve a learning culture for improvements at work. The environment has to be healthy. It should enable people to feel safe, productive, and worthy of their efforts. There have to be fair and equitable rewards and benefits.

The employment recruiting, hiring, compensation, retention and promotion, and separation (voluntary or involuntary; retiring, layoff, or firing) policies and practices have to be carefully planned and implemented. Above all, management decisions and actions must appear reasonable or "justifiable" from the perspectives of people below, and they must be acceptable to others all across the organization.

When the work environment is physically safe and "accident proof," people are not afraid to work. Good and carefully planned physical layout, appropriate lights or sunlight, safe equipment, easy to operate machines, appropriate tools, good and well-maintained buildings and machinery, easy access to computers for information, and other "right" physical support affect the quality of human efforts in a beneficial way. In addition to such physical elements, employment policies and practices dealing with individuals' financial and psychological aspects significantly affect the quality of human productivity. Financial support and other internal activities for employee training and skill developments improve corporate competitive strengths.

When management fails to create a healthy, learning, and productive work environment, business suffers. The challenges of the global market become difficult to meet.

Disastrous Employment Policies and Practices

Recent economic crises and business failures shed light on the existence of unhealthy work environment, particularly in large corporations. The contemporary business environment of layoffs; firings; frozen salaries, bonuses, and promotions; rising work-related accidents and medical emergencies; cuts in vacation and sick days, diminishing health care benefits, elimination or reduction of employer's contribution toward employee retirement—among others—is indicative of the quality of work conditions that have evolved over the years.

Each time there is an economic crisis, highly educated and experienced corporate managers use the current economic situation to shrink employee benefits further. They justify their cost-cutting measures on competitive grounds. If these austerity programs are business necessities, one wonders why executive compensations and benefits have continued to rise over the years.

In relative terms, the benefits for operational managers and workers at levels below the CEO and his/her top executive lieutenants have shrunk significantly. In contrast, the size of compensations—salaries, monetary bonuses, stock options, health care benefits and other perks, employment signing bonuses, severance packages, etc.—of these corporate managers has been going up and up. There are instances of some executives having doubled or tripled their compensations each year in recent times. In 2006, after a short tenure of 12 years only, one Exxon leader earned a severance package worth almost $400 million.

Because corporate managers have no stockownership long-term stake in the firms they run, they use their management positions to maximize their personal compensations as quickly as possible. Consequently, their decisions and policies contribute to business disasters and economy-wide crises.

To earn high compensations quickly, corporate managers formulate and implement fast revenue-enhancing measures and operational plans and policies that lead to drastic cost-cutting. In the process, they weaken relationships with customers and distributors (poor product quality/service), as well as with workers (job insecurity, inadequate financial incentives, and equipment breakdown caused by lack of maintenance). They put pressure on suppliers to cut price and seek out inferior materials. Furthermore, corporate investments are cut, temporarily postponed, or altogether dropped and scratched out for product and market developments for the future—in such areas as R&D, plant modernization, employee training and development, etc. In essence, self-compensation-driven management actions, instead of helping business in the long run, become dangerous to corporate long-term security, growth, and survival.

The shortsighted and self-serving management behavior may improve corporate sales as a result of low product prices from cost-cutting for the moment, and subsequently, the corporate profitability may perhaps improve. In reality, though, such management actions compromise the organization's competitive strength due to resulting customer dissatisfaction. Poor quality in product or service does not build a customer base. Product quality suffers when low-cost inferior material is substituted. Poor pre- and postpurchase service may result either from the absence of sales efforts altogether or from the delivery of slow or bad service.

Unhealthy working conditions affect employee motivations to perform well or excel at work. Less than enthusiastic work efforts are not good for business or its competitive position in the global marketplace. Cost-cutting measures not only reduce individual financial security and benefits but they often result in loss of individual flexibility and creativity in the workplace. When employees are not empowered with some flexibility in work-related decision-making, there is no incentive to experiment or innovate. If there are no adequate financial and psychological rewards for contribution toward process improvements, work processes do not improve for future gains in cost and quality. In other words, cost-cutting measures affect work ethics and employee morale.

When work conditions deteriorate, employees may exert minimal efforts just to get by and hold on to the job. They may waste work time while pretending to work. Highly motivated and productive individuals, like scientists and skilled professionals, leave at the first available opportunity elsewhere when they are bypassed for well-deserved promotions or are not appropriately rewarded in salaries and merit bonuses for their good performance and real contribution. Good workers slow down in the absence of "real" financial rewards and career progression; they are not fooled by the "superficial" job titles or certificates of recognition and appreciation while the management continues to derive all the concrete financial benefits. The work environment is also affected when corporate managers withdraw decision-making authority from lower levels, centralize or recentralize, and consolidate power.

Basically, fast-result-producing management policies and practices cause major adverse effects in three areas:

1. Employee "intrapreneurship"—like entrepreneurship, risk-taking by employees for product and service improvements through creativity and inventiveness, meaning through process and product innovations
2. Unethical and/or illegal work-related behavior and conduct—false advertising, misleading prices, falsification of financial records, rewarding of unproductive team players, supervisory misconduct like encouraging illegal behavior, misuse of authority and power, and workers' violent and desperate actions such as shooting and killing at work—abusive bosses and peers in particular
3. Loss of excellence in human efforts from lack of productive motivations

In short, in pursuit of quick corporate profitability, corporate managers create unhealthy working conditions inside and across the supply-distribution chains. When corporate leaders implement cost-cutting and revenue-enhancing measures, they adversely affect economic security and motivations to perform well—honestly and productively. Workforce reductions, salary cuts and freezes, unfair and inequitable career promotions and financial rewards for productive workers, favorable treatments of team players and management loyalists, unsafe and harmful physical facilities, lack of training and development, and a number of other unhealthy work situations threaten the corporate competitive position and its success in the long run.

In order to improve immediate profitability, when corporate investment speculators and managers use their positions, powers, and authority, unhealthy conditions are bound to occur. Gains may be accomplished for the needs of these self-serving individuals. For others, though, the shortsighted operational policies and practices are detrimental in the long run because the management's actions threaten the core competitive strengths and advantages of business.

What we have experienced in the past two decades is the result of disastrous leadership performance. Unhealthy work environment has become the central feature of the contemporary corporate world.

How Leaders Create Unhealthy Working Conditions

Sometimes the causes of human performance problems originate with the board directors who seem to represent diverse investors' interests, none being stronger than their own and corporate executives' interests and influences.

In theory, though, corporate owners or stockholders have direct control over corporate policies and practices, and they could affect working conditions depending on their financial and other objectives. Corporate founders with majority stockownership usually continue to exert their power and influence to maintain flexible and creative working conditions for long-term business gains. They are not likely to compromise corporate security and survival for quick gains. Their ownership and active interest ensure the security of a healthy work environment.

When stockownership is acquired by a group of nonfounding long-term investors, the work environment does not change significantly. However, when large and strong speculating investors acquire the stockownership for fast and high return on investment, unhealthy conditions are likely to emerge. They may exert pressures on their managers to take shortcuts for profit improvements and stock-price appreciations.

Many powerful investors/speculators often acquire controlling ownership interests through business mergers and acquisitions—sometimes through leveraged buyouts, stock swaps, or some other creative financial strategies. Because their interests are strictly monetary, for profit or return maximization, they follow business strategies of quick fixes that involve immediate improvement of corporate profitability, followed by divestiture (sellout) with big returns, irrespective of any other consequences for the corporation or its other stakeholders. Some of the U.S. corporations have been infected with speculative investment bugs, causing unhealthy working conditions and untenable employment policies, adversely affecting human motivations, productivity, and performance—and overall success over the years to come.

In case of organizations with widely dispersed small stockowners, sometimes in millions worldwide, and with no single powerful and controlling ownership influence, the ownership interests are largely in the hands of the corporate board or its executives. Only once in a while, someone takes a lead, tries to unite diverse powerless small stockholders, and fights to gain control over corporate policies through proxy fights and representation on the corporate board to preserve ownership interests. Their investment fate, otherwise, rests with their board representatives and top administrators. Their power to influence corporate policies and practices are essentially very much limited.

Many of the existing corporations are characterized by worldwide and diverse small stockownerships with no single powerful voice or force. As a result, their long-term interests for dividends and stock price appreciations are compromised by the preoccupation of their corporate board and corporate executives. Basically, individual small stockholders have very little or no influence over corporate business policies or affairs, and they are not in position to influence the work environment.

Labor unions with their weakening power over the years have no major influence on corporate stockholders, on board directors, nor on corporate managers or their policies.

Corporate directors, as explained in Chapter 6, "Corporate Board Governance," in reality, have failed in their fiduciary responsibilities and have essentially tended to represent corporate managers more than small stockholders or any other stakeholders. With corporate managers, they pursue their own financial interests, too, and they do not interfere with management plans or policies. They approve management actions without any closer supervision or guidance. Only when there are strong protests from employees or labor unions, they show some concern; otherwise, they remain indifferent to employment conditions.

Essentially, professional corporate managers—CEOs and executives in collaboration with their top staff, outside consultants, advisors, and other team players—are left in charge, unchecked, to exploit and use corporate resources for selfish pursuits. These self-serving individuals recruit, retain, reward, and use their "club" members for mutually beneficial pursuits and individual gains. In the meantime, the interests of everyone else (see Chapter 8, "Management Club") get disregarded and compromised. Unhealthy conditions emerge as a result.

The current conditions are ripe for increasing labor union memberships. Labor unions with unskilled and skilled professional individual memberships in large numbers may emerge as countervailing power against corporate management power in the future, stronger than ever in recent years.

Conclusion

In conclusion, lack of best human efforts for personal and greater good at the workplace is not good for business. When the work environment deteriorates, business cannot succeed in the long run. Bad working conditions threaten the organization's competitive advantage in the marketplace. Ineffective human resource management sabotages improvements and progress in product and service gains over the rivals. When highly capable and motivated individuals leave for competing firms because of lack of good working environment, the business firm can no longer continue to remain competitive and exist for too long. Eventually, financial resources and business opportunities diminish, and the organization has no choice except to get acquired or shut the doors permanently.

The current business and economic crises are the result of self-serving corporate managers. Executive greed for personal gains underscores bad business decisions and disastrous employment- and work-related policies. The shortsighted management actions have tempted or forced good-intentioned managerial and nonmanagerial individuals in positions of power and influence to carry out unsound, unethical—and sometimes unlawful—conduct. It shows how blind loyalty and team-playing can be dangerous to business health, and to the stakeholders' economic interests at large, beyond the organization's stockholders. What we have experienced in the past two decades is deteriorating work conditions as a result of corporate management greed.

A few decades ago, at the early stage of the computer revolution, there was a concern for the high probability of income with fewer hours of workweek and greater leisure time for most people. Instead, the work environment has deteriorated to the point where today most families have to work hard and longer just to survive—and barely at that, with diminishing health care and retirement benefits. Economic insecurity is at an all-time high with rising health care costs. Most families need two paychecks to hold on to their homes and to maintain average standards of living.

In contrast, corporate major investors and their professional and collaborating managers continue to enrich themselves. There is upward movement of concentration of wealth in the hands of fewer and fewer people while unhealthy conditions at work continue to multiply. The working middle class, with lower income and lower purchasing power, keeps expanding, and more people with jobs are moving rapidly in the direction where some sort of assistance from government and/or charitable organizations will become essential for survival.

The reality is, human greed at the top in corporate world is no good. Individual greed is not healthy for the corporation, neither is it good economically for the society at large. It corrupts human values that could eventually affect our judicial and political processes. Instead of contributing toward the well-being and advancement of civilization, corporate leadership greed takes us back toward the path of destruction of civilization!

CHAPTER 14

Reckless Strategic Financial Behavior: Ill-Conceived Financial Management

Corporate management's primary responsibility is to protect the stockholders' long-term ownership interests in financial security and growth. But, in the pursuit of their own personal financial interests, the CEO and his/her top executives and advisors jeopardize their organization with their imprudent financial strategies and practices. Instead of implementing effective business policies and approaches, corporate leaders undertake risky financial behavior and focus on the organization's current profitability and fast maximization of return on investment. They ignore the corporate strategic market advantages and potential for long-term cash flows. They disregard the cash problems and corporate security in the years to come.

The short-term financial aim of corporate managers is to reduce business cash drain through fast cost-cuttings and also to improve the cash inflow through sales increases. In other words, corporate leaders focus on operational income. For corporate executives, this goal is of utmost importance because their personal compensations depend on immediate profitability, not on what happens in the future. The long-term consequences of their operational decisions, in sales and financial terms, are not their primary or major concern for the present. Such thinking in the competitive global marketplace is imprudent and extremely dangerous and risky. It could lead the organization to the path of disaster.

In addition to operational tactics, corporate managers use some other risky financial strategies—namely, reckless leveraged or debt financing. This type of financing is preferred over other techniques, because it is relatively cheaper in cost and generates higher returns if successful.

Even though debt financing (financial leverage) could help increase profits, it could turn out to be dangerous in times of cash shortages or liquidity problems. Business may not be able to pay its maturing debt or other financial obligations if there is serious decline in sales and profits and credit sources dry up. Insolvency could result in takeover by other firms, bankruptcy, government bailouts or forced takeover, or total failure with doors closed permanently.

Contemporary Financial Scene

Such business and financial realities have become evident in the current economic crises worldwide. What we have experienced in the past few decades is reckless business leadership conduct, underscoring self-centered financial motivations of "professional" corporate managers in large industrial corporations and major financial institutions, along with the management's collusive or cooperating collaborators.

There is no intrigue or mystery as to what corporate managers with no long-term financial stakes in corporate financial well-being have done or do. The business troubles or failures of many major U.S. corporations [Chrysler, General Motors (GM), etc.] and financial institutions [Citibank, Bear Stearns, Lehman Brothers, American International Group (AIG), and others] underscore unsound business philosophies and practices.

The faulty leadership strategies are not the by-product of lack of business knowledge and experience. The vast majority of corporate managers possess considerable business experience as well as formal management education; some even hold MBAs from prestigious business schools. In spite of corporate leaders' presumably good understanding of financial concepts and strategies, they practice what is reckless and risky. Their business actions may be in their personal or individual best interests, but are certainly not good for the financial well-being of their corporations and, most importantly, not good for most of their stockholders, employees, suppliers, distributors, creditors, customers, taxpayers, and the public at large.

To improve their personal financial benefits—salaries, money bonuses, stock options, severance packages, other frills and perks—corporate professional managers follow a fast financial track. They watch capital markets closely and follow what happens to their company stock prices on daily basis. They love to watch their firm's stock prices move upward high and fast, and they try their best to influence the stock price rise. They are cognizant of the fact that their periodic financial reports, especially quarterly or annual, move stock prices up or down, depending on the levels of corporate profits they have earned or expect to earn in the next quarter or year. Their management performance is evaluated on the basis of their periodic achievements—not on what they do for business to succeed in the competitive global market in the long run. How their performance is perceived in the financial markets determines their executive compensations and opportunities for career progression in the firm or elsewhere with higher personal benefits.

So the upward movement in stock prices (stock price appreciations) for personal financial gains and career objectives becomes the driving management force behind corporate decisions, plans, and policies, and practices are designed with the underlying motivation of influencing stock prices through corporate gains as quickly as possible, and in any manner necessary—if required, unethically or unlawfully to be far ahead in the financial markets relative to others, and stay there for personal compensation maximization. The stock market dictates corporate policies and operational targets.

Not unlike speculators, corporate leaders become more preoccupied with current corporate valuation or market capitalization than what is good for all stakeholders in the long run. Their thinking and behavior, as recent economic events show, contribute to corporate or business disasters.

Management Financial Shortcomings

To accomplish their immediate personal goals, corporate managers overlook their fiduciary duties and obligations to others concerning long-term corporate financial security, survival, and growth. They focus on operational performance or income and rate of return on investments (ROI) on a quarterly or annual basis. They overlook or underemphasize capital investments for long-term corporate strategic strengths and advantages that could secure corporate financial worth and liquidity. Their actions may sound appropriate in the short term, but they may lead to serious financial problems from the related marketing problems in the future.

For immediate financial reasons, in addition to sales increasing and cost-cutting tactics, corporate managers employ a variety of financial approaches or window-dressing profitability and liquidity techniques. Among them are the following:

- Debt financing for operational expenses (including R&D, if any, salaries, overhead, etc.), for a few required strategic investments (broken equipment replacements), and for cash dividend payments to stockholders and other obligations—corporate credit, commercial papers, lease financing, bond issues, etc.
- Delayed payments to suppliers and creditors; easy credit to unworthy customers yet restricted/tightened credit for loyal customers and employees, favorable treatments for team players, and other similar practices
- Aggressive measures to collect account receivables
- Longer retention of past earnings without distribution to stockholders; reduction or elimination of dividends
- Issue of "treasury" or new stocks to improve cash balances. "Creative" accounting practices to defray expenses and recognize unearned sales revenues and income

Furthermore, to influence their company stock prices, instead of cutting or eliminating dividends when faced with liquidity problems, corporate managers increase stockholder dividends, and/or they do not issue "treasury" or new stocks that may reduce or dilute stock value and prevent desired stock price appreciations.

Sometimes knowingly and unethically, sometimes illegally, using corporate guarantee or reputation, corporate leaders push worthless investment schemes onto unsuspecting investors worldwide.

In the thrust for fast improvements in corporate liquidity and/or profitability, there are two prime motivations: (1) executive compensations, fringe benefits and perks, not neglecting the possibility of having the severance package rewritten and enhanced and (2) potential opportunity to earn huge personal financial/career rewards by enabling the organization to become an ideal candidate (takeover target) for corporate merger and acquisition (M&A) and serving as "broker" to the resulting marriage.

It is not unusual for corporate managers to acquire another entity as additional financial and/or marketing strategy. The underlying purpose usually is not strategic in the long run. The union has underlying different motivations for fast gains in the short run.

When the organizational union—one corporation acquiring another entity or two—occurs, the acquiring parent merges and consolidates the acquired organization. Alternatively, the acquiring parent manages its acquisition as a separate and independent enterprise under tight parental guidance, supervision, and control.

When the underlying motivations are predominantly short term in nature for fast personal executive gains, the subsidiary option is a preferred choice. The subsidiary structure makes it easy to sell off the subsidiary at profit in the near future and severe the relationship altogether. Or the acquiring parent may spin off the subsidiary as a separate entity with its new stock offerings, continue to maintain majority ownership control with stock holding, and use the cash flow from the new stock offering for other purposes. Later on, the divorcing organization could—and often does—sell the stocks, usually at a high price, make huge financial benefits, and walk off. The divorced subsidiary would usually be left on its own to face its subsequent emerging cash flow problems that may have resulted from the past imprudent operational decisions.

Leveraged M&A Financing and Consequences

M&As are common occurrences in the corporate world. Instead of internal expansions through strategic product and market developments to raise corporate financial valuations in the capital markets, professional corporate leaders put their businesses on fast track. To corporate leaders, once again, current corporate worth or market capitalization is more important than sales and profits in the long run. Simply to maximize their personal financial gains, they carry out M&A to secure current products and markets. They do not worry about or carefully develop better products and business processes for market captures and developments. They prefer, instead, the M&A route, which usually benefits few and not most stakeholders at large.

The history of M&A is not good for most stakeholders. Most M&As usually benefit speculative investors and the corporate managers of the uniting entities. Financial strategies for the union between the two or more business firms is accomplished frequently with a small amount of cash payment, partial stock swaps, and/or a heavy use of leveraged buyout—in other words, debt financing, which is referred to as "bootstrap."

In leveraged buyout transactions, various corporate assets are used as collateral to borrow. The secured legal credit papers or bonds are usually perceived by financiers as less than investment grade or riskier, and thus, they bear high interest rates resulting in higher acquisition cost for the acquiring firm. The paper could receive the perception and reception equivalent to that of a "junk" bond. High cost and borrowing pose additional market problems, such as higher product costs affecting competitive position; high costs lower profitability or return on acquisition investments, too, if the financial leverage eventually becomes less favorable from inadequate product sales—and/or efficiency improvements from business activities consolidation and eliminating seemingly unnecessary duplications in efforts or resources.

Each M&A corporate entity reaches the decision and consents to partnership, because the weaker partner is left with no other alternative for survival and growth—or it wants additional competitive strengths and advantages faster in one or more business areas, namely, marketing, technological, R&D, manufacturing, and financial. The synergy through the partnership is pushed as beneficial by the acquiring corporate leaders, even though personal motivations are more predominant than organizational interests or the interests of less powerful stockholders and other stakeholders.

The stronger, acquiring parent is usually able to negotiate much more favorable merger terms and hold the ownership and management power over the other partner(s). While the negotiating management leaders may get personally beneficial terms, their other stakeholders may pay the heavy price—sooner or later.

Usually the acquired party's employees, suppliers, distributors, and the community at large are adversely affected by the subsequent integration efforts—such as consolidation of various activities, functions, divisions or branches, and affiliations, as well as human and financial assets across the supply, production, distribution, and marketing chains. As different positions and operations are downsized for marketplace efficiencies, people lose work hours or jobs, and the local community loses the sources of income for economic well-being and community growth.

Customers may lose as quality suffers initially from competitive pricing pressures and later on from the lack of or inadequate desired product improvements and innovations. Higher prices may emerge, as the stronger company dominates weaker competitors and dictates terms with financial and marketing muscles, exerting monopolistic power and influence. Corporate monopoly or market power often is misused by corporate managers for selfish reasons, and not typically for greater good.

As soon as the acquisition transaction is completed, the acquiring parent company focuses on fast operational success in the marketplace through integration. Its leaders aim to utilize all the available synergy and integrated efforts to prove to the market that the merger has turned out to be successful—at least in appearance so that they could further pursue personal gains at a higher speed. Pressures for efficiency and immediate operational profitability mount. Once again, personal greed causes risky financial behavior and tactics to continue, with some changes via greater force and less caution. The use of debt financing is expanded for greater profits and opportunities for further M&A activities for quicker stock price appreciations in the near future.

Following the completion of the acquisition process, the acquiring parent may pursue an alternative strategy. Its corporate managers may aim forcefully for immediate synergy and resulting profitability so that, instead of aiming for further growth, they could break up the company shortly after acquisition for quick corporate financial gains. They may decide to sell off divisions or branches to other interested corporations that have their own buying power or capability for leveraged buyout.

In lieu of selling off a division or two or some part of the organization to someone else, the corporate executives may establish each division or unit as a separate and independent enterprise with its own stock and corporate identity. They may issue an initial public stock offering (IPO) to investors and create a totally new corporation with its governing management under the direction of new stockholders and their representatives and essentially in complete charge of management responsibilities. The issuing parent may maintain its stockownership control in the new firm in the early stage, but it may dispose of its stockownership in the new company and give up all the ownership and management control over its creation. The executives of the divorcing corporation may manage to secure with the new entity lucrative consulting contracts (paid, nonelective board appointments) for themselves in the years to come after their departure from their current position or simultaneously with their present employment situation.

The IPO breakup route is followed especially when the financial market conditions are favorable to command a high IPO price. It is not followed unless the investors perceive each breakup unit to be worth more as a new entity than as part of the larger corporation.

The stock price of the severing company appreciates with the IPO news, especially if there is market acceptance and the price of new stock offering is expected to be high and well deserved.

As the parent firm severs the relationship completely and claims its stock earnings, the new enterprise is left on its own without the resources of its severing parent. It is faced with its own fate—not to mention the problems and struggles of most smaller and newer firms related to survival and growth. Now the new enterprise is faced with a much higher probability of failing than succeeding. Its credit and capability to borrow are not as strong, neither is its capability to issue additional stocks for cash flow improvement. Both its debt and overall cost of capital would rise. Without the strengths of its former parent company, its financial position is weakened. Similarly, in many other such business areas as marketing, it no longer enjoys strong advantages of having access to resources of the larger firm.

As soon as the parent company disposes of its stockownership in the new corporation at the peak of the IPO price, or shortly afterwards, it recovers all of its investment at huge profit from new investors. It hands over the management power. The parent claims the cash and severs the relationship with its former unit—leaving the new enterprise fairly cash dry and heavily in debt or dependent on borrowing, credit financing, or additional new stock issues at lower price, and thus diluting the stockholder value, or to some other fate.

If a firm was acquired using the leveraged buyout, the acquired firm may be left on its own later on, loaded heavily with secured debt that would make its survival and growth less certain subsequently.

But the corporate managers of the acquiring parent walk off with huge financial rewards and their individual financial security for a brighter future. The managers and employees of their acquisition ventures and several other stakeholders, on the other hand, are faced with a shaky new fate that would be determined by their new corporate stockholders and their preferred managers or representatives.

With the heavy use of debt financing, sometimes, corporate managers use a technique known as "management buyout," with intent to turn the company "private." They may issue some stockownership for "private" equity financing. The motivation for "privacy" is to minimize public disclosure of vital information, close public scrutiny, and undesired pressures on management for results from outside. This may be a preferred approach if there is something to "hide" in ethical or legal terms. Without much open accountability, it becomes easier for the managers to pursue, if so desired, riskier business strategies for greater profitability and financial gains.

Conclusion

Evidently, as the corporate reality of unjustifiable executive compensations and business disasters in the corporate world suggests, "professional" corporate managers adopt reckless and risky financial behavior to maximize their personal financial gains. They deploy several financial techniques that have potential for disasters in the long run. However, these techniques may provide immediate improvements in corporate cash flows, profits, and stock price appreciations; in many instances their impact in the long run is the weakening of the corporate financial security and stability. Various forms of leveraged or debt financing and unsound investment strategies—including secondary buyouts; mezzanine capital; private equity; investments in uncertain or speculative areas in infrastructure like energy, secondary investments, and own or self investment for speculative returns—indeed represent high risk as well as potential for significant financial losses in the future. Yet, they take precedence over sound strategic marketing and financial planning for corporate gains in the long run through product and market developments and meeting the managerial fiduciary responsibilities and obligations toward economic interests of different corporate constituencies.

In reality, each corporate management financing technique and acquisition, integration and consolidation, and disinvestment represents consequences that may become unpleasant and unbearable for the community at large and may disrupt thousands of families and their lives, causing them financial hardship.

Most financial acquisitions are not very sound for business survival and growth in the years to come.

In the early years of the twenty-first century, the number of leveraged buyouts has increased significantly. The situation is not very much unlike in the 1980s when the United States was faced with business crises, such as unsound real estate financing by savings and loan institutions. Not unlike in the 1980s, there have been several mega leveraged buyouts, each involving hundreds of billions in heavy debt financing. Not until the subprime crises surfaced in the later part of 2007 and early 2008 did the rate of mega leveraged acquisitions begin to slow down.

One major financier of leveraged buyouts has been Citigroup, which recently wrote down some of its investments to reflect their market worth.

The history of executive-greed-based mergers and acquisitions is not very pleasant. Creative, clever, and often dishonest financial strategies and tactics continue to emerge periodically for fast gains in the marketplace. They become industry practice for a while afterwards based on some immediate financial rewards of such techniques. Not until their serious adverse consequential effects spread widely, nationally, and perhaps across the globe requiring governmental bailouts and regulatory controls do we become concerned and question the logic and legality. Until then, there is silent approval or indifference toward self-serving management thinking, focus, and behavior.

PART V

Conclusion and Recommendations

CHAPTER 15

Concluding Remarks and Recommendations: Unveiling Causes of Recent Business Crises

Overview Summary

Product and market innovations are inevitable in the global marketplace. To remain competitive and grow, a firm has to innovate or adapt, change, and do what is essential and prudent for business. It does not matter whether the firm is small or large. There are other choices for business too: it can continue to maintain status quo, ignore the market forces, adhere to current or old practices, disregard sound financial principles, and/or follow imprudent and bad business strategies and practices. None of these other choices, ultimately, is without some disastrous consequences in the long run. Recent business crises clearly provide some evidence to this fact.

The most serious crisis (subprime) in decades—a huge number of financial institutions and other business corporations, such as Bear Stearns, Merrill Lynch, General Motors (GM), Chrysler, American International Group (AIG) are struggling for survival or have already failed—gives us insights into bad management practices of "professional" corporate leaders and their selfish motivations for personal financial gains in compensation. Similar self-serving bad management practices were behind the other two preceding economic crises, the dot-com bubble and the savings and loan (S&L) scandal. Each economic or business crisis is evidently much more severe and longer in duration than the one preceding it.

It has become clear that the recent economic crises are the result of shortcomings of corporate managers, especially in large organizations. These firms are run by "professional" managers, who have good education and good past management experience but no significant stockownership as founders or investors.

Because professional corporate leaders have no long-term stake in the firm they manage, their management behavior is driven by their compensation-based motivations. Their short-term business decisions and actions have one major primary purpose: to immediately maximize personal compensation as much as possible—salary, money/stock options bonus, severance package, and other financial benefits and perks.

These corporate managers' fast pursuits for personal gains have put their firms on the path of certain or probable financial disasters and business failures. While they use their management positions, powers, and corporate resources to enrich themselves, their actions harm the interests of most other stakeholders such as stockowners and investors, creditors, employees, distributors, suppliers, and the community at large. Taxpayers often pay the price in terms of government bailouts and financial assistance in order to save jobs and income in the community.

Clearly, corporate professional managers seem to ignore their long-term fiduciary duties and obligations to their stockowners, and to everyone else with some stake in the corporate welfare and well-being. Instead of looking after long-term corporate interests, these managers have incentives to focus on short-term corporate results by implementing tactics of sales revenue enhancement and cost-cutting.

It is not difficult to understand why they do not pay attention to strategic investments for the development of future corporate competitive core strengths (skill, knowledge, technology, etc.) and products. The simple reason is that their individual compensations are based on what they accomplish today in profits or stock price appreciation, and not on whether or not they have improved the corporation's competitive position in the marketplace for the future through careful planning and resource allocations.

When corporate managers do not allocate adequate resources for core organizational competencies, they jeopardize their long-term corporate security, survival, and growth. In essence, they weaken their organization and create a very serious competitive disadvantage for their business.

For high and immediate corporate gains, which enable managers to earn high compensation personally, the CEO and his/her lieutenants employ several policies and practices. Many of their actions often turn out to be very unsound and risky, like cutting research activities and reducing key "productive" workforce. It is not unusual for corporate managers to use very risky but potentially profitable financial tactics, such as highly leveraged (debt) financing for investment purposes. For instance, when they expand production facilities or acquire another firm, corporate managers tend to use excessive and burdensome borrowing, which causes problems in the event that the firm experiences decline in sales revenues and cash flows.

There are corporate leaders who carefully plan immediate sales growth and cost-cutting in order to make their firm an attractive target for takeover by another firm. Such maneuvers usually produce many personal rewards (lucrative higher management positions, consultancy contracts, stocks or options in the acquiring firm, money bonuses, huge severance packages, etc.) to these individuals when the firm gets acquired on the basis of its good recent performance in profitability and return on investment.

In search of support for self-serving management decisions, plans, policies, and practices, corporate leaders look for team players inside the organization and other collaborators who are in a position of power and influence elsewhere. Corporate managers use their own authority and power inside to solicit loyalty, support, and cooperation. Those who are outside join the "management club" to enhance their own personal financial interests and influence. Together, the club members behave like "fraternity" members—all for one and one for all, helping out one another as and when called for.

The "management club" members include corporate executives and staff, various divisional presidents or managers, operational managers and supervisors, outside management consultants, marketing research firms and planners, lobbyists and public relations (PR) firms, rating agencies and law-enforcement agencies, politicians and legislators, lawyers, public accountants, investment bankers, business acquisition brokers, advertising media executives, industry leaders, competitors (perhaps unlawfully), and any one else of influence and knowledge who can contribute as a worthy club member.

When corporate leaders recruit individuals for management positions in the firm, they inquire of candidates as to whether or not they are capable of being good "team players." The firm wants to fill positions with team players, not someone who could not fit in or is a troublemaker. Candidates' references and backgrounds are carefully evaluated through the leadership's own network of friends and acquaintances. Even consultants and advisors are carefully investigated for special tasks before they are engaged and paid very "decent" fees and other financial favors. Anyone who does not wish to play the "game" has no place in the management club, and he or she is not considered worthy of important tasks.

While pursuing their own self-interests, the team members cooperate, collaborate, and collude. But they are careful and avoid undesirable collisions, conflicts, and confrontations that are not in self-interests. They try to keep their actions under the law as much as possible, but if necessary, they do not hesitate to resort to unethical and immoral conduct or bend the law. Occasionally, an individual may go beyond, cross the legal boundary and break the law. When other members become aware of any misconduct or violation of the law, they tend to look away and ignore until their own self-interests are in serious jeopardy. They try to protect one another up to a point, but after that everyone is on his/her own.

Team players get fairly rewarded. As they act more and more as team players, other stakeholders' long-term interests essentially are compromised; the organization may be put at greater and greater risk.

When the time comes, the CEO, his/her top team players, and outside collaborators move on. They find another organization, a different setting. A different individual may take charge at the top. Role reversals are not uncommon. Some team members occasionally swap their management or staff positions among themselves, or switch roles with one another, their previous roles for the new ones, in different position titles and with different responsibilities and tasks. Cross-memberships in two or more teams are common too to protect mutual interests. Playing different roles occasionally is part of the necessary game moves to preserve the group's overall financial interest, influence, and power. As the game continues, each member may contribute in some way toward the same mutual self-serving goals.

The club membership or network grows with time by recruiting eager, willing, and cooperating individuals. People prefer to join the club; they do not want to be left behind in career or business. The list of players becomes longer and longer as the network extends its claws, forcing and converting nonplayers into players and nonconformists into conformists. Eventually, everybody understands the rules of the management game, whether written or not, whether spoken and conveyed or not. One way or another, the basic message gets across, delivered and understood, forcing conformity for self-survival, and some illusive benefit in the name of team-playing and greater good.

On an ongoing basis, while the top players and their collaborating top lieutenants, both inside and out, derive and rip off great personal benefits, others are looked after with as little as possible, without crossing the dangerous line of dissatisfaction or revolt by other stakeholders. Once in a while, the greed at the top gets out of control. Uncontrollable desires for greater personal gains quickly take over. Some team captains and major players ignore the established norms and carry out a few unusual plays—usually lawful but economically extremely unreasonable and disastrous. When the negative consequences of extreme executive greed begin to spread and cause domino effects, the community at large notices and may be forced to act with financial bailouts and other government actions.

Not surprisingly, team-playing compromises the interests of everyone else. The subprime crisis suggests what happens when the club members look after each other's interests. Evidently, many individuals at the top in corporate hierarchy, creditors and investors, independent certifiers and raters, consultants and advisors, legislators and regulators—and others—have acted like collaborators by ignoring or endorsing bad financial and marketing practices in major financial institutions and other big corporations.

Corporate collaborators have no long-tenure interests in a specific organization. They are more interested in maximizing their personal wealth and gains from their present leadership or management position than in securing their job or their corporation's security and survival. Given their personal motivations, it is not difficult to understand why they focus on short-term corporate profitability and improvements than on long-term corporate security and growth. It is easy for them to talk about corporate vision and long-term destiny than to put their words into actions.

It is not difficult for us to comprehend why they hop from one corporate position to another, from one organization to another, achieving quick, unsustainable gains, seeking or using organizational resources and their own positions of power, seeking and working with collaborators—other executives, staff, and operational managers, outside business associates, etc.—who are willing and accommodating management supporters, all pursuing their own selfish interests.

Corporate speculators and management collaborators aim for immediate financial gains and stock price appreciations. They grab whatever they can quickly, and move on. They use their financial muscles and other powers to squeeze out whatever is possible. In contrast, the organization suffers, and its other stakeholders lose in the long run.

When corporate leaders elsewhere within the same or immediate industry, and their management collaborators and speculators, pursue similar self-serving goals, the whole industry becomes an oligopoly. All firms within the industry together exercise collective power and implement monopolistic practices in the marketplace. They imitate one another in their marketing policies and tactics, without trying to shake up their respective competitive positions and status quos. The level of operational profits may be overall satisfactory across the industry so that there is no undue pressure or incentive for technological or product innovations. Everyone tries to derive the maximum benefits out of their existing investments in products, manufacturing equipment, plants, and facilities. R&D and technological innovations are low in industry priority. The U.S. auto industry remains undoubtedly a classic case in study.

This industry-wide collaboration goes on for a while until somebody from within the industry deviates in a major way. It may go on until some competitor or competitors from abroad, or outside the direct industry at home, emerges and challenges the status quo, threatening the local industry and attempting to break the monopoly over the marketplace with better products or market strategies.

As the new industry entrants become successful, they alter the nature of market and often change customer expectations and requirements. The old players, who are more concerned and interested in their status quo than change, or who are too slow to change and adapt appropriately, start to lose out.

Sometimes, it is too late for some to adapt and survive. Their predicament makes them good targets for acquisition. If there is no one interested in acquiring a firm with serious declining sales, that business eventually fails and the corporation as an entity vanishes. Its stakeholders lose.

A business organization fails. It is not unusual for the whole industry to fail and be replaced with the new one with different organizations that continue to fulfill the basic needs of customers as well as their other desires more effectively and efficiently.

The ongoing transition in one industry may have undesirable effects or repercussions across other industries, and the domino effects may lead to economic recession nationwide, in more than one country or globally. Each cycle of adverse effects may be more serious than the previous one depending upon the severity and time duration across industries and throughout national economies. Governmental or public policies could affect and alter the cyclical effects.

What we have seen over the past two decades are the cycles of business failures, organizational growth, and emergence of new corporations. We have seen the cycles of some industries declining and some new ones emerging with new products and technologies. What we have seen are the cycles of economic declines and growth. We have observed stock market price gyrations and other financial maneuvers—often with wealth being transferred upward from one group to another, faster toward the top from financial speculations, investments, high compensation, and financial earnings by corporate managers and others high in social and political powers and hierarchies.

What we have observed is growing corporate dependence on governmental bailouts. Unreasonable risk-taking has become a part of the big business strategy because of the readily available government intervention and economic assistance. Government bailouts have increased in numbers over the years, at each business cycle. What we have observed is growing political and judicial corruption with aggressive business lobbying and campaign contributions. What we have experienced are the cycles of business regulation, deregulation, and superficial "reregulation."

In 2010, almost one year after the government bailouts of major financial institutions and government takeover of GM, executive greed has become more apparent than ever before. Some major banks, which had received billions from the U.S. government in order to continue to survive, were reported to have set aside recently in excess of $150 billion in compensation—mostly in bonuses for their executives and staff at higher up. Apparently, these firms have no shame. It is especially appalling to think that the decision-makers of these firms used the taxpayers to enrich themselves in some way while millions of people were faced with unemployment and home foreclosures caused by the misdeeds of the same executives and their colleagues in the industry. What about the government that helps the Wall Street before it does the main street? Niall Ferguson describes the contemporary financial scene as the "Wall Street's New Gilded Age" in which "financial capital" and "political capital" are "rolled into one." (*Newsweek, September 21, 2009, pp. 52–55*)

Yes, indeed. All efforts toward regulatory reforms had not moved forward in months to make any significant difference, in spite of the fact that for more than a year, one party had been in control with both the White House and the U.S. Congress. Regulatory actions had been stalled by aggressive lobbying by business interests.

To protect the general public from predatory financial policies and practices, there was a movement to create a government agency referred to as Consumer Financial Protection Agency. But within weeks though, the movement was in serious jeopardy in the U.S. Senate Banking Committee. There was a lot of political and regulatory posturing, but no substantial progress toward reforms. There had been no antitrust actions to break up the big financial institutions that are too big to fail.

To show that the government was doing something to prevent similar economic crisis in the future, an impartial and independent commission was set up. The 2008 Financial Crisis Inquiry Commission had been mandated to investigate the extent of knowledge of the regulatory and law-enforcement agencies and their subsequent actions, if any—in other words, what and when did the Department of Justice, the Federal Bureau of Investigation (FBI), the Federal Reserve Bank, the Federal Deposit Insurance Corporation, and other regulatory authorities know, what did they do or did not do, and whether any of their actions did contribute toward the crisis.

Within weeks after its formation, the Commission had interviewed a number of responsible and knowledgeable witnesses from various levels of government. Many of these individuals in positions of some regulatory authority blamed the lenient system for regulation and the Fed's failure to heed numerous warnings about fraud and reckless lending dating back to year 2000. After detecting widespread fraud in the subprime mortgage market, in 2004 the FBI had sent out warnings about the likelihood of serious economic crisis in the near future. Many state regulators found themselves incapable of enforcing the state laws due to certain federal government policies, actions, or inactions.

Before the Commission could finish its investigation, there had emerged sufficient evidence to underscore the failure of the regulatory environment in one way or another as a major contributing factor toward the most serious economic crisis in decades.

Any time soon in the future we are not likely to see any major changes. Even though politicians, legislators, and regulators profess to be working for the people, they depend on businesses and their financial support for their own self-interests. Their personal as well as financial success depends on their cooperation and collaboration with business, on their membership in the management "club," where everybody is part of the "team." For the public policy-makers, protecting business interests is self-preservation. So it would be naïve to expect significant reforms.

Large corporations are aware of the power of their financial muscles. They prefer the status quo of regulatory loopholes, lenient regulations, and lack of law enforcement. They do not mind flexing their muscles when necessary. If they have to, they would spend millions to influence the legislative and political processes.

Even the U.S. Supreme Court did not hesitate to show its support for business corporations. In 2010, by overturning the century-old laws about campaign financing, the U.S. Supreme Court awarded the big corporations unrestricted power to use their financial resources to affect political processes and governmental policies.

In some way, as the Wall Street bonus decisions suggest, big businesses have no regard for any regulatory threats. Their message is clear: "Public be damned!"

If the elected representatives and regulators are unwilling to stop executive greed, what about the corporate board of directors who represent millions of their corporate shareholders and their interests? Forget it. In large corporations, most nonemployee board directors receive hundreds of thousands in annual compensation for their few hours of part-time work each year. In a recent survey of 491 large and important companies by *Fortune*, as summarized by Carol J. Loomis ("Directors: Feeding at the Trough," *Fortune*, January 18, 2010, p.20), the average board member compensation for the year 2008 was $213,000. The survey closely looked at 23 firms and found that the average in these cases exceeded $400,000. In one firm, a director was paid in excess of $1.5 million.

In light of such exuberant compensation findings, Loomis questions the independence of corporate directors and their judgments and writes: "How does a board member challenge a CEO when the . . . (director's huge compensation is) . . . important to his or her lifestyle?" (p.20)

The three major economic crises in the past two decades, with significant losses each time in jobs, incomes, stock values, and retirement funds, and shrinking middle-income class in the United States and elsewhere, show the "real" or "actual" contribution of professional corporate leaders. While the corporate managers continue to enrich themselves with their rising compensations, everybody else is forced to get by barely with their low income, depleting savings, and diminishing purchasing power.

Each time, the major economic crisis underscores executive greed. Each time, it underscores the fact that our society is suffering from the disease called "management delusion," from the lack of clear comprehension about the "real" or "actual" economic contribution of corporate management (executives, board directors, and others at the top) in the context of benefits for others who are not part of top management. We are all suffering from the illusion of too many myths about corporate leadership, which are advanced by the corporate leaders, management gurus and consultants, and business schools. The actual contribution of our business leaders is not clearly understood by the society at large.

The concentration of wealth in the hands of small and elite corporate management class is not a result of worthy innovation or creativity of "professional" corporate managers. Professional corporate leaders are not among the real business innovators or wealth creators. They are not like Sam Walton, Bill Gates, Steve Jobs, Jeff Bozos, and Henry Ford. Professional managers are greedy and use their position, power, and networking relationship to maximize their own personal gains.

The scientists, engineers, creative individuals, risk-taking entrepreneurs—who make "real" economic contributions with their innovations, ingenuity, hard work, many years of sacrifice in personal or family comforts—deserve all the riches from their success and accomplishments. They are not like professional managers. They earn, and thus deserve success and wealth. They come up with new ideas, insights, technologies, and processes for economic efficiency and better products. They create new products and organizations. Their efforts help open up opportunities for employment and income, which stimulate economic growth. They add real value in economic gains and wealth creation. Unlike the contribution of professional managers, their contribution is not superficial.

Each economic recovery is a result of new organizations and industries that emerge with product and market innovations and different business models and plans. As long as these new businesses are run by their creators and remain under their creators' close scrutiny, they continue to prosper and add economic value for others too.

But after some time, when these innovators and entrepreneurs sell their business, or lose their ownership interest and management control because of speculating investors or some other reasons, "professional" managers begin to take over major business decisions and policies. As a result, underlying business motivations change. Consequently, the organizational life cycle accelerates directly in proportion with the speed in the pursuit of quick returns and higher personal compensations by short-term, speculative major investors and professional managers.

The faster pursuits lead to quicker declines in corporate sales, profits, security, and stability. Usually, the organization's high but unsustainable gains ensue with operational maneuvers, followed later on, however, by deteriorating sales, deteriorating competitive market positions, and decline in profits, resources, and foundation stability. Ultimately, the inevitable happens: employees lose jobs for good and business closes its doors permanently. Under professional managers, the organizational life gets shortened through a hostile takeover or the organization becomes extinct.

Periodic business cycles, organizational failures, and serious business problems are inevitable, as a result of perpetual individual greed for self-gains for money and power at the top—in high positions of authority and responsibility in business, in government and other organizations, and even in academia (university and public school administrations) and in health care (particularly hospitals and large institutional service providers—for example, health care "payers" such as employers and government, and health care insurers). This is the corporate reality.

Highlights of Corporate World Realities

At this point, let us highlight some key economic realities of the corporate world:

- Each economic or business crisis seems to be much more severe and longer in duration than the preceding crisis.
- As our ability to search and communicate improves, the global market becomes more integrated and competitive, and each national government's ability to regulate the economic affairs within its jurisdiction diminishes.
- Pressures and processes for deregulation and economic cooperation have become stronger in the past two decades than ever before. Consequently, there has been considerable deregulation worldwide.
- Free and capitalistic market forces have become less capable of functioning properly under the deregulated, legally underenforced, and unenforceable (usually in practical terms) laws across the national borders, or under politically corrupt environment. (The post–Soviet Union Russia and the United States are good examples.)
- Unsound deregulated business environment encourages bad business practices, motivated by unchecked personal greed for financial gains and other benefits.
- Executive compensation has become the driving force behind "professional" corporate management short-term-oriented focus and behavior.

- Professional managers in large corporate businesses tend to focus mostly on immediate corporate profitability while overlooking or disregarding the long-term consequences of their operational, short-term decisions and actions concerning revenue increases and cost-cutting.
- For corporate professional leaders, whose compensations are based on current corporate profitability and improvements, long-term business vision, growth, and destiny become low in priority. Strategic planning and implementation become lower in priority and get less proactive attention, and the required periodic long-term investments are put on hold or underfunded rather than funded in time as previously planned. R&D and useful market research and analysis for planning purposes are de-emphasized. Budgets for maintenance and modernization of technology, equipment, buildings, and physical facilities are reduced. Human training and developmental programs are halted, or reduced in scope, and face budget cuts. Status quo strategies are stressed over product and market developments and business expansion strategies.
- Acquisitions for growth and expansion are sometimes pursued by corporate management when the potential for personal financial gains and benefits is particularly very high.
- Selective and relevant financial and market data are sought out, collected, and/or manipulated to support specific management decisions. Leadership decisions are not based on careful analysis of pertinent and reliable strategic planning and marketing and financial data.
- To achieve fast operational results, top corporate leaders get directly involved in operational matters and practices, start dictating operational policies and procedures from the top, and begin micromanaging lower-level activities. Authority and decision-making get fairly centralized. Empowering of people below and allowing freedom for creativity and flexibility or choices at low levels diminish. Tighter controls are implemented. Employee learning and experimentation for productivity or quality improvements are discouraged. Cost of product or service quality becomes major concern over quality of service. Relationship management at all levels (customer, employee/labor, supply, distribution, etc.) becomes less important, and relations are allowed to deteriorate. There is low concern for creating productive and motivating work environment. Positions are consolidated and reduced, people are laid off, compensations and promotions get cut or frozen, and other employment policies are implemented without much concern for employee morale. Excellence in corporate performance at all levels for the future is not at the center of corporate priority. Immediate gains in corporate profits take precedence over everything else. Quality management becomes less important, and product costs are reduced through material substitution, elimination of complimentary warranties and services, and other measures.
- Fair and equitable performance evaluations and merit payments (salary raises and job promotions) are ignored to provide greater rewards for the "team players"; capable and productive members of the organization

across all levels do not enjoy the rewards they have earned and which they deserve.

- For the board of director positions, trustworthy personal acquaintances and management collaborators are nominated, and their election is influenced in many subtle ways. Other outside team players and collaborators (management consultants, bankers and financiers, brokers and agents, market researchers and analysts, and so forth) are actively sought, utilized, and financially rewarded for their cooperation.
- When necessary, as a corporate entity or as part of the industry-wide attempt, lobbying and "bribing" pressures are utilized in order to influence political, legislative, regulatory, and judicial processes.
- Contemporary corporate management compensation practices are not aligned with the business leadership fiduciary obligations and duties in the context of preserving corporate resources and utilizing them effectively for future growth and prosperity over the years to come.
- Executive compensations encourage and lead to irresponsible and risky—often unethical and immoral and sometimes criminal—management behavior.
- While greedy executives and big speculative investors enrich themselves, other stakeholders bear the heavy cost; small stockholders, employees, suppliers, distributors, customers, and the rest of the society at large suffer the consequences of business disasters, as do individual retirement funds.
- Most serious business problems are not the result of management incompetence. Rather, they are related to executive greed. Most professional corporate managers are highly educated and experienced. Many hold advanced degrees in business (MBAs) from prestigious schools; some have professional certification, such as CPA or CFA.
- Many large businesses have not been able to survive or prosper without the increasing government interventions and financial bailouts, and without the strict regulatory supervision and law enforcement. Government aid or assistance to business has become more indispensable over the years in order to protect income and jobs and provide economic stability and expansion.
- The growing number of large business failures is evident in business acquisitions, bankruptcies and restructuring, downsizing, or permanent door closings.
- Recent economic crises suggest that economic stagnations or declines are not as much consumption-based as they once were several decades ago. The recent problems essentially are related to executive greed and to management's irresponsible and risky business decisions, policies, and actions. The level of consumer spending on products and services is simply manipulated by greedy corporate managers until it reaches its breaking point and customers can no longer be squeezed more for corporate profits and executive compensations. Once the breaking point is reached, the economic decline begins and, ultimately, some forms of government interventions are essential to stop the further decline and reverse the trend.

- There have been upward movements and concentration of wealth (ownership power and/or investment decision-making control) in the hands of fewer and fewer individuals—especially in the United States, the UK, and the Middle East. There have been much more disproportionate distribution of national incomes and economic and political powers.

Recommendations

Unless we tackle the root cause (executive greed) of our economic and corporate crises, no government intervention or financial bailouts would be able to shorten any existing economic crisis or prevent future periodic economic crises. Business problems are the result of management failure in its fiduciary duties. Serious business difficulties are preventable; they are not very much related to extraneous environmental variables. Business problems are internal and corporate-based. No governmental interventions without the long-term regulatory controls over corporate executive compensations would succeed in the long run.

Executive compensations must be tied to long-term business growth and profitability. High salaries, high cash bonuses, bonuses in stock options with fast vesting at low prices, and high severance packages are not appropriate incentives for corporate managers. Instead of ensuring business success in the long run, they harm corporate future growth and prosperity. The current practice of compensations is not appropriate—especially in light of the fact that on average, the tenures of top professional leaders are shorter in duration, less than ten years, sometimes just a few months, a year, or two.

In essence, we have to keep in mind that most of corporate managers do not deserve their high rewards for their short-term operational decisions or quick corporate profitability that is unsustainable over the years. Most organizations succeed, grow, and prosper over a long term because of their people across all levels of business, and across the organizational supply-and-distribution chains. No organization is capable of accomplishing anything without the productive contribution of its people inside and business associates outside. Leadership contribution is vital, but it is not the sole determinant of business success. However, business failure is largely a function or by-product of management failure. Because of bad management, business may cease to exist as an independent corporate entity.

This reality is not limited to just one or two corporations. It has spread across the corporate world with the growing professional management class. Most corporations—especially large ones—are characterized by millions of stockholders across the world with no "real" ownership power or control over the "professionals" who run the firm. The wide stockownership empowers the corporate managers to pursue their own self-interests without proper control and supervision.

There are still business organizations—mostly small- and medium-sized enterprises or SMEs—that are closely controlled and managed by their entrepreneurial founding stockholders or owners. These firms are not likely to be characterized by the reality of executive compensation problems.

The corporate creators and management policy-makers, whether the firm is small or large—individuals like Bill Gates (Microsoft), Jeff Bezos (Amazon), or Steve Jobs (Apple)—are proud of their creation and success. They closely monitor and direct their managers who are in charge of important operational matters. They do not want to put the fate of something they love in the hands of disinterested management professionals or practitioners, who seemingly have no vested long-term love or serious financial interests in the corporate future in the years to come. These entrepreneurial guardians check their managers' performance carefully. As long as these founders control and directly supervise their enterprise, there is no aim to maximize profits quickly or achieve fast financial gains at the expense of the enterprise's future competitive market strengths and advantages.

One of the reasons why Ford Motors has managed to be financially in better shape than their counterparts, GM and Chrysler, is that the Ford family still maintains some control and influence over the corporate policies and actions in important business affairs. The firm has not been too reckless with the corporate resources or financial management for liquidity.

Many large corporations in today's economy have lost their true entrepreneurial spirit, love, and control of their creators. They are no longer as much committed to their business' long-term growth. The corporations have been handed over to their professional leaders for managing by their millions of small investors worldwide and other stakeholders, who have no significant influence on management and demand only good long-term results. The small stockowners have no control on executive compensation.

In the United States, we have observed the S&L crisis and its economic consequences, followed by the dot-com bust with greater adverse effects just a few years later. Less than a decade afterwards, the subprime crisis has led to unprecedented economic problems and crises worldwide since the Great Depression of the 1930s. When the next cycle will be or how severe and harmful it will be is anybody's guess.

One primary cause of such cycles, undoubtedly, is executive greed in big businesses. Unless we find some effective system of compensating professional managers on the basis of their individual contribution in the long run toward the corporate "actual" gains and accomplishments over many years, our business problems are not going to be effectively resolved.

To reverse the current course, the time has come for the corporate world to make changes. Several remedies have been pointed out already through the book. Listed below are just a few major ones worth reiterating:

- The executive compensation system that frequently uses operational performance (current or recent corporate quarterly profits and stock price appreciations) as the major management performance criterion for executive financial rewards and retention decisions should be changed.
- Performance criteria must underscore corporate gains (or losses) over a long time, resulting from the quality of executive *strategic decisions*, not

just management operational decisions and tactics for quick results. Management decisions and actions should be evaluated in terms of accomplishments, both in the short run as well as their implications for outcomes in the long run.

- Executive performance rewards should be tied to corporate periodic gains over the next 3, 5, 7, 10, 15, and 20 years, and perhaps beyond, depending on the nature of decisions and the impact of decisions on the outcomes over the years. For instance, plant investment decision has greater impact in the long run than do policies on employee training and development. R&D investment is much more important in the long term than actions on some efficiency gain immediately.

- The basic or initial salaries should be sufficient enough to attract qualified individuals. However, they should be comparable to salaries elsewhere within the industry—and to some extent, within the organization itself. Periodic or annual salary increases or performance rewards should be internally more equitable and fair, and they should reflect the individual "real" contribution in terms of long-term corporate profitability and growth. Money bonuses, stock options, retirement benefits, severance packages, and perks and benefits should be restricted and handed out, or vested, in annual installments, depending directly on the corporate profitability and market positions at a specific point of time in the future. Executive performance rewards should be proportional to actual future results or outcomes of past executive decisions, policies, investments, and actions. They should not be out of proportion internally in relative terms, in comparison with the rewards for others across the organization based on their individual contributions.

- The level of executive rewards or compensation in the severance package must depend on the length or duration of individual tenure within the organization; the longer the tenure, the higher the rewards. There should be no lump-sum money rewards in the executive severance package unless the individual is retiring after his/her many, many years of service to the firm.

- Most restricted rewards should be in the form of corporate stock options, with periodic vesting in different amounts each time at different exercise option prices. The periodic amounts of vested stock options should vary from low to high, year after year, slowly increasing in amount each time. The periodic exercise stock option prices should range from high to low, reducing gradually as time moves forward.

- The hiring and compensation of the CEO and his/her immediate few lieutenants should be subject to the corporate board approval as well as to the approval of the vast majority (60 percent or higher) of corporate stockholders. In some cases, major corporate creditors must approve too.

- Likewise, all members of the board of directors must be elected by the vast majority (60 percent or higher) of corporate stockholders. Nominations by top corporate executives should be discouraged, and there should be absolutely no top management influence in the board's election process to minimize conflicts of interest.

- Compensations of board directors should be subject to the approval of the vast majority (60 percent or more) of the corporate stockholders—and, in some cases, also of creditors.
- The selection of many outside major business associates (collaborators)—specifically, management consultants, public accounting firms, investment bankers and financial advisors, business acquisition agents and brokers, marketing research firms and analysts, major advertising agencies and media, lawyers and PR firms, lobbyists—should be subject to the approval of simple majority (more than 50 percent) of stockholders. The fees paid out to these associates should be clearly conveyed to stockholders, in addition to the disclosures required by the government. The disclosure to stockholders should be straightforward, with major compensations or contractual features highlighted.
- Executives should be allowed to nominate outside business associates for the stockholders' approval. However, each nomination list must have at least three candidates for a specific appointment. The corporate stockholders should not be presented only with a single candidate as choice.
- Performance of major outside business associates should be carefully appraised periodically for future retention decisions.

Concluding Remarks

As the above points clearly suggest, all stockholders—especially small stockholders with long-term investment interests in dividends and stock price appreciations and overall investment returns—need to become more active. They must get more involved in corporate affairs and preserve their interests.

Proactively, all corporate stockholders have to assume certain responsibilities and take actions immediately. Among them are the following:

- All stockholders must minimize the conflicts of interest between their board directors and corporate managers and their collaborators.
- They have to closely monitor and scrutinize executive decisions, plans, and actions, and take appropriate measures as quickly as possible.
- They should insist on and demand from their executives the development of long-term corporate strengths, advantages and competitiveness that would secure corporate survival, growth, and success in the years to come.
- They must closely watch corporate budgets and spending for human resource development, plant and equipment maintenance and repairs, R&D, equipment and facilities purchases and modernization, information and organizational processes upgrading, and efficiency improvements.
- They have to closely watch executive motivations, compensations, and self-centered pursuits for personal gains that could harm the corporation in the long run. They must minimize executive dominance over decisions on compensation and severance packages for individuals at the top in management.

- They must sanction and harshly disapprove any and all executive actions that are unlawful or that could corrupt the political, legislative, and judicial processes.
- Above all, they must become aware of and recognize the real or actual executive "contribution" toward their organization's profitability, success, and failure—not just in terms of current or immediate accomplishments but over a long period of time in the past and also apprise themselves about the executives' plans for the same organization over the years to come. They must evaluate their corporate executive's performance in terms of their long-term fiduciary duties and obligations to the corporation and its stakeholders—including themselves, employees, and the community at large.

In essence, corporate stockholders must take charge of the organization in which they have a vested ownership interest. They must serve as countervailing, strong and legitimate power against the damaging and self-serving influence and power of their professional corporate managers.

The executive operational-performance-based compensation system appears to be at the center of the unprecedented worldwide business crisis in many decades. The disastrous impact of executive compensations on so many large, well-established, decades-old household names suggests that we are faced with a management crisis in the corporate world.

In conclusion, the professional management contribution toward business success is a mirage, and we have to understand this business reality. We have to recognize the management's delusion and crush it. We have to understand the illusory importance of the leadership's unique quality for business success and growth. No individual in business is indispensable. We have to separate the creative and founding entrepreneurial managers from the professional corporate leaders.

If the corporate managers believe that they deserve what they earn in compensation, it is time for us to ask them some important questions: Why do we have so many serious business problems? How significant is your contribution, in comparison with others in your organization? Where did you get your last five worthy ideas for profitable corporate actions? Why are you preoccupied with the day-to-day problems, and don't think long term and have a broad strategic focus and approach? Where are your concrete plans and actual resource allocations for your company's competitive strengths for the years to come—specifically for the next 5 years, 10 years, 15 years, and perhaps longer? Not just talk, but where is the actual funding dedicated for specific long-term goals? What specific competitive problems do you foresee today and where are your specific plans to overcome them?

We must not be fooled by their pet answers, such as "We have a committee looking into our future problems, and they are supposed to have their report soon," or "I plan to have my staff look into such matters after they have finished up with their next year's budget allocations." We must not be fooled by figures that can not be backed up or by sophisticated but meaningless terminologies and jargons.

Corporate managers know politically correct answers and many business school "buzzwords." Education and training in business is useful, and it can teach rational approaches to business decision-making. However, we must understand that managing effectively for long-term organizational success continues to remain an "art"; management is not a science. Controlled classroom learning and simulated exercises and right words and answers cannot teach entrepreneurship, creativity, inventiveness, or moral conduct. The clever use of right words and phrases does not produce right and moral marketplace conduct.

Over the years, the author has observed an interesting phenomenon: the number of instances of "unethical" management conduct has increased in proportion to the growth in business courses and classroom lessons on "social responsibilities and ethics."

Business education has become an industry, not unlike other industries—certainly a profitable one in recent years. The number of business study programs has mushroomed in the past decade or two. To generate revenues, even prestigious business schools do not hesitate to offer degree programs and certificates that are dubious in value. There are now graduate business courses no longer than one weekend in duration. Instead of enhancing good knowledge in business and teaching "ethical" behavior, many programs essentially boost their students' individual egos and arrogance, and they provide networking contact for self-serving purposes. Yet, the leaders in business education pretend that their programs are noteworthy and that the high fees are highly justified. For many universities and faculty members, business education has become a "cash cow."

Business school is a strong advocate of team-playing and collaboration. The problem with team-playing and collaboration is that they lead to self-serving behavior.

Some teachers in business schools have found an easy way to spare their time and effort from their teaching responsibilities. They have learned how to ignore their "real" academic obligations. Instead of spending hours preparing for their classes and actually teaching, they divide their students in class into small groups of three or four. Then they let their students use a large portion of class time to discuss business cases, incidents, and exercises among themselves in their individual groups. The group sessions are justified as good "team-building" experiences for students, where students learn to work together for a common purpose. This is one of the few approaches that students prefer too.

On the surface, this approach seems to be an effective teaching tool. The problem is that most of these young adults and inexperienced students—who already did or do belong to various sport teams and social and "fraternal" groups for years, and already know how to work in groups—are forced to learn about business concepts and strategies from one another in the group, especially from someone who knows as much or as little as everyone else. One wonders as to what the students really learn at such sessions other than perhaps something superficial, without any depth or any critical thinking! Or, perhaps, they learn nothing other than the importance of being a team player for self-preservation and success!

We have to recognize that we are forced to learn and pressured into being team players in many ways. Furthermore, we have to recognize the dangers of management team players and their self-serving and personal-compensation-driven game playing. We have to understand the existence of the "management club," its characteristics, its members and their individual contributions. We must recognize the management collaborators—particularly the CEOs, their immediate lieutenants, and their other allies outside the organization and across all levels and circles of the society. We have to understand and recognize the extent of management network involving rich and powerful individuals in business communities and societies at large across the national boundaries.

Together, our business leaders and their allies play global social, political, and economic games for personal financial gains and power. They grab important positions of power and influence. They continue to play and usually win. In cases of some temporary setbacks, the situation is not a serious problem for them. Financial losses are bearable and can be recovered fast in the near future. Occasionally, a few key players drop out of the games for various reasons. Overall, in order to stay ahead, most players continue to recruit new members to expand their networks, their power bases, and extend their influence.

While the game playing goes on, the corporate leaders intentionally or unintentionally cause periodic cycles of business failures and new business births. They contribute toward economic recession and recovery. Periodically, the adverse consequences of their collaborative actions are enormous.

Because of the global interdependence, the rest of the world pays the price one way or another. But not the rich and powerful at the top in the hierarchy. This has become evident in the upward movement in the concentration of wealth and power. Over the years, the rich have become richer and more powerful. Most other individuals and families have experienced a downward shift in their "true" incomes, in their savings and retirement funds, and in their "real" standards of living.

The self-serving behavior of the corporate CEOs and other professional managers in positions of power and authority has been identified by some scholars as one of the "destructive" globalization forces in the long run. Given our intergenerational and interdependent global political economy, all of us have a moral responsibility and obligation to overcome or prevent any and all destructive forces. We cannot let the evolving global order for resource- and knowledge-sharing be destroyed by individual greed at the top in corporate management. Our global security, survival, peace, harmony, and good health depend on the kind, considerate, and cooperative human spirit!

Appendix 1: Suggested Readings

Anderson, Chris. "The End of Theory." *Wired*, September 2008.

Ansoff, H. Igor. *Corporate Strategy*. New York: McGraw Hill,1965.

Begley, Sharon. "The Science Wars." *Newsweek*, April 21, 1997, 54–57.

Bennis, Warren G., and Philip Slater. *The Temporary Society*. New York: Harper & Row, 1968.

(Numerous articles and books, specifically on motivation and leadership.)

Birkinshaw, Julian. "Paradox of Corporate Entrepreneurship." *Strategy and Business* 30, Spring 2003, 46–58.

Bradley, Bill. "A Proposed Framework for Analyzing Organizational Failure." AMDS 2005 proceedings, Atlanta, Georgia. January 23–24, 2005, 1–10.

Carroll, Paul B., and Chunka Mui. *Billion-Dollar Lessons: What You Can Learn from the Most Inexcusable Business Failures of the Last 25 Years*. New York: Penguin, 2008.

Chandler, Alfred D. *Strategy & Structure*. Cambridge, MA: MIT Press, 1962.

———. *The Visible Hand: The Managerial Revolution in American Business*. Cambridge, MA: Belknap Press, Harvard University, 1988. (Numerous other articles and books.)

Charan, Ram. "Why Executives Fail." *Fortune*, June 21, 1999.

Christensen, Clayton. *The Innovator's Dilemma: When New Technologies Cause Great Firms to Fail*. Boston: Harvard Business School Press, 1997.

Cohen, Wesley M., and Daniel A. Levinthal. "Absorptive Capacity: A New Perspective on Learning and Innovation." *Administrative Science Quarterly* 35, 1990. 128–152. (Also, A New Tool for Resurrecting an Old Theory of the Knowledge@Wharton. http://knowledge.wharton.upenn.edu/article.cfm?articleid=1480.)

Collins, James C., and Jerry I. Porras. *Build to Last: Successful Habits of Visionary Companies*. New York: Harper, 1997.

Deming, W. Edwards. *Out of the Crisis*. Cambridge, MA: MIT Press, 1986.

(Many other articles and books on quality, too. Most widely known for his 14 points for enhancing management effectiveness. Product/service quality improvement is at the center. Personal greed is the primary cause of declining quality, and thus competitiveness, leading to failure.)

Domet, D., and R. Kimber. *The Logic of Failure*. Boulder, CO: Perseus Publishing, 1996.

Farber, David R. *Sloan Rules: Arthur P. Sloan and the Triumphs of General Motors*. Chicago: University of Chicago, 2002.

Ferguson, Niall. "Wall Street's New Gilded Age." *Newsweek*, September 21, 2009, 52–55.

Gardner, Burleigh, and Sidney Levy. "The Product and the Brand." *Harvard Business Review* 33, March–April 1955, 33–39.

George, Michael, and Stephen Wisdom. *Conquering Complexity in Your Business*. New York: McGraw-Hill, 2004.

Ghosshal, S. "Bad Management Theories Are Destroying Good Management Practices." *Academy of Management Learning and Education* 4, no. 1, 2005, 75–91.

Gillis, Tamara. The IABC Handbook of Organizational Communication, San Francisco: Jossey-Bass, 2006. (Especially the section on corporate fallacy on "Synergy" from mergers and acquisitions.)

Hamel, Gary. *Leading the Revolution*. Boston: Harvard Business School Press, 2000.

Hamel, Gary, and C. K. Prahalad. "The Core Competence of the Corporations." *Harvard Business Review*, May–June 1990, 79–91.

Hammer, Michael. "Reengineering Work: Don't Automate, Obliterate." *Harvard Business Review*, July–August 1990, 104–112.

Hammer, Michael, and James Champy. *Reengineering the Corporation*. New York: Harper, 2001.

Handy, Charles. *The Age of Unreason*. Boston, MA: Harvard Business School Press, 1989.

Hart, Paul. *Groupthink in Government: A Study of Small Groups and Policy Failure*. Baltimore, MD: Johns Hopkins University Press, 1990.

Henderson, Bruce. "Strategic and Natural Competition." *Perspectives*. Boston: Boston Consulting Group, 1980. (Many books cover his BCG 2x2 Growth/Share Matrix, "experience-curve" and other perspectives. See: Stern and Deimer.)

Johnson, Gerry, and Kevan Scholes. *Exploring Corporate Strategy*. New Jersey: Prentice Hall, 1997.

Juran, Joseph M. *Quality Control Handbook*. (1st ed., original), New York: McGraw Hill, 1951.

Juran, Joseph M. and A. Blanton Godfrey. *Juran's Quality Control Handbook*. 5th ed. New York: McGraw-Hill, 1999.

Kantor, Rosabeth Moss. *Men and Women of the Corporation*. New York: Basic Books, 1977.

Kaplan, Robert S., and David P. Norton. *The Balanced Scorecard: Translating Strategy into Action*. Cambridge, MA: Harvard University Press, 1996.

Kim, W. Chan, and Rene'e Mauborgne. *Blue Ocean Strategy: How to Create Uncontested Market Space and Make the Competition Irrelevant*. Boston, MA: Harvard Business School Press, 2006.

Koch, Richarch. *The 80:20 Principle: The Secret to Achieving More with Less*. New York: Doubleday, 1999.

Loomis, Carol J. "Directors: Feeding at the Trough." *Fortune*, January 18, 2010, 20.

Mahler, Walter. "Every Company's Problem: Managerial Obsolescence." *Personnel* 42, July 1965, 8–10.

Malone, T. W. *The Future of Work: How the New Order of Business Will Shape Your Organization, Your Management Style, and Your Life*. Boston, MA: Harvard Business School Press, 2004.

———. "Is 'Empowerment' Just a Fad? Control, Decision-making, and Information Technology." *Sloan Management Review* 38, no. 2, 1997, 23–35.

McCraw, Thomas K. *Prophet of Innovation: Joseph Schumpeter and Creative Destruction*. Cambridge, MA: Harvard University Press, 2007.

Mintzber, Henry. *The Structuring of Organizations*. Englewood Cliffs, NJ: Prentice Hall, 1979.

Nutt, P. C. *Why Decisions Fail: Avoiding the Blunders and Traps That Lead to Debacles*. San Francisco: Berrett Koehler Publisher, 2002.

Pinchot, Gifford. "Innovation through Intrapreneuring." *Research Management* 30, no. 2, March–April 1987.

Porter, Michael E. *Competitive Strategy*. New York: Free Press, 1980. (Also, dozens of Porter's articles and books on the subject of corporate competitiveness.)

Reason, James T. *Managing the Risks of Organizational Accidents*. Burlington, VT: Ashgate Publishing, 1997.

Roberto, M. A. "Lessons from Everest: The Interaction of Cognitive Bias, Psychological Safety, and System Complexity." *California Management Review* 45, no. 1, 2002, 136–158.

Riles, Al, and Jack Trout. *The 22 Immutable Laws of Marketing*. London: Harper Collins, 1993.

———. *Marketing Warfare*. New York: McGraw-Hill, 1986.

Rivkin, Jan W., and Nicolaj Siggelkow. "Organizing to Strategize in the Face of Interactions: Preventing Premature Lock-In." *Long Range Planning* 39, 2006, 591–614.

Russell-Walling, Edward. *50 Management Ideas You Really Need to Know*. London: Quercus, 2007.

Schumpeter, Joseph. *Capitalism, Socialism, and Democracy*. London: George Allen & Unwin, 1976. (Numerous groundbreaking publications on economic development, innovation, entrepreneurship, and democracy.)

Sloan, Alfred P. Jr. *My Years with General Motors (with John McDonald)*. New York: Doubleday, 1963.

Stern, Carl W., and Michael S. Deimler, eds. *The Boston Consulting Group on Strategy*. Hoboken, NJ: John Wiley, 2006.

Taylor III, Alex. "GM And Me," Fortune, December 8, 2008, 90–100.

Zhang, Xiaomeng, K. M. Bartol, K. G. Smith, M. D. Pfarrer, and D. M. Khanin. "CEOs on the Edge: Earnings Manipulations and Stock-Based Incentive Misalignment." *Academy of Management Journal* 51, no. 2, 2008, 241–258.

Appendix 2: Bad Economic News—Some Recent Examples and Facts

In the first four months of 2009, the number of U.S. bank failures had reached 22. North Carolina experienced its first bank failure since 1993. In 2008, there were 25 bank failures in the United States. Among these bank failures were big banks, such as Washington Mutual and IndyMac.

The Federal Deposit Insurance Corporation had identified over 250 banks and thrift institutions or Savings and Loans (S&Ls) that were in serious financial difficulty in 2008. The rescue cost was estimated at $65 billion by this government agency.

General Motors (GM) and Chrysler too had to be rescued by the government loans. To save the firms from collapsing further, the government demanded huge concessions from the firms' creditors. For instance, the U.S. Treasury Department demanded of GM creditors that they accept a smaller amount of GM stocks in exchange for the company's $29 billion in debt. The government had asked Chrysler's creditors to forfeit 85 percent of $7 billion in debt in order to receive government loans to save the company from total collapse.

In April of 2009, there were reports of nearly 1.2 million debtors who had filed for bankruptcies over a period of one year. In other words, 4 individuals and/or businesses for each 1,000 in population had filed for legal protection from their creditors. The rate of bankruptcies had doubled in two years. Between March 2008 and March 2009, in California, the number of bankruptcies jumped by 82 percent, from 9,308 to 16,917. In a smaller state Delaware, the bankruptcy filings rose by 127 percent. Many affluent individuals were forced to seek protection when they lost jobs as a result of the subprime crisis.

The Indian government auctioned off ownership of Satyam Computer Services Ltd. and charged its former CEO and eight other individuals with cheating, forgery, and falsifying records. The top management had faked financial data to make the company revenues and cash balances look stronger. The company's two independent auditors from Price Waterhouse were accused of being part of the financial conspiracy. Satyam, which was the fourth largest software services company in India, is now a scandal-tainted outsourcing group.

Joe Nacchio, former CEO of Qwest, was convicted for insider trading and sentenced to a six-year prison term.

Bernard Madoff was sentenced to a 150-year prison term for defrauding thousands of investors of billions in investment through his Ponzi scheme.

Bank of America is being investigated for its failure to disclose Merrill Lynch's $3.6 billion in compensation bonuses just before the government-arranged takeover of Merrill Lynch by Bank of America.

Goldman Sachs CEO Lloyd Blankfein, whose annual compensation was estimated to be around $43 million, suggested a need for executive compensation overhaul and government oversight over hedge fund and Wall Street investment activities. His company received $10 billion in government bailout money.

Rewarding executives "for short-term, high risk gains with negative long-term consequences" is a dangerous practice.

Ignorance was not the primary factor in the financial meltdown. It was greed. Solution: break up large companies. Don't let firms grow big and gain in prominence to the point that they could have devastating influence worldwide.

The past three major economic crises—the S&L scandal of the 1980s, the dot-com bubble of the 1990s, and the subprime crisis of 2000s—have a common thread. The two real-estate crises were caused by imprudent lending by financial institutions and the dot-com bust was related to unwise speculation. All these crises underscored human greed for quick financial gains, a greed that was harvested by the unchecked or unregulated business environment.

There are about 2,600 state and municipal pension plans for approximately 22 million public employees. Their retirement funds are valued at approximately $2 trillion. These pension funds have lost 40 percent in value in recent months. The declined assets are a cause for concern. Some assets have to be liquidated to get the cash needed to meet obligations. The loss in asset values is expected to exceed $1 trillion. Many retirement plans have thus become about 50 percent funded. The situation is regarded as alarming. Police funds that provide early retirement with full benefits are particularly in a precarious position.

Consider the recent business phenomena: socialization of losses and privatization of gains; imprudent risk-taking; and high compensation for quick gains with negative long-term consequences.

Ban financial instruments or derivatives that are complex and are not easily understood by investors. All financial instruments must be subject to some government oversight and scrutiny. Ban issuing of financial instruments unless they are examined and approved by a government agency. All financial instruments should be controlled just like all new drugs—subject to government approval.

Make all media financial experts liable for false advice and recommendations—just like malpractice for physicians and medical practitioners.

PartyGaming, an online British gaming firm with a stock listing on the FTSE 100 Index, admitted to committing bank fraud and contravening other American laws. The company paid $105 million in fine to avoid prosecution.

Mutual funds share blame for excessive executive compensation and greed. The funds managers align their own personal interests with executives' and tend not to represent their investors' best interests.

A headline in *WSJ*, April 8, 2009: "More Investors Say Bye-Bye To Buy-and-Hold."

Because of financial problems, many people do not get their prescriptions filled.

Index